AGAINST
ALL ODDS

AGAINST ALL ODDS

A mother's fight to prove
her innocence

Angela Cannings

with Megan Lloyd Davies

TIME WARNER
BOOKS

First published in Great Britain in 2006 by Time Warner Books

A CIP catalogue record for this book
is available from the British Library.

ISBN-13: 978-0-316-73304-5
ISBN-10: 0-316-73304-0

Typeset in Sabon by M Rules
Printed and bound in Great Britain by
Clays Ltd, St Ives plc

Time Warner Books
An imprint of
Little, Brown Book Group
Brettenham House
Lancaster Place
London WC2E 7EN

A member of the Hachette Livre Group of Companies

www.littlebrown.co.uk

Time Warner Books is a trademark of Time Warner Inc.
Used under licence.

This book is dedicated to our children.

To Jade, without whom Terry and I could not have survived. We hope the telling of our story in our own words will help her to fully understand the past when she becomes an adult.

And in memory of our precious babies, Gemma, Jason and Matthew.

ACKNOWLEDGEMENTS

Terry and I would like to give our deep and heartfelt thanks to the following:

Our family and friends for their continuous love and support.

John and Sandy Walton for their friendship, compassion and belief.

Dr Barnes and the staff at Salisbury District Hospital who showed us care and concern; I. N. Newmans Ltd, the funeral directors who treated us with complete compassion; Chris Howard-Jones at Victim Support and the Salisbury Mental Health Team for providing a lifeline for Terry; Louise Fountain, clinical psychologist, for her support in helping me cope; the late John Pook, of Wiltshire County Council social services, for his professionalism and concern for us as a family.

Rose, who gave me the will to fight on. I will be forever grateful.

Bill Bache, Jacqui Cameron, Kath Buckley, Jo Briggs and Michael Mansfield QC, my legal team, for their belief in me and their tireless efforts to see justice done.

The medical experts who gave evidence in my defence; the schools who have supported and encouraged Jade throughout; the doctors, counsellors and other medical professionals who are still caring for us; the people of both Salisbury and Saltash who have shown nothing but kindness and concern for us as a family.

John Sweeney for his invaluable investigation and all the

journalists who brought our story to the attention of the wider public; Penny Mellor and her family for their invaluable support; Susie, whose bravery in giving evidence at my trial was never underestimated by me; Meat Loaf whose songs have helped us through so much.

All the members of the general public who wrote to me while I was in prison – your faith and support kept me going during the worst of times.

John Batt for his advice and generosity during the writing of this book, and all those who gave us invaluable feedback.

Ivan Mulcahy, my agent, for convincing me people would want to hear my story.

Elise Dillsworth, my editor, and all the team at Little, Brown Book Group for enabling me to tell it.

Richard Madeley and Judy Finnigan, Lorraine Kelly, Jenni Murray, and Richard Branson for their support.

Tom and Marion Mendham, Clare Saunders and Toby Atkinson for their hospitality.

Terry and Gill Chambers, our close friends and lifelong Southampton Football Club supporters (like most of the Cannings family), who presented us with a lasting memorial to Gemma, Jason and Matthew by setting their names in stone at the football ground.

Megan Lloyd Davies who has laughed, cried and supported us throughout the writing of this book and without whom this story would not have been told.

To all those I have not mentioned, please know I am forever grateful.

FOREWORD

This book chronicles a journey of courage and commitment, from the turmoil of tragedy in hospital corridors, through the surreality of crowded courtrooms, along oppressive prison passageways to eventual and final vindication. Here is an ordinary citizen, and her supportive family, refusing to be overwhelmed by the odds stacked against her by the system as a whole and who is determined, for the benefit of all, to pursue the path of truth wherever it may lead.

The odds stacked against her start with the undoubted prejudice arising from the mere number of allegations. In the words of Oscar Wilde's Lady Bracknell – "To lose one parent, Mr Worthing, may be regarded as a misfortune; to lose both looks like carelessness." Professor Meadow, the paediatrician, notoriously converted the thrust of this sentiment into a statistical calculation in the trial of Sally Clarke – 1 in 73 million. By the time of Angela's trial this evaluation had been thoroughly discredited by the Court of Appeal and was, therefore, not admitted in her case. Nevertheless, the odour had not been entirely dispelled.

On top of the searing distress caused by losing three of your children, Angela was faced with the formidable task of proving a "double negative". It is difficult enough in the circumstances of a normal trial to demonstrate, as a defendant, that you did not commit the crime. In this instance the issue goes beyond that, to asserting no crime had been committed at all. It's not so much a "who dunnit" as a "what dunnit". The authorities had a simply stated hypothesis – smothering. Angela could do little more than say, "I didn't do it, but I don't know what did." This presents a serious predicament and challenge for any adjudicator or juror. It requires substantial rigorous intellectual scrutiny and integrity. Although the criminal justice system has its bedrock based on two well-known principles – the onus of proof resting on the prosecution and the standard of proof entailing a certainty beyond reasonable doubt – everyone realises that, in practice, there is an enormous burden placed on a defendant in cases like this to provide an alternative explanation. Nature abhors a vacuum. Human nature hungers for the satisfaction of grasping something that will displace the void of not knowing.

In an endeavour to meet this need, an impressive array of medical expertise was engaged by the defence to search for potential explanations suggesting a variety of natural causes. Gemma was 13 weeks old, Jason was 7 weeks and Matthew 18 weeks. The highly skilled pathologist dealing with Gemma and Jason in the first place recorded the cause of death as "natural", being Sudden Infant Death Syndrome (cot death). This is often referred to by the acronym SIDS. It means that after careful and thorough investigation, no natural, or unnatural, cause of death can be ascertained. In other words, we know what it isn't, but not what it is. What is still not fully appreciated is that the single largest category of infant death (under twelve months) falls within this definition. There are no satisfactory clues – as there were not in the Cannings cases. Although over twenty experts from a broad range of disciplines applied their minds to the possibilities, they could do no more than touch the edge or frontiers of current scientific development.

None of this however adds up to murder. To employ a Rumsfeldism – "the absence of evidence is not the evidence of absence". While this has little relevance to Iraq, it does have resonance in scientific method. There could well be a cause yet to be identified and recognised.

It's an ill wind . . . as they say and ultimately Angela's incarceration and continued protestation of innocence not only blew good but also generated a wind of change few could have predicted. The Court of Appeal judgement quashing her conviction has become a benchmark of how cases of this kind should be approached in the future and is a pinnacle in judicial reasoning.

As a final footnote, Professor Meadow, who played such a pivotal role in Clarke, Cannings and others in the family division, was struck off by the GMC. In February 2006 this decision was successfully challenged in the Administrative Court on the basis of public policy immunity for expert witnesses.

Should this prove to be the final position, it will be ever more incumbent on individual experts, professional bodies, prosecuting authorities and courts themselves to ensure a much stricter control on the ambit, competence and admission of expert evidence.

Michael Mansfield QC, London 2006

PROLOGUE

It started like any other day – and how I wish it had ended that way. How many times through the intervening years have I imagined putting my baby son Matthew safely to bed and kissing my three-year-old daughter Jade goodnight before turning out the light? Of padding softly downstairs, pouring myself a glass of wine and cooking some food? Of snatching a couple of soaps on television before going upstairs, cuddling up to my husband Terry and falling asleep? Of being just an ordinary mother.

But however many wishes I have wasted, 12 November 1999 did not end with the four of us sleeping peacefully under one roof. It was the day that ripped the heart out of our world. It was the day that sent us spinning into a nightmare from which we have still not fully woken up. And it was the day that made us the family we are today.

I woke in the pitch black of a dark November morning. Terry's alarm had gone off at 5.40 a.m. and he struggled out of bed to start the day. He was used to the early starts as a supermarket bakery manager but I lay clinging to the last cosy moments before the warmth seeped from his space on the mattress beside me. Next door I heard Matthew beginning to stir. Contentment washed over me as I thought of him lying in his cot in the room he shared with Jade. His birth had brought a peace to our life we had feared we would never know. In the ten years before Matthew was born, we'd endured more pain than most parents could imagine – the loss of two babies to cot death. But then Jade was born in 1996, and three years later Matthew had completed our happiness. We finally had what we had dreamed of – a normal family life.

As I tiptoed into the children's bedroom, my heart, like every other mother's would, gave a familiar tender lurch. Maybe mine always gave an extra pull when I gazed at my two children because it was a sight that for so long I had feared I'd never see. Quietly I picked up Matthew out of his cot and took him into our bedroom where I gave him a bottle. I always enjoyed that time – holding him close while he stared intently up at me as he fed.

A few minutes later, like every morning, Jade came into the room and I flicked on the television cartoons she so loved before wrapping the duvet around the three of us so we could snuggle up together. It was always a special time as I cuddled my children, still slightly drowsy from sleep and not yet caught up in the chaos of the day. We would sit in bed, warm and safe together, as Jade stared at the colourful screen and eighteen-week-old Matthew settled himself after his feed. As sleepiness slipped from her, Jade turned to the brother she adored and asked me to make a nest for him in the duvet. As she smiled and cooed at Matthew, his eyes followed her every move – each seemed equally enchanted with the other.

'C'mon, let's get you some breakfast,' I said after about ten minutes and the three of us went downstairs.

I put Matthew into his seat and sat Jade down at the kitchen table before giving her some toast and spooning porridge into my son's eager mouth. The health visitor had advised me not to start him on solids until he was twelve weeks old, but I'd had to two weeks early – he just wasn't settling properly and needed more food. Like every other baby, Matthew didn't necessarily stick to timetables. After getting dressed, we left the house at about 8.45 a.m. for the journey to pre-school. Usually we walked from our Salisbury home because I liked to get some fresh air into the children and it was a nice route that took us through a park, but because it was a cold morning and Matthew had seemed off colour the day before, I drove.

'Bye, Jadey,' I said as I bent down to give her a kiss.

My lips had hardly touched her cheek before she rushed into the crowd of children. Jade was a very sociable little girl and loved the three mornings a week she spent at pre-school.

After driving home, I got ready to start my morning chores. I'd gone back to my part-time job at Tesco, where Terry also worked, about a month before and I did four nights a week. It meant I had to be extra organised when it came to running our home, and while Terry was great – he'd feed and bathe the children and put them to bed – I was always keen to get things done.

That morning I had lots to do – I wanted to wash my hair and needed to organise the huge supermarket shop I'd spent £140 on the night before. I also wanted to prepare Matthew some of the puréed vegetables I'd fed Jade as a baby.

I took Matthew upstairs at about 9.00 a.m. and put him to bed for his morning nap. He slept on a mattress placed on a pad attached to an apnoea alarm – a device that detects a baby's breathing motions and activates an alarm after a pre-set time if they stop. Sometimes it would give a high-pitched shriek if Matthew rolled off the mattress or if the battery was low, and whenever I heard it I ran to his bedside with a rush of metallic fear bursting in my mouth.

Matthew had the apnoea alarm because he, like Jade before him, was considered at increased risk of cot death after we had lost our thirteen-week-old daughter and seven-week-old son. The doctors had never been able to explain to us why Gemma and Jason had died. They described their loss as Sudden Infant Death Syndrome – our babies had gone to sleep and never woken up. Two more tiny victims of cot death.

Everyone we met reassured us there was nothing we could have done to prevent their deaths but still I couldn't help wondering. I think it's something all mothers share: the desire to protect your child and the automatic sense of blame if you feel you haven't. We were even reassured after Jason died by a kindly professor of pae-diatric pathology who was a leading expert on cot death. He too urged us not to blame ourselves and told us of other families who had suffered multiple cot deaths.

His words comforted us and Terry and I had followed every piece of advice he gave. We'd moved house, stopped smoking and left a long gap to allow us to heal before trying for another baby. Five years later Jade was born and it had signalled a whole new start for us. She too had slept with an apnoea alarm and was part of the Care of Next Infants Scheme, which gathered information about babies whose siblings had died of cot death.

Of course there was an unspoken apprehension somewhere in the back of both Terry's and my minds and it was brought into sharp relief when Jade suffered breathing problems at nearly three months old. I had found her struggling for breath in her cot and she was taken into hospital for two weeks. I just couldn't calm down. Jason had suffered breathing problems just before he died and I was terrified something might happen to Jade after a brain scan, 24-hour heart monitoring, urine and blood tests and sleep monitoring. The doctors could find nothing wrong, but I was unable to quell my fears.

The medical staff were kind to us and even offered to keep Jade in hospital for three months to monitor her but we decided that we must get back to real life and, as our little girl flourished, the shadows of fear gradually melted away. Slowly Jade grew into a healthy and happy little girl and my anxieties withered. The arrival of Matthew convinced us we could finally put the past to rest.

It hadn't all been plain sailing, though. The morning before he was born I had felt milk dribbling down my chin as I tried to eat breakfast.

'Mummy, your mouth looks funny,' Jade told me. I ran to the mirror to see the left side of my face dropped and frozen like a stroke sufferer's.

The doctors told me I had Bell's Palsy – a virus that affects the facial nerves – and it wouldn't interfere with the birth. The only thing that might improve it was steroids, and a week after

Matthew was born I started taking them. It meant I had to stop breastfeeding him, which I didn't like. But I was also anxious to do whatever I could to improve the palsy. I'd never been vain but I was only thirty-six years old and my eye didn't close properly, my taste and hearing were affected and the smile I'd always used to great effect for a laugh and a joke was strangely lopsided. Slowly my face improved but my confidence had been severely dented. I felt that I looked like an old woman.

Any difficulties though were far outweighed by seeing Matthew and Jade together and I felt happier as each day passed. We got into a routine at home, and went on our first family holiday together to a caravan park in Devon. I watched my son fill out from a tiny newborn into a chubby, happy baby. Finally I felt complete – I had a healthy son and a daughter.

But a shadow of concern flickered in the back of my mind on the morning of 12 November. A week earlier the alarm had rung its piercing shriek and I found Matthew gasping for breath in his cot. My mind a blur, I rang an ambulance. By the time he arrived at Salisbury District Hospital Matthew was back to normal, gurgling and looking around as if nothing had happened, while I sat numbed by the possibility that the unimaginable had almost happened again.

Knowing our history, the doctors had run every test possible but nothing had shown up.

'He's bright, alert and contented – there's no reason he can't go home,' they assured us.

And so, after a night in hospital, they sent Matthew home and told us not to worry. This, of course, was impossible, but we'd been reassured so many times by different doctors, and Jade was absolutely fine, so I guarded against becoming overprotective and stifling my children with my maternal fears.

On the eleventh, Matthew seemed lethargic. Terry urged me to wait a few hours before calling the doctor. He too was anxious not to become overprotective.

'He's fine,' said Terry, as he gave me a cuddle when I got back from shopping. 'He's eaten and is asleep. There's nothing to worry about.'

I told myself not to be silly.

'Jade is healthy, Matthew is fine now and every possible test has been done,' I said to myself as I pushed my worry to the back of my mind.

I tucked Matthew into his cot, turned on the apnoea alarm and waited outside the door for a few moments to check that he settled himself. Once everything was quiet, I turned and left my son asleep.

CHAPTER ONE

The piercing shriek of the alarm cut through the background hum of the television. Gasping, I threw myself through the kitchen door before running up thc stairs to my son's room.

It was just four steps through the bedroom door to his cot where he was lying still on his front. Trembling, I turned him over and saw he was not moving.

He looked blotchy and his lips were purple.

Meningitis, I thought for a split second as I looked down at him. But the thought drained from me. I knew at once we had lost Matthew. Panic filled me. How could this be happening a third time? It was unimaginable. We'd left those dark days behind, hadn't we? Jade was healthy and Matthew too. He couldn't be gone. It just couldn't be happening.

But even as my mind struggled to deny what my eyes could see, I knew my son was dead. This was the third time I had found one of my children with the life drained from them. I froze.

Blindly, I ran to the phone and called Terry at work – I had to have him with me. Once again I was on my own when I found my lifeless child and I couldn't bear to be alone again – facing the black wave that was poised to come crashing down on us.

As I waited for him to arrive, I put Matthew on his sister's bed and started trying to give him mouth-to-mouth resuscitation. But my mind went blank as I struggled to remember what

1

I had been shown by doctors at the hospital. Fear, terror and disbelief crowded into my brain. I had to help my son, try to bring him back, but I just couldn't remember what I was supposed to do.

I heard banging on the front door and ran down to open it.

As Terry rushed upstairs he asked me, 'Have you phoned for an ambulance?'

'No,' I sobbed.

'Why?' he demanded.

'I just wanted you here.'

'Phone an ambulance,' he shouted back at my stepdad Brian, who had driven him home from work.

Terry ran with me into the children's room and looked at our tiny son.

'Look at him, look at him,' I said. 'I think he's gone.'

With one glance, he too knew that Matthew was dead. He disappeared wordlessly from the room and dully I heard him smash a blow into a cupboard door.

Brian came in and passed the phone to me.

'Put the baby on the floor,' the operator told me. 'Puff gently twice then press with your two fingers on his chest. Open his clothes up and look at him. Is he moving?'

Tears streamed down my face as I tried to follow what the voice was telling me. Over and over it asked, 'Is he moving? Is he moving?'

And each time I knew he wasn't.

We followed the ambulance to the hospital and were taken into a relatives' room where we sat and waited with a nurse. Fear clenched tight around my heart – a crushing sensation I was all too familiar with.

Soon Dr Barnes, a senior paediatrician we had met after Jason's death, came into the room. He wanted to know everything that had happened that morning. What Matthew had eaten, how he had seemed, what time he went down to sleep, what position he had been in.

2

'Attempts at resuscitation are continuing,' he said quietly, before leaving us to sit and wait.

'What did I do wrong?' I cried, as Terry repeated again and again, 'Why us?' We both sobbed thinking of Matthew alone in a room as doctors tried to breathe life back into him.

'Do you know we've already lost two children?' Terry asked the nurse. He sounded confused, disbelieving that we were once again in hospital.

'No, I didn't,' she replied softly.

'Our babies. They were called Gemma and Jason. Now we've got a daughter Jade, who's nearly four. She also nearly died. But the doctors saved her.'

Through the fog of my disbelief I heard Terry turn to me.

'Why did you ring me before you phoned the ambulance? I can't understand why you did that,' he asked.

'I panicked,' was all I could say.

Silence fell on the room once more.

'I'm sorry I can't show more emotion,' Terry said as he turned to the nurse. 'But we've been through it twice before and I feel empty and dried up.'

Soon she left to go and get some tea and Dr Barnes returned.

'Terry and Angela, I'm sorry to say there are still no life signs in Matthew and the resuscitation has been prolonged. If we continue, in the very unlikely event of success, the chance of severe brain damage is likely. I'm very sorry. I need to ask you if you would like us to continue trying to resuscitate Matthew?'

Terry and I sat dazed, tearfully staring at Dr Barnes as he confirmed what we already knew – our son was gone.

Terry looked at me.

'No, no,' he said, utter shock on his face – as if a stranger had walked up to him in the street and punched him in the stomach. 'Just let him go.'

Some time later, unknown to me, Dr Barnes would whisper to him: 'I'm sorry to tell you this, Terry, but you're going to have to expect crap in your lives now. I'm going to have to inform the police.' But I knew nothing of this as we were taken into another side room where a nurse handed Matthew to me. Tears rolled down my cheeks, and my heart lurched for a second as I looked at him wrapped in a blanket. He's only asleep, I thought. I've got it all wrong. He's just sleeping.

Matthew looked so peaceful lying in my arms and I hugged him close to me, desperate to deny what was happening. But the truth kept pressing down on me, edging its way around the corners of my hopes. I knew this was goodbye.

After a few minutes a nurse came into the room to tell us he needed to be taken to the Chapel of Rest. But I couldn't let him go, not so soon, he'd been smiling at me only a few hours ago and now this?

'Not yet,' I told her, as I held onto my son and lowered my face to his.

I was hardly aware of Terry and the nurse leaving the room and our close friend Terry Chambers arriving. I looked up at him, utterly bewildered that I was here again.

'What am I doing wrong?' I whispered as I held onto Matthew.

'You're doing nothing wrong, Angie,' he told me. 'It's just nature.'

But his words meant nothing to me. All I could do was cuddle Matthew for the final time, drinking in his physical presence. I knew that soon my arms would be empty once again.

'It's a long walk through the hospital,' the nurse said gently when she eventually returned to take us to the Chapel of Rest. 'We'll have to go past a lot of people. How do you feel about that?'

She moved as if to take Matthew from me.

'No,' I whispered. 'I'll hold him. I want to take him.'

'Do you want to clean yourself up, Angie?' Terry Chambers asked me.

There was a moment of silence as I stared at my son.

'I should do,' I answered, aware of tears covering my face. 'Can you hold him please?'

Gently Terry took Matthew from my arms as I quickly scrubbed at my face with a paper towel before taking him back again and clutching him to me.

It seemed to take for ever as we walked through those long

4

corridors while all around us people went about their normal day. Nurses bustling their way to wards, white-coated doctors looking purposeful, people going to visit relatives and friends. Bright lights, vending machines, name plaques on doors, the quiet murmur of the waiting areas.

I felt absolutely separated from it all – as if an invisible glass box had been built around me, enclosing me and cutting me off from reality – because as people got on with everyday life, our world was crumbling around us.

I could only stare blankly at passers-by who smiled good morning as if it was an ordinary day and I was an ordinary mum carrying her baby wrapped in a blanket. They opened doors and waited for me to go through, stood aside as I walked slowly down the corridor. Some might even have smiled at the tiny bundle I held in my arms – that sudden expression of joy which greets a new life. But it all passed me in a blur.

I was on my final walk with my beloved son.

Matthew, who had signalled the end to our dark days, who made Jade's face light up when she came into the room and Terry grin with pride at his ferocious appetite. The baby who had brought a peace to my life because his survival meant we had finally defeated fate.

Every step carried me closer to having to let him go and I never wanted that walk to end. When the nurse moved towards me to take Matthew away, I clung onto him – not wanting to feel his weight lifted from my arms, knowing that when I let him go I would never feel him against me again.

Never hear his giggles when I nuzzled under his chin, smell his skin with a dusting of baby powder on it, feel him grasp my finger when I fed him. Never again see Jade make her brother smile as she played with him, or turn my head in the car to see the two of them strapped into their seats behind me.

I held tightly onto my baby, pressing his cool skin to mine, burying my face in the blanket wrapped around him, feeling his weight in my arms for the last time.

Later that day my father would also go to the Chapel of Rest to see Matthew – crying as he rocked his grandson and covering him in kisses as he said goodbye. There were many people who mourned our son.

The next thing I remember, Matthew was gone and Terry and I were walking blindly out of the hospital.

It was the hardest thing of all that day to leave him in that massive building where only strangers would look at him.

As Terry and I drove silently away one word screamed inside through the numbness: 'Why?'

Arriving home, our thoughts immediately turned to Jade. We were at a loss what to do. She adored Matthew.

I remembered the first time she had seen her brother after he was born by caesarean weighing 9 pounds 2 ounces. Terry and I were keen for her not to feel pushed out by the new arrival and had wracked our brains about how to make her feel secure.

The day after Matthew was born I drew the curtain around my bed and made a nest of blankets for him in the middle. When Jade pulled back the curtain with Terry behind her, her new brother was lying there waiting to meet her.

'Who is this, Jadey?' I asked, as she peered at the bundle of blankets. 'This is your little brother.'

She climbed straight onto the bed and asked me to put him on her lap.

Just to make doubly sure she accepted the new arrival, we'd also got a present for her 'from' Matthew to say 'thank you for being my big sister'. Terry and I knew just how persuasive presents can be to a three-year-old.

That was just eighteen weeks ago.

It's a situation unimaginable to any parent – how to tell one child that another has died, how to help them understand why someone has suddenly gone, without scaring them.

I was incapable of making any decisions. Numb with shock, questions raced around my head: did I use too much teething gel? Had I used the wrong washing powder? Was his bedroom too hot, or too cold? Had I failed to notice he was ill? Everyone else I knew had healthy children and so all I could think was that it must have been something I'd done wrong. I desperately wracked my brain for any clue to what it might have been.

As I sat silently, Terry decided that because Jade knew she had had a brother and a sister who had gone to sleep and were now stars in the sky, we would tell her Matthew had gone to join them.

My mum and Brian were also with us and we agreed we should pack up Matthew's things and tell her he had 'given' her her room back. That night Jade would have to sleep in the bedroom they had shared only that morning. We didn't want her to go to sleep surrounded by the day-to-day stuff of her brother's life – the cot, the changing mat, the bottles of lotion – which suggested everything was the same. It might, we felt, confuse her when we told her Matthew wasn't coming back.

I've often wondered since if it was the right thing to do, whether our actions triggered the suspicion that was to dog me for years to come – that my behaviour was cold and 'unnatural'. But all I can say is that in the immediate hours after we lost Matthew, we did the best we could and we did it full of love and concern for Jade.

Deep down part of me didn't want to start bagging up his things and dismantling the cot. I wanted them to stay in the room because somehow it meant he hadn't yet left and I could still hold onto him. But I thought of Jade and carried on helping as the cot was taken apart, clothes and toys were bagged up.

'Where should the cot go?' I asked.

'Let's just put it in the garden by the shed for now,' Terry replied.

I couldn't bear to part with it all just yet and so we kept some of Matthew's belongings for Jade to have – some cuddly toys, a few bits of clothing, so that he wouldn't have disappeared completely. I also wanted some to touch as I grieved. I kept the tiny cream trousers and top I'd bought him to wear to my sister Tina's wedding when he was just a month old. I kept some of the footless all-in-ones that had kept him cool in summer. I kept the padded navy all-in-one he'd worn when the weather got colder.

And I kept his Southampton football club teddy – given to him because his dad was a massive fan.

My sister Claire arrived home with Jade at about 2.30 p.m.

As my daughter burst through the door in a rush of blonde hair and blue eyes, she gave me a smile and a hug – a hug which somehow melted through the numbness and showed me there was a spark of hope, because we still had Jade and we had to get through it as best we could for her.

Quietly I took her upstairs and knelt down in front of her.

'Where's Matthew?' she asked, as she looked around the room.

'He's gone to sleep, darling, and not woken up,' I said gently. 'He has gone to heaven now with Gemma and Jason and is the brightest star in the sky.'

I thought my heart would break as she started to cry. Clutching Jade, I sobbed silent tears for all that we had lost, for our shattered dreams.

Terry too looked completely broken and when, a couple of hours later, he said he wanted to take Jade up to his mum's, I knew he needed to go somewhere safe to cry.

I was in the house with Claire and her fiancé Kevin when the doorbell rang.

'Hello, Mrs Cannings,' said a man standing on the doorstep. 'I'm Detective Sergeant Findlay from Wiltshire Police and this is Detective Constable Gill Dawson.'

We'd had a visit from a police officer after Jason's death. He'd dropped into our home for a few brief minutes to ask a couple of questions. I assumed these officers just wanted to get all the details – like the doctors had done that morning – and so I let them in. After we'd chatted briefly downstairs, they asked to see Matthew's room.

'Of course,' I said and took them upstairs. 'We've taken the cot down and put it in the shed,' I told them numbly as they looked around. 'We thought it was best.'

I walked towards the wardrobe and opened the door. 'We've packed all his clothes into bin liners and they're downstairs,' I added.

8

It didn't seem strange that they were looking around. I questioned nothing as I went through the mechanics of that visit. I felt cut off from it all, as if life was happening around me. While my body was part of it, my mind was far away.

'We'd like you to come with us to the victim support suite at Salisbury police station if that's possible,' DS Findlay told me after we'd gone back down to the kitchen where I had pointed out the batteries I'd taken out of the apnoea alarm as we were packing things up. Another thing we wouldn't need any more. 'We just need to ask you some questions about today.'

I hardly registered their request as I went to phone Terry at his mum's.

'The police are here and need to ask us some questions,' I told him, as we arranged to meet each other at Salisbury police station.

I didn't know then that a tight knot of fear budded in Terry's mind the moment he heard those words.

Just before half past five we were taken into what looked like an ordinary house at the back of the station. We were shown into a living room – complete with sofa, armchair, TV and coffee table – with a kitchen off to the side and stairs going up to a second floor.

Terry and I sat beside each other on the sofa as a man introduced himself as Detective Constable Graham Fisher, from the Child Protection Unit. Gill Dawson was also there, with two women from Wiltshire Social Services.

Soon a stream of questions started about Matthew, Terry and me and our family life. I wasn't intimidated – everyone seemed pleasant and sympathetic – and, as each question took an age to filter into my shocked brain, I answered as fully as I could.

DC Fisher then said he was going to take Terry upstairs and I should stay with DC Dawson and a social worker. Why are they separating us? I wondered. But there was no time to answer my own question as the social worker started asking me others.

What was I like as a mum? Did I love my babies? What was I like to them? Did I have any concerns about anything? What was my relationship with Terry like? Did I have problems coping?

She was tall, with short hair and glasses, in her early fifties. There was now none of the sympathy which every other doctor, nurse and professional had shown to Terry and me after we lost Gemma and Jason. I was bewildered by her interrogation, confused by all the questions, which I thought I'd already answered.

But in the wake of Matthew's death, I could hardly manage to focus on what was happening as I answered their questions and sipped the tea they offered me in breaks.

Later Terry came back into the room with Graham Fisher.

'Where is Jade? We need her back,' he asked anxiously.

'We won't be long,' came the only reply. 'We just need to go and have a chat.'

All Terry and I could do was sit and wait as the officers and social workers left the room.

'Ange, what have you said to them?' Terry asked quietly as he turned towards me. 'You should be careful what you say.'

He was acutely aware there might be a darker interpretation of what had happened that day but I had no idea what he was talking about. I sat there stunned, my ever-present questions running through my head. Had I wrapped Matthew up too warmly? Should I have left a window open? Why hadn't I listened to the doctors and put him on his back? He would never settle like that but I shouldn't have put him on his front? What kind of mother was I?

I said nothing.

It was about quarter to eight when they came back into the room.

'We need to get Jade back,' said Terry urgently. 'We've been here for hours and I need to pick her up.'

Through the fog I heard a voice say that no criminal action would be taken against us. I looked blankly around the room as the voice continued and I heard the words 'at-risk register' and 'care order'. I had no idea what they meant.

'Jade cannot be left alone with you tonight,' the voice said.

'You'll have to make arrangements for her to stay somewhere else.'

The only thing that registered in my mind was that we would not be able to have Jade back home with us. I was appalled. We stood up and I looked at Terry in a daze. What were they saying? Why couldn't we have her? What were they doing?

During all that happened over the next four years, that night was the one and only time Terry allowed rage to get the better of him.

'How can you do this to us after what we have been through today?' he screamed. 'We have lost a child and you are going to deprive us of Jade? How on earth will she understand why we haven't picked her up and taken her home? It's barbaric.'

I realised I was sobbing once again. I didn't understand what was happening but I had crumbled as soon as I heard that Jade would not be allowed to come home with us – we had lost Matthew and now they wouldn't let us have our daughter.

The tension in the room reached breaking point as Terry shouted, 'Well, if you've finished with us, we need to go home now.'

We left the room.

Some might wonder why we agreed to go home without Jade, why we didn't stay and fight for our child. But all I can say is that Terry and I had been brought up to respect authority, to obey the law and structures we believed were only there to protect us. We had no idea what to do in that moment when they turned against us, made us outsiders looking in. We felt utterly powerless to challenge those representatives of everything we'd been taught to obey.

Of course we didn't realise then, as we stood in that room and those strangers stared at us, that it was the start of a long fight against everything we had been taught to believe in. In the space of just a few hours, the systems we trusted – police, social services – had turned against us.

It was so dark and quiet when we arrived back home. The life had gone from the house.

'I'm just off down the shop. I won't be a minute,' said Terry.

I took off my coat. Numbly I sat down, questions racing through my brain while all the time my heart was slowly freezing. Why were they doing this? It must all be a mistake. Why wasn't Jade with us? It just wasn't fair. We needed her. When would she be coming home? For now she was staying with Terry's sister Jenny but it wouldn't be for more than a couple of days, would it? It couldn't take more time than that to sort out, surely?

I so desperately wanted to hold her and feel her warmth against me, reassuring me that everything would be all right, that she was still here and one day we would smile again.

Terry walked back in, slamming the door.

'I'm sorry, Ange,' he said, as he threw a packet of cigarettes on the table. It had been eight years since I last smoked. We'd stopped on doctor's advice and had never weakened. Terry opened the packet and handed me a cigarette before taking one for himself and lighting them both.

I took a deep breath of pungent smoke and slowly exhaled, the rush of chemicals making me feel sick. Wordlessly, I watched the smoke curl above me as Terry and I silently smoked cigarette after cigarette, lost in our thoughts and unable to talk about the awful events of that day. Much later we climbed the stairs to bed and took the sleeping tablets our GP had given us earlier in the day.

My heart ached for Jade. Depriving us of our daughter that night is something I still have not forgiven and the one thing I think I never will. It was the final kick in the teeth on the worst day of my life and all I could think about was how on earth she must be feeling when Matthew had gone and now Mummy and Daddy had too. But as I lay there waiting for the tablets to take effect, asking myself over and over again why they'd done this, I still had no idea what it all meant.

As the questions turned over relentlessly in my mind and I searched for any clue as to what I had done wrong that day – after all, Matthew had depended on me – it never crossed my mind that someone, somewhere might think I had deliberately harmed my son.

CHAPTER TWO

Almost fifteen years to the day before we lost Matthew, I had left home to start a new life with Terry. It was November 1984 and I was twenty-one.

'No!' I shouted, as my dad came running out of the house after me. 'You're not going to make me stay. Just remember it's because of you that I'm doing this.'

My dad was beside himself – outraged that his eldest daughter was having a relationship with a man nearly ten years her senior. Not only that, Terry Cannings was a father to two children and getting divorced from his wife. To my Irish Catholic dad it was a scandal and the constant shouting matches had forced me to move out.

As the neighbours twitched their curtains and I piled my belongings into my beloved Mini, my father raced after me.

'What are you doing? It's a disgrace,' he said angrily. 'Look what you are doing to your mother.'

But I was determined to go. I had a choice to make – Terry or my dad – and I knew in my heart what I had to do.

'Bye,' I called, as Mum stood on the doorstep crying. Behind her my younger sisters and brother stood and watched.

With a lump in my throat, I started up the little car that had sig-nified my first step on the road to independence when I bought it with money saved up from my wages. As the engine rattled into life, my dad gave me one last glance before going back into the house.

For a moment I almost faltered when I caught a glimpse of my mum in the mirror – sadness etched on her face. Soon she would have to go back inside to face my dad. But even though I felt sad, this was a journey I wanted to make. Sighing, I eased the car into first gear and started driving away – leaving behind my childhood home for a new future with the man I loved.

My dad had arrived in Salisbury in the late 1950s. Aged eighteen, he left County Kildare for England and ended up in Wiltshire because his older sister lived there. Handsome, game for a laugh and full of charm, Steve Connolly was a novelty in the small market town, and sure enough a local girl soon fell under his spell.

My mum Mary Sheppard could hardly believe his cheek when Steve – who was working as a hospital porter – chatted her up as she recovered from having her appendix out. But the approach summed up my dad. Always willing to chance his luck, he captivated Mary, who'd grown up in Winterslow, a small village outside Salisbury, and was considered quite a catch after winning the local carnival queen competition.

'He could talk the birds out of the trees,' my mum would say.

After a stormy courtship my parents married in 1962 and, unsurprisingly, their wedding also boasted a touch of drama when my dad's parents refused to attend – outraged because my mother was not Catholic and their precious son was marrying in a Protestant church. Maybe they would have made a different decision if they'd known that within three years my mum would convert to Catholicism and bring up all her children in the faith of their Irish forebears.

I arrived in May 1963, followed by Tina, Claire and Andrew by the time I was seven. Our childhoods were steeped in the church. In every aspect of our life – from prayers before sleep to mass every Sunday – our mum passed onto us her devout faith. Every Saturday we would all troop to St Gregory's church for confession where I, slightly puzzled and certainly scared about what might happen if I defied the priest who so influenced our

14

lives, would struggle to think of something to say. If I didn't confess my eight-year-old 'sins', the priest would refuse me communion the next day, and that was a fate far worse than any wrongdoing I had committed.

'Bless me father because this week I played with matches,' I would solemnly reveal in the hush of the confession box. Or, 'I've been horrible to Tina.'

The Catholic faith also dominated our schooling and at St Osmond's Junior, where I started aged seven, a nun called Sister Catherine ruled with a rod of iron.

'Her hair must be cut,' she told my mum when I arrived with hair three-quarters of the way down my back.

Mum dutifully took me home and chopped four inches off my blonde hair.

'Not enough,' said Sister Catherine when I returned to school.

And so another three inches came off and I went back to class with shoulder-length hair. The shock, I'm convinced, turned my hair from blonde to the dark brown it is today.

If Catholicism was one constant theme of my childhood, family was the other. My mum's eleven brothers and sisters meant there were aunts, uncles and cousins dotted all around the Salisbury area and weekends were spent visiting them. My uncle Bert and auntie Sylvia's farm in Winterslow was a particular favourite, and the four of us would run riot jumping in the hay stacks and playing games in the fields with our cousin Lorraine. In the countryside around the farm we would go blackberrying, my mum using the fruit to make pies, and it was during those weekends that we had time with Dad.

My parents' marriage was very traditional in many ways. For my mother, her children were her life and she was a constant presence – strict but loving in equal measures. She ran our home, everything from paying the bills to decorating, like clockwork. She cooked pies, knitted for us, put ribbons in our hair, used her wedding veil to make a canopy for a doll's cot, and made sure we didn't stretch the limited household budget too much by giving us one bath a week to save on immersion-heater costs.

Mum was very much a practical homemaker and wasn't one

for cuddles – I don't think she had enough time because there were so many of us – but I certainly felt loved.

My dad, like most fathers, was not around as much because he was busy at work during the week. After his spell as a porter at Salisbury Hospital, he got a job laying roads with fellow Irishmen and would come home each day filthy from work before cleaning himself up for tea and going out with his workmates. For him, making sure there were meals on the table and the bills were being paid were the cornerstones of his role as a father. He was the head of the family and commanded our respect.

He wasn't just an authoritarian, though, and he encouraged us with our interests – me and hockey, Andrew and his pet rabbits – before making us shriek with laughter at his jokes. I was always a bit of a daddy's girl – aware that my father had a soft spot for me, his eldest child.

When I was about nine, Dad got a job as an ambulance man and suddenly, excitingly, we had a telephone so he could be contacted. He also sometimes brought home his shiny cream ambulance. I can remember staring wide-eyed at it parked on the road outside our house, marvelling at how huge it was.

Up the hill and unknown to me, Terry was growing up with his parents and he too would notice the ambulance on the odd occasions it was parked at our house.

A couple of times the reality of Dad's work crashed into our cosy home when he returned with his shirt covered in blood. My mum got the boil wash on and Dad never talked about it. But we knew that he had gone from working on the roads to a responsible job and he took pride in his uniform.

The highlight of every year was in July when Dad packed up the car and drove us down to Weymouth where he dropped us off at a caravan park near the sea. He'd then head back to work in Salisbury and we would spend a week on the beach with my mum's brother Parry, his wife Roberta and their two children, Jacqueline and David, who travelled down from their home in Glasgow, occasionally joined by Roberta's parents and my uncle Bert and auntie Sylvia.

The holiday always followed a comfortingly familiar routine

as every day around lunchtime the men disappeared to the betting shop for an hour before returning to allow the women to make their way to a nearby cafe for a cream tea. Meanwhile we would play in the sand and swim – always returning to the same spot by the lost-children hut where we set up year after year.

And always, without fail, Scottish flags would be posted up on the windbreakers so that if we did get lost we'd find our way back to the family.

'Thank you for your application. But we regret to inform you that due to current height restrictions you are not eligible for police service.'

Another letter dropped on the doormat from another police force I had written to asking about becoming an officer. All of them had told me that at 5 feet 2 inches I wasn't tall enough to patrol the streets on the lookout for criminals, and that put paid to my career dream.

Joining the police force, becoming a nurse and working with animals were all jobs I was interested in doing. But mostly my passing career aspirations were sacrificed for my love of sport. Hockey, netball, tennis and athletics, I loved competing and was over the moon when I won the school's sports girl of the year award.

On the academic front I never shone brightly and left school aged sixteen with a couple of O levels and four CSEs. Undeterred I signed up for retakes at Salisbury technical college until the penny finally dropped that I was never going to shine academically when I failed the lot. My mind then turned to the realities of the world of work and, because I needed a wage, I got a job on the fruit and veg department at Tesco where I'd already had a Saturday job for a couple of years.

Soon I was enjoying the freedom of my first wage packet and, while I hadn't been that keen on working in a supermarket, I actually started having fun. I had a great bunch of friends and with cash in my hand began to discover my independence. I loved

17

going out and would spend night after night at the Conquered Moon pub near my home where a big group of boys and girls congregated. Sport and church went by the wayside as I worked hard and played even harder. Abba, David Cassidy and Slade were my heroes. My friends and I spent most weekends dancing and drinking in pubs. I'd inherited a good sense of humour from my dad and was always quick with a joke. He'd also passed on to me some of his charm, which meant I got on well with people and was always up for a laugh – I never went crazy but I wasn't scared of a bit of teenage rebellion. At sixteen my heart was broken when my first boyfriend dumped me, the following year I discovered sex and there were a couple more romances after that. But they never lasted more than a few months – I was too interested in enjoying my independence to get tied down like many of my school friends had been.

I soon realised that in order to really strike out I needed a car. After passing my test, I marched into Barclays bank to ask for a loan.

'We need to know that you'll be reliable with your repayments,' the bank manager sternly told me.

And so for three months I dutifully saved a part of my wage packet – which amounted to the princely sum of around £50 a week – to show I was a worthwhile candidate. The bank manager was convinced and I put my dad in charge of my precious £300 loan.

He went off to a car auction, plumped up my meagre funds a bit, and I came home one day to find a black Morris Mini 850 parked outside our house.

It was my pride and joy. I'd made a best friend at Tesco called Ally and we had a ball. After a hard week's work, we'd head off to Bournemouth to the Academy nightclub, the Mini groaning under as many friends as I could fit in.

By the time I started working full-time at Tesco, I'd known Terry for about three years.

When I was fifteen we'd moved to Primrose Road and my dad

had become friendly with Terry and his then wife Maureen, who lived three doors up. He came round to our house at times and soon I was earning extra money babysitting for the couple's sons, five-year-old Martin and Stephen, three.

I never gave Terry a passing thought. He may have been just nine years older than me but it might as well have been five hundred to the teenager I was then.

The babysitting trailed off when I went full-time at the supermarket – I was leaving pocket money behind for a wage packet – but I still saw Terry around Tesco, where he managed the bakery. Wearing his whites, he would say hello and was always the happy-go-lucky joker.

Soon I was promoted to be a supervisor on the fruit and veg department and as time went on I saw more of him. We'd bump into each other in the canteen during tea breaks or stop for a quick chat around the store and gradually our conversations got longer and longer. Terry and I are both great talkers and we'd chat for hours about this and that, the music we liked, the people at work, the holidays we were hoping to go on.

It might seem odd to some – I was still young after all and he was nearing thirty. But it seemed the most natural thing in the world at the time and because we instinctively trusted each other the age difference didn't seem to matter.

Terry and I understood each other in the most important ways. He too was Salisbury born and bred and had grown up in a loving family with his mum Doreen, dad Derrick and sister Jenny. His father too had worked hard while his mum stayed at home to look after the kids. Fundamentally we shared a common outlook on life – no one owed us a living, whatever we wanted to achieve we had to work for, and if you wanted others to treat you with respect you had to show it yourself.

Over the months we became firm friends and gradually Terry started confiding in me about the problems in his marriage. It didn't seem strange because he had been on the periphery of my life for many years and by then I counted him as a good friend. Inevitably the canteen gossip started and by the time Terry separated from his wife in the summer of 1983 everyone thought we

19

were having an affair. It annoyed and frustrated me but I knew people had tunnel vision and hoped they would soon forget their misplaced speculation, so I mostly just ignored the talk.

In fact, I was quietly amused that people would think I'd run off with him because, while a lot of my friends had gone off with men and got pregnant or married, I wanted nothing to do with all that. I was having a great time at work and even more fun out of it. I didn't need to get tied down. But as the days, weeks and months went by, my feelings for Terry moved beyond friendship as chats in coffee breaks at work became the odd trip out to the pub and I found myself thinking about him more and more.

Here was a man who didn't seem to be interested in me just because he was attracted to me – in fact, I didn't think he was at all. He wasn't after one thing and we were great friends. He wasn't like any man of my own age. Whether it was because he was a lot older than me I don't know, but Terry was somebody who would sit and listen – like I sat and listened to him. I struggled with my new feelings, though, because I knew he had only just come out of a marriage and I didn't want to push myself on him for fear he'd laugh me off.

Then one day in early 1984 he walked up to me at work and said, 'Ange, would you like to go for a drink tonight?'

Nervously I said yes. We'd been out socially before but something seemed different. Terry too seemed on edge.

That night we went for a drive to the New Forest and in the soft blackness he stopped the car before leaning across and kissing me.

The doubts started the next day. What had I done? Here I was a twenty-year-old and he was twenty-nine with a soon-to-be ex-wife and two kids.

But Terry gave me one of his smiles when I saw him at work and I knew I wanted things to last.

Six months later, we moved in together – much to many people's concern. As well as my dad's opposition to the relationship, Ally was also worried.

'What are you doing, Ange?' she had asked one day as we sat in her house drinking tea. 'You're having so much fun and now suddenly you're involved with Terry – he's too old and look at all the baggage he's got.'

'But I want to be with him,' I replied. 'I don't know what it is, I can't explain it but I feel good with him and I want to be with him.'

It was the only time that Ally and I almost fell out. But I was insistent and, like the good friend she was, she eventually accepted that I was happy.

At times even Terry questioned why I was in the relationship. I knew he was conscious of the age difference and whatever I did I couldn't seem to convince him I was serious.

A month after we'd moved in together, Terry was offered a job at a new Tesco on the Isle of Wight. As one of their top bakery managers, they wanted him to work his magic, and I decided to go with him. Life started well when we moved. We were put up in a hotel while we hunted for a flat and a heavy fall of snow saw Terry leaping around like a five-year-old. But barely three months later he decided he must return to Salisbury because his younger son Stephen was desperate without his dad and had started running away and playing truant from school.

One night Terry sat me down.

'As much as I want to stay here, I'm going to have to go back to be nearer Stephen,' he said.

I could tell he was worried about his son and felt sorry for him – he desperately wanted to make his new life with me work but deep down knew his responsibility was to Stephen, who was just ten.

'If that is what you feel then you must go,' I told him.

A year into our relationship, my understanding of his situation convinced Terry that I was with him for good. Until then, he couldn't quite comprehend why a young woman with no ties would fall in love with him, older, separated and a dad. But I never questioned his resolve to be with his son – it was part of what made me love him – and that, he said, showed him he could finally trust me.

After a transfer to Tesco in Cosham, near Portsmouth, Stephen

21

was still unsettled and so we went back to Salisbury where Terry got a job with an independent bakery and I worked in the adjoining shop.

A year later in January 1986 it was decided that Stephen was going to come and live with us. Martin wanted to stay with his mum but we'd agreed that Stephen would live with us during the week and return to his mum's at weekends. At twenty-two – just twelve years older than him – I was scared about becoming a stepmum.

'Is he trying to tear us apart?' I'd anxiously ask Terry.

'He's my son, I can't turn him away,' he told me.

Knowing I had a choice to stay or go, I decided to stick with it.

Stephen arrived with a small bag of clothes and, because we were in a one-bedroom flat, he was installed in a bed in an alcove in the sitting room. I can vividly remember the first meal I cooked for him. It was a roast dinner complete with broad beans, carrots and swede but Stephen obviously wasn't impressed.

'I don't like that and I'm not eating that,' he said as he stared at his plate.

Sternly, Terry replied, 'Right, son, if you are going to live with us then you will eat what we eat and if you don't like it you will go without.'

Silently Stephen ate his food without further complaint.

But while he might have eaten his greens, I was still worried. I'd never had anyone to look after full-time before, the responsibility felt daunting and I was unsure how to handle the situation. But I fell back on the only thing I knew – the lessons my mum had taught me in childhood – and so I ironed his uniform, polished his school shoes, made sure he washed his neck, packed up his lunch for school and took an interest in his schoolwork.

As the months wore on, even though I nagged him a lot and there were times he'd scream that I was not his mother, we learned to get by, and after that we learned to get on. Stephen lived with us for seven years and to this day still sends me a card every Mother's Day to thank me for what I did. I will always be proud of my 'son'.

*

Smiling, I pressed my swollen belly against Terry's back. It was July 1989 and I was eight months pregnant with our first child. Sometimes I'd put Terry's hand on my stomach so he could feel the baby move, but on other occasions I would wrap myself around his back in bed so he could feel the kicking.

'Eergh,' he said and wriggled away. My moving stomach always scared him a little.

It was 5 a.m. and Terry was just about to get up for the start of another twelve-hour shift at the bakery in a new Tesco store that was set to open in a couple of months. He was busy training staff and setting up equipment while I was on maternity leave, counting down the days to the birth.

Earlier that year we'd moved with Stephen into a two-bedroom council flat in Winterbourne Gunner, a village about three miles outside Salisbury, and I was busy nesting – spring cleaning, clearing out cupboards and stocking up on baby supplies. I was so excited.

Early the previous year I'd suffered a miscarriage and the experience had left both Terry and me saddened. I was rushed to hospital in an ambulance after starting to bleed heavily at home when I was ten weeks pregnant.

But now we were about to start a new life with a new baby and I couldn't wait.

We'd married on 21 March 1987 – booking an early slot at the registry office so Terry and his friends wouldn't miss the afternoon horse racing on television. Even his best man Steve Crouch was the manager of the local bookies. To this day, Terry still puts a bet on every day.

He was the one who had wanted us to marry. I'd been happy to carry on living with him and could stubbornly see no point in changing things when we were so happy together and Terry had only just come out of a marriage. But he had a traditional outlook on life and was anxious for us not to 'live in sin'. Then, as now, he was a traditionalist who wanted to live his life according to what society expected of him. My dad, who had continued to disapprove of my relationship with Terry while we lived together, changed his opinion as soon as we got engaged. After the distance between us, he couldn't do enough and I welcomed him back. But old habits die hard and even in the car on the way to the wedding he told me it wasn't too late to turn back.

'No, Dad,' I replied. 'I love Terry and I'm going to marry him.'

It wasn't a big wedding. We couldn't afford much and there were just twenty-one guests who went back to Terry's mum's house for a buffet lunch. The whole thing must have only cost £250 but it sent us into the red at the bank for the first time and I had to start married life by confessing to my new husband that I'd got us into debt. He moaned, groaned and then laughed. But it was a great day, and I loved every minute of married life.

Terry and I just clicked. I looked up to him, admired him and felt protected by him. I loved his clear blue eyes, his easy smile and his loving nature. The way he would wrap me up in his arms in the privacy of our home and the cups of tea he'd bring me in bed on our days off. It was never wine and roses, Terry wasn't a big romantic, but I felt safe with him.

Our holidays abroad were our most special time because then we could leave work behind. I'd never travelled before and each year we had two weeks together somewhere new. They were the highlight of our year. We lay on the beach in Benidorm, swam in the clear Aegean sea of the Greek islands and travelled to the pyramids. We were always laughing together and nothing could stop us – even when I forgot one of our suitcases on a holiday in Cyprus and had to make a dash back for it from the airport.

Back home, we had a good network of friends and family, a happy life and I couldn't wait for our first baby to complete it.

On 14 August 1989 I gave birth to our first daughter, Gemma.

It was a long labour. I was in hospital for almost twenty-four hours before the doctors decided to give me an emergency caesarean. But Terry's reaction made it all worthwhile. He was in cloud cuckoo land when he set eyes on his first daughter, and Stephen was the same. He was fourteen and loved his baby sister. I remember staring at the three most important people in my life and feeling so proud.

Gemma was a healthy 8 pounds 12 ounces and I had no trouble feeding her so after spending a week together in hospital we went home. I was a bit nervous about looking after a baby on my own but I made sure I listened to my mum and the midwives who came to visit. Gemma was a contented baby so life soon got into a routine.

Terry couldn't take his eyes off his daughter and even after a long shift would light up when he saw her.

During those early weeks I went out for a walk every day with Gemma in the buggy and Cindy our dog guarding the pram. We'd walk through the countryside on hot summer days and I would sometimes have to pinch myself, unable to believe my luck. I had given Terry a daughter, we had a nice flat and Stephen adored his new sister. Life was good.

But like any first-time mother, I was also anxious. I worried about whether I was doing things right – if Gemma was getting enough milk, whether she was warm enough, if she was gaining enough weight. It was a jolt to suddenly have a tiny, helpless baby who was wholly dependent on me, and it could at times make me feel anxious and a bit low.

The one area where I knew my mothering skills were less than perfect was monitoring Gemma's nappies. I loved washing them and hanging them out to dry to get the fresh air through them. Strange as it seems, glancing down from the kitchen window and seeing all the white terry towelling nappies hanging in a line and blowing on the breeze would fill me with a silly pride. I had brought another human being into the world. But my sense of smell has always been awful and unless my daughter was centimetres from me, I would never detect a dirty nappy. Terry and Stephen would take the mickey out of me mercilessly and deep down I felt a bit guilty – what kind of mum can't smell her babies' nappies?

But they would tease me out of my worries. I shouldn't doubt myself – I was doing okay.

It was a cold winter morning on 14 November 1989.

Terry had left early to start work and Stephen had gone to catch the bus to school.

I put Gemma into her baby sling and, carrying her close to me, got on the bus into Salisbury to do some shopping. Winterbourne Gunner had only one small shop and I needed to stock up on fresh vegetables. We got back around 10.30 a.m. and about half an hour later I put Gemma down for a nap in her cot in our bedroom before getting on with the housework.

About two hours later I went in to have a look at her. I don't know why I went in. Maybe I had a feeling, I just don't know, but I crept into the bedroom to check on my daughter.

Gemma was lying on her back completely still. I reached out to touch her because I thought she was asleep and with that one movement knew something was terribly wrong. She was very pale and not moving.

Panicked, I rushed into the living room and rang an ambulance before phoning Terry and telling him to come home.

It felt like an eternity as I waited for help to arrive. I had no idea what to do and even to this day, I cannot remember exactly what happened. It's all a blur, fuzzy.

I'm sure most mums would think they'd remember every second of such awful events, that the day they lost their baby would be etched on their memory for ever. But throughout everything I have never been able to. Maybe it was because I was in a state of shock, maybe it's because it was so long ago – seventeen years – or maybe it's because I didn't want to accept what was happening then, and still don't deep down, so I've blocked it all out.

These are the flashes of what I can remember.

Feeling absolutely helpless because I had no idea what to do.

Praying that everything would be all right and somewhere still thinking it would be.

The ambulance arriving and Gemma wrapped in a blanket being carried into it.

A room at the hospital. A cold, old-fashioned room with big windows.

Terry and my parents waiting with me in the room until a doctor came in to see us.

Just flashes of that awful day are all that remain.

'Gemma has died,' the doctor told us. 'There was nothing you could have done. Do not blame yourselves. It was Sudden Infant Death Syndrome.'

I'd never heard of SIDS – or cot death – before but the doctor explained that some babies went to bed, stopped breathing and no one knew why. I was utterly confused. How could a healthy baby go to sleep and never wake up? In 1989 cot death had nowhere near the profile it does now. There were no information campaigns and I was simply astounded the doctors were saying, 'Yes, your healthy baby has died but no we can't tell you why.'

Then a nurse asked if we would like to see our daughter and we went into a side room with a screen at the end of the bed. Behind it was a wicker moses basket, like the one we'd had for Gemma when she was first born, and she was in it looking so peaceful – as if she was asleep. Only one feeling overwhelmed me when I looked at her – I just wanted to take her out of there, take her home and say, 'It's all right, you're back with us now, where you belong.'

The hurt and bewilderment on Terry's face was one of the hardest things to bear. That morning he'd gone to work and kissed his daughter goodbye. Now we had lost her, and all we could do was walk away and leave her in that room. It wasn't our room. It wasn't where she was supposed to be.

The next time I saw Gemma was in the Chapel of Rest. I was with my mum and sister because Terry couldn't bear to go. She looked so different, lying in a white coffin with a white net over the top, wearing a white outfit, with red on her lips and cheeks. Gemma didn't look at all how I remembered her. Maybe she's okay, maybe I can take her home, I thought to myself before realising where I was and knowing that I never could.

I placed a silver bracelet Terry and I had bought Gemma into her coffin and Claire and Mum also put mementoes inside before we turned, went home and started the awful process of trying to come to terms with how much we'd lost. Losing a baby isn't just about losing that tiny person – it's about losing your dreams, your hopes for the future, and your faith in yourself as a parent when no one can explain to you why they died.

Eight days later we buried Gemma in the cemetery of St Mary's Church in Winterbourne Gunner. It was a tiny church and our family and friends were packed inside. Days earlier, our local vicar John Walton had come to our flat to talk to us. We weren't church-goers but John was unfailing in his empathy, guidance and kind heart, and was to become one of our greatest friends and supporters during the years that followed.

We walked from the flat to the church and I remember holding onto Terry every step of the way, my eyes blinded by tears. As we approached the grass path leading up to the church gate I could see friends lined along it and beyond was the church door where I saw the funeral car pull up.

As it drew to a stop I saw Gemma's tiny coffin in the huge black hearse and it seemed so out of place, this miniature white box which contained my beautiful daughter. It couldn't be happening.

Later, after the funeral service, my dad carried the coffin out to the graveyard and we said prayers at the graveside before each throwing a single white rose into the grave and seeing Gemma lowered into the earth.

As I stood at the graveside, the only thing I could think about was God. I'd grown up, given up so much of my young life to the church and any anger I felt was directed at Him. He dominated my thoughts and even as the earth closed over my precious daughter I couldn't bring myself to fully accept that she had gone.

I had never felt so empty.

CHAPTER THREE

I lay in the bath and stared as the warm water closed over my cae-sarean scar – the bright red gash was all I had left of Gemma. In the weeks and months since her death, Terry and I had tried to get back to normal, but the death of a baby rips a hole into your life that nothing can ever truly repair. I felt hollowed out, stripped of my motherhood and everything I had looked forward to. In one day, our little family had been destroyed and I had no idea how we would ever recover. I felt bare, separated from everything. I had been a mum and it was all gone.

The doctors had told us there was nothing we could have done for Gemma – her death was inexplicable, a cot death, a bereave-ment which had torn through our life with no rhyme or reason. But I found the not-knowing the hardest thing and constantly wondered what I had done wrong, replaying time and again events leading up to our daughter's death. Tiny little happenings kept nagging me – the injections Gemma had had the day before she died, the stinking nappy I'd changed. But despite going over it time and again, I could never come up with a conclusive expla-nation for the chasm that had opened up in our lives.

The doctors don't know why we lost her, so why should you? I told myself as I tried to quell the constant questioning. But deep down I felt I had failed as a mum because I was the one person who should have been able to tell why my baby had died and I couldn't.

Terry and I returned to work within weeks of losing Gemma – anxious to retreat into the reality we'd known before her birth. But we knew it never could be so and we spent hours pouring out our grief to John Walton. He didn't come with a religious view to push down our throats or a message to drive home. Instead he simply sat and listened quietly as we talked and talked about the death of our child, seeking comfort from each other and a way out of the maze of our grief. I needed Terry then more than I ever had and, as I had always known it would, my love for him sustained me.

Stephen was also heartbroken. My dad had told him the news about Gemma when he arrived home from school on the day we lost her. Terry and I had both gone to see our mums and the fourteen-year-old schoolboy put a brave face on it when my father spoke to him. But as soon as Terry put his arms round Stephen later in the day, he burst into tears. I knew he missed his sister deeply.

Gradually as the months passed, I started to function again, and as time slowly slipped by I realised I wanted to have another child. Terry had awoken in me a powerful maternal instinct and I was anxious to provide for him the loving family environment we had both been brought up in. Terry was hesitant about trying again but he could see I was desperate to be a mum. Nine months after Gemma's death I discovered I was pregnant.

'So what would you say was the optimum baking temperature in my oven at home?' the surgeon asked as he peered over the screen shielding my stomach.

It was 25 April 1991 and I was lying in Salisbury District Hospital about to have a caesarean. I had been desperate to deliver my second baby naturally but the doctors had said it would be a risky breech birth. As Terry sat beside me, the medics enthusiastically sought his advice on their baking endeavours as they started the operation. All I could feel was tugging behind the screen as they chatted until suddenly a baby's bottom was lifted towards me.

'You have a son,' the nurse said. 'Do you have a name for him?'

'Yes. Jason Terry,' I proudly replied, as Terry took his son in his arms and, for the first time since Gemma's death, I felt almost whole again. I had nurtured my baby, carried him for nine months and here he was. He was part of me and no one could take that away. Once again nature had worked her fascinating magic and I looked proudly on as Terry cuddled our son.

I started breastfeeding Jason as soon as we got back to the ward and the apprehension that had tinged my hope for the previous nine months melted away. It was as immediately natural with him as it had been with Gemma. For me, breastfeeding my children was always one of the defining moments of my motherhood because they depended on me to nurture them. I never did it for long because my milk went quickly, but for those first few weeks of my children's lives, I knew I was giving them a good start. I had met women in hospital who said they could never do it, while to me it was the most natural thing in the world. But everybody is different and I found it fascinating to see the various ways in which women mothered their children.

After a week in hospital we returned home. Jason had been diagnosed with loose hips and had to wear an Aberdeen splint – a plastic contraption that fitted over his nappy and forced his legs into a Y-shape. We were given our first apnoea alarm and I found having it comforting. Everyone kept telling me that if anything happened I would be alerted. I had also been shown resuscitation techniques, although I'd found it hard to take them in – flashes of Gemma kept stealing into my mind as I looked at the dummy. But the information, plus constant reassurances that we wouldn't lose another child to cot death, meant I had gone some way to quietening the constant worry that had been with me throughout the pregnancy. I made myself stop asking too many questions once Jason was born because I didn't want to become paranoid. I realised I needed to draw a line between everyday life and managing the worry. You put it into a box at the back of your mind because otherwise you know it will be too much, and instead you concentrate on the little milestones towards normality – the moment when Jason was in my arms, when he breastfed for the first time, when he came home. The worry was there, of course, but I tried as hard as I could to let it go. Jason, I told myself, is healthy and happy. Finally our family life could begin again.

Just five weeks later I heard the apnoea alarm sound its high-pitched wail. I was in the garden pegging out washing and it was as if I had suddenly been thrown into ice-cold water – the quick sucking in of breath as your body reacts to shock. I started running up the garden, desperate to reach the alarm and make it stop. I had put Jason down for a sleep in our bedroom earlier that morning.

I ran in to find him pale and still. Switching off the alarm, I picked him up and lifted him onto the bed. Panic gripped me, rendering me unable to respond. I tried to remember what I had been shown but as I stared at him I heard a car and went to the window to see our health visitor Gloria Peacock getting out. She had been due to visit that morning and I ran to open the door to her – Gloria had arrived, she was my health visitor and I went to her for help. Everything was going to be all right.

'It's happened again,' I said as I opened the door.

As Gloria rushed into the bedroom, she told me to go and call an ambulance and I ran into the sitting room where I dialled 999 before ringing Terry. Those next few minutes are a daze. All I can remember is watching helplessly as Gloria gave my tiny son mouth-to-mouth resuscitation and feeling Jason in my arms after he started breathing again. There is so much I cannot recall, so many details that have been lost – such as the fact that I apparently ran to the bathroom to retch after Terry arrived. I can only imagine that terror overcame me as it seemed the unimaginable might be happening again. But, like the day of Gemma's death, much of this day is a blank.

The next thing I remember was the paramedics wrapping Jason in tin foil as Terry and I climbed into the ambulance with my mind screaming: this cannot be happening, it just cannot be happening.

He was rushed into the recovery room and about twenty minutes later the doctors came in to see us. All they could say was that his body temperature was low and he must have picked up a bug. By now the panic had subsided and I was blaming myself for what had happened, but the hospital staff kept telling me he would be fine, that I had had a shock and there was nothing I could have done. Like all the times before and after, until the day of Matthew's death, I was treated with absolute compassion when one of my children was taken into hospital.

Two days later the doctors told us all the tests had proved negative and we could take Jason home. But however hard I tried to quell my fears I knew something was not right. He just wasn't the same baby as before. He was not feeding properly and looked distressed every time I winded him. He was off colour and seemed out of sorts.

I told myself not to be paranoid but, however hard I tried to stifle the fears, they kept returning. Increasingly I felt as if I was failing Jason because I knew something was wrong but could not pin down exactly what. Call it maternal instinct, call it sixth sense, but I – like most mothers – knew my baby. Even Terry could see there was something wrong and I felt strangely reassured when he commented on how off colour Jason seemed.

Three days later I tried to talk to a visiting midwife about my fears.

'There's something terribly wrong,' I said as I broke down into floods of tears. 'I just know there's something wrong.'

'Angela, he's fine,' she cooed at me. 'It will take a while to get his system back to normal but there's really nothing to get upset about. I know you're worried after losing Gemma but this time it's different – it won't happen again. You must stop worrying yourself.'

I told myself that I would talk to the doctors when I took Jason in for a check-up in a few days' time. But however much I kept telling myself I should listen to the experts, my gut instinct said something was terribly wrong, and for one awful week I could only wait anxiously, convinced something was going to happen to my child.

*

I was having breakfast when I heard the alarm go off – the second electronic scream to rip open my world in a week. It was 13 June and Terry had already left for work. As I ran into the bedroom, I saw the red light flashing on the apnoea alarm and turned Jason over to find him completely floppy and drained of colour. There was nothing. No movement at all.

'No, Jason, please don't do this to me,' I whispered, as I ran with him into the living room.

Whereas the week before I had frozen, this time I was determined that Jason would not die as Gemma had before him. Everything else fell away as I crouched over my baby and began mouth-to-mouth resuscitation. Over and over I put my mouth onto his and pressed my two fingers into his tiny chest. Each time I could see his chest rise and each time I thought he was going to start breathing on his own, but then he would be still again and I would reach down once more.

Why isn't this working? my mind shrieked. I've got to make him all right again. I've got to.

Angrily, I wiped away tears that blurred my vision and breathed once again into his tiny mouth before watching for signs that he was responding. I would not give up. I would not lose. Jason was not going to leave me. I was not going to be left alone again.

But panic filled me when I realised he was not responding. Just like the previous week, I went to pieces as I stared down at Jason and saw he wasn't breathing.

Sometime during those awful minutes Terry rang home and I cried at him to call an ambulance. I returned to Jason. How long I was there I do not know. The world had closed into that one fixed point between me and my son. Dimly I was aware of the paramedics arriving and, as they tried to move towards us, I refused to allow them near.

'I'm looking after him.' My mind screamed. 'He's mine and I will make him all right again. Don't touch him, he's mine.'

One of the men came to my side and tried to pull me to my feet.

'Let us deal with this now,' he said. 'We need to carry on.'

I heard Terry's voice behind me.

'It's no good, Ange,' he whispered. 'He's gone. You've got to come away.'

Wordlessly I ran into the bathroom, where I crouched down in front of the toilet and vomited. It had happened again. As a cold sweat settled lightly over my skin and I slumped to the floor, I could hear the thump of a helicopter propeller overhead as an air ambulance arrived to take Jason to hospital. Then there were the noises of the paramedics as they desperately tried to breathe life where I knew it had drained hopelessly away.

The weeks and months after Jason's death were a horrifying repetition of what had happened to us before. We mourned him in the same church where we had mourned Gemma, we buried him in the same plot where she lay, my father carried the coffin and we laid white roses, and once again our family, friends and doctors told us there was nothing we could have done.

But all I could feel was an overwhelming sense of failure because yet again I had not protected my child from harm – something had killed my babies and, while the medics could not tell me what it was, I believed I should have been able to save them.

Terry and I moved blindly through life, comforting each other as best we could and drawing closer together, but unable to forget the awful loss we shared. Once more we were a couple when we should have been a family and this time I found it very hard to return to work. It felt as if there were mums and babies everywhere I looked and the pain stabbed deep inside me. I should have been like those women – at home looking after my baby, out shopping with my baby, going for walks with Cindy and my baby – and instead I was working. I had given birth to two beautiful children and yet I was alone.

Once again my anger was directed at God and, although I had long stopped going to church, I returned to my faith in quiet moments only to rail against what He had allowed to happen. Sometimes, as I walked Cindy in the fields near our house – the same fields where I had once walked with Gemma and Jason in the pram – I would talk to Him out loud, hurling the same questions repeatedly.

'Why are you doing this to me? What did I do so wrong? Why do we deserve this hurt?'

It's difficult to describe but I no longer felt whole inside. I was spiritually broken and I retreated into myself to survive. I searched and searched for a reason why I had lost my children. I think to this day that if somebody had given me one I would have dealt with my grief differently. I believe part of you dies with your child, and when we lost Jason I knew, as I had with Gemma, that I had lost a part of myself I would never get back.

Six months later we were visited by John Emery, a professor of paediatric pathology at the University of Sheffield, who also did work with the Foundation for the Study of Infant Deaths. A kindly bearded man in his sixties, he was considered one of the country's leading experts on cot deaths. We spent an entire day talking over what had happened.

'There are things you can do to help decrease the odds of ever losing a child again,' he told us. 'You should stop smoking for a start and move house. But most importantly you should give yourselves a proper amount of time to grieve. I'm talking about three or four years in which to recover from Gemma and Jason's deaths before trying for another baby.'

Importantly, Professor Emery also told us that we were not alone – that other families had also lost two or more children to cot death. No one could tell us it wouldn't happen again, but at last we knew we were not the only parents to suffer such losses and it was a huge comfort to me. Until then I had believed we were unique and it had added to my sense of failure. His visit also helped Terry greatly. After Jason's death he felt he could never have a child again, could never put me or himself through the grief of another bereavement. But Professor Emery was the first medical person to offer Terry hope that we could do a lot to help ourselves avoid tragedy for a third time – and convinced him that we might have a future.

Through the years that followed life moved on and we had to move with it. Losing even one child is something you never forget, but as time passed we gradually learned to live with our loss. There were low days, of course, but Terry and I drew on each other and became closer than ever – our love strengthened by the fact that the other was the only person in the world with whom we truly shared our pain. In a strange way we became quite selfish in those years. We consciously indulged all our pleasures and enjoyed holidays, nights out and time with our friends and family in a way we knew we never could have done if our children had lived. It was almost a rebellion against the pain – we'd lost Gemma and Jason but were determined to enjoy our life because, despite it all, we were still together. It was our way of moving on – abandoning the selflessness that children require and concentrating on living life to the full. Other things fell into perspective, too, and whereas money and financial security had always been important to us, our experiences told us it wasn't everything. Terry continued to work long and hard but it wasn't all consuming in the way it had been at times in the past. I knew he felt guilty because in Gemma and Jason's short lives he had put work first, and he vowed it would never happen again.

On Professor Emery's advice, we sold our flat and bought a three-bedroom house in Durrington – another village 12 miles outside Salisbury – and spent a lot of time doing it up, fixing the double-glazing, having a patio laid and redecorating all the bedrooms.

We also spent a great deal of time with our friends Terry and Gill Chambers – holidaying in Cyprus in 1993 and spending weekends with them. They were like us in many ways – there was a ten-year age gap between them and Terry Chambers had also been previously married, so we had a lot in common. They were great for us during those years and we had so much fun with them.

We filled our time in other enjoyable ways too – going to see Terry's, and also by now my, beloved Meat Loaf play in London, Brighton and Birmingham, spending nights in the pub playing skittles and watching Southampton football team play. We also fell in love with *The Rocky Horror Picture Show*, so much that we organised a coach to take all our work friends and family to see it. We all got dressed up in stockings and suspenders – all except Terry, of course, who said he'd never find a suspender belt big enough to fit him – and shrieked with laughter when Nicholas Parsons and the man from the Gold Blend adverts appeared on stage.

Things also changed for the people we loved. Stephen met his future wife Kellie and their first child Shannon was born in May 1994, followed by Lindon two years later. Other events were not so happy. My parents split up in 1996. As their children got older, the distance between them had become more apparent and, to be honest, I'd felt sorry for Mum because I believed she deserved more care and attention than my father gave her. But I also knew it was up to them to work it out, and I loved my dad so I didn't confront him. There was huge upset though when he moved in with a woman called Katherine, who was thirty years his junior, soon after the split. It was difficult to accept and I didn't really speak to Dad for about six months because of what had happened. Andrew in particular took the whole thing very hard. He was still living with my parents when they split up and had to finally become fully independent. They both remarried within a couple of years – Dad to Katherine and my mum to Brian. I felt they'd both got a new lease of life and was happy for them.

As for me, losing two children had left a mark which I feared would never heal. I never spoke openly about it but deep down felt different because I had had – and lost – two babies. Whereas my sister Tina had had two sons and our friends like Steve and Anthea Crouch and Steve and Jane Grant were all watching their family grow, Terry and I were not. No one showed any embarrassment or awkwardness about it, but I felt very conscious that we weren't following the natural path of life and I should have been with Gemma and Jason.

A sense of family had been instilled in me by my childhood, our extended family and looking after Stephen. And so while I knew that children weren't the be all and end all of life, mine didn't feel complete without them and I desperately wanted to give Terry a child – he was the man I loved and I felt a family would seal our relationship. We would watch our children grow as we grew old together.

Four years after Jason's death, Terry and I started to talk about having another baby. We knew we had done everything Professor Emery had advised us, and finally we began to dare to hope for our future. For a long time I had felt like a failure because I had brought babies into the world and they had been taken. But as the years passed a sense of deep emptiness once again opened up inside me and, while I was apprehensive, I also knew we had done everything asked of us. We deserved a future together. Terry and I had been happy together as a couple for more than ten years and I felt it was time to try again.

Jade was born on 15 January 1996 and I cannot describe how happy we were to have her. Terry was off work for the first few weeks of her life and it was a really important time for us. The doctors were also great and Jade was part of the Care of Next Infants scheme for a year. It meant an extra-special eye was kept on her and she was seen by health visitors fifteen times in the first two months of her life alone. We were also given open access to the children's ward at Salisbury District Hospital and I filled out a daily diary for some six months about her progress.

Her admission to hospital when she was three months old after I found her gasping for breath struck fear deep within us. Once again, we were reassured she was fine, but in the following weeks I felt a familiar terror rise up inside me that we were looking into the abyss of losing another child. But I consciously kept my fears under control and, when Jade was taken off the paediatrician's register after reaching her first birthday, it felt as if we had been given a green light to believe in normal family life once again. A new child can never replace another and I knew my grief would always be part of me. But I truly believed we had moved on at last.

The first two years of Jade's life were about enjoying her, watching her grow and letting the worry of cot death slowly ebb from our minds. She gave both Terry and me so much pleasure that eventually we started to talk about having a brother or sister for her. We didn't want Jade to be alone.

Matthew was born on 5 July 1999 and once again the doctors offered to make him part of the CONI scheme. But we thought better of it. I had found it so stressful with Jade – a constant reminder of our sad past – and now we had to look forward, be normal once again. Life was finally complete. Terry, I and our two beautiful children were a family at last.

For a split second when I woke on the morning after Matthew's death, I thought my world was still complete. In those first waking moments of 13 November 1999, as I hovered between a fitful sleep and wakefulness, I was in the life I should have been living. My two children were sleeping in the bedroom next door and I was waking up to another day as their mother. But then I realised Jade had not run into the room, I could not hear Matthew's gurgles, our home was utterly silent – and reality flooded back in. The constant background hum two young children create had disappeared and Terry and I were alone. I felt completely empty.

All I could think about was Jade. How was she? When would we be able to see her? Would she ever understand why Mummy and Daddy had left her on the day her brother died?

And then I thought of Matthew, alone in that huge hospital with only strangers to look at him.

'I've got to go and see him,' I said to Terry, who was downstairs smoking a cigarette, looking as shell-shocked as he had the night before.

'I know Dad went to see him last night and the formal identification is done but I must see Matthew.'

I didn't know it then but Tina and Andrew had gone up to the mortuary with my father only to be told not to approach or touch Matthew. All I was aware of was a desperate desire to visit my son – somewhere I think an irrational part of me believed that if I did so I would be able to bring him home and normal life could start again. Peace would be restored instead of this unbearable charade.

'I'm sorry, Ange, but I can't. I just can't go,' Terry replied.

Silence fell between us before he added, 'Jade's going to stay put with Jenny.'

Jade always liked going to stay with Terry's sister, who had picked her up the night before.

'She'll be back with us on Monday once the police have done what they need to do and when she is I'll be making a complaint about all this.'

I knew he was right. As much as we wanted Jade home with us, it was better to let the police finish so that she could return to a peaceful home. After all, everything would be sorted out soon enough.

'Okay, I'll go up to the hospital with Claire. She wants to say goodbye,' I replied, before finally daring to whisper the question that had hung between us ever since I had found Matthew lifeless in his cot. 'Terry, how could this have happened again?'

'I don't know, Ange,' he replied. 'I just don't understand anything any more.'

'But I must have done something wrong,' I said. 'It must be me. Must be something I do.'

'You did nothing wrong,' were the only words Terry could muster.

His silence scared me. When we had lost Gemma and Jason we had talked endlessly about it and Terry had told me time and time again that I had nothing to blame myself for. But now what else was there for him to say? We'd been so sure that we had finally found happiness after Matthew was born that I'd been sterilised.

I'd suffered a setback when I'd contracted an infection following the operation in October. It had laid me low and, as I struggled to get better, I'd tearfully wondered if I could cope with a baby and a lively toddler. The doctor had prescribed me an anti-depressant but I'd taken only one before deciding they were not for me. Terry and I had always worked through our problems and we'd do so again.

Now it seemed as if we were being punished for a third time for believing we had a right to a normal life. It was too shocking for us to try and put into words. We instinctively knew we could never begin to explain it. During those first few days after Matthew's death we simply existed. No more.

As I left the room, paranoia and disbelief crowded into my brain and a voice – which would accompany me for months to come – started echoing in the back of my head.

'It's happened again,' it intoned. 'When will you accept that you and Terry just aren't supposed to be together? Everyone said it all those years ago and now they're being proved right. What's wrong with you? How can you carry a baby for nine months with no complications and no problems for this to happen again?

'There must be something wrong with you, with your body. It's got to be you. You'll never be allowed the family you want because someone up above is saying no. Just accept it – you're never going to be allowed happiness.'

The lift doors opened with a dull thud to reveal a long, cold corridor and we silently stepped out onto the shiny floor. I was back at Salisbury District Hospital with Claire and Gill Dawson, the policewoman we'd met the night before, who was our family liaison officer – there to help us while the police finished their enquiries. Claire and I had planned on going up to the hospital to see Matthew alone but Gill had insisted on driving us.

'I'll take you,' she said, as we stood in the living room. 'It's no problem at all. The car's just outside.'

We went into a waiting room where a softly spoken nurse guided me towards a door leading into a tiny side room. On my right was a small frosted window and on the left a high table with a cross and a moses basket on it. Claire began to cry when she saw the basket and her sobs came faster and faster as she reached over and looked down at Matthew. Instinctively I took her hand, clicking into the protective big sister role I'd always played with her, desperate to soothe her wracking sobs.

'Why?' she kept saying. 'Why did this happen? He's so beautiful, Ange.'

Every part of me resisted looking into that basket and I concentrated on comforting Claire, grateful for a diversion from what we were in that room to do. But as I did so I realised Gill Dawson was standing slightly behind us in the corner of the room with a notebook and pen and, staring silently at me, she looked down and started making notes. I glanced confusedly at the nurse who looked back at me, unable to explain with a glance what Gill was doing. I just didn't understand it. My sister was sobbing for her dead nephew and she was taking notes? I was standing in front of the body of my child and she was writing things down? I had absolutely no idea why she was doing it but a wave of nausea washed over me as I realised she was recording this moment in the crisp white pages of a police notebook.

I lowered my eyes to Matthew and as I looked down an overwhelming sense of love jostled with anger inside me. My other two babies had died when they were tiny but at eighteen weeks old Matthew had moved past being a newborn and started to develop his own personality. How could he be gone? I was here to take him home again, wasn't I?

A hot rush of rage filled me – the first real feeling to flood my senses since finding Matthew lifeless in his cot. But still I resisted the undeniable truth of that moment. Desperate to escape it, I would not allow myself to touch my baby and feel the physical proof of what my heart could not accept – the marble cool of his once warm skin. All I wanted to do was reach out, pick him up and take him home. But as I stood in that tiny room listening to Claire weep, I finally realised Matthew was never coming home and for a third time I was going to have to bury one of my children. I started to cry.

For the rest of that weekend, I went through the motions of 'real' life. Family visited, I made cups of tea, Terry and I looked at each other in confusion and I broke down every time Matthew or Jade's names were mentioned. But I was frozen inside – simply going through the mechanics of living when everything had drained away inside me. Gill Dawson came to see us again and so did the child protection officer Graham Fisher, who took another statement from Terry. The police had taken some of Matthew's things away, like his all-in-one, and when our relatives wondered out loud what they were doing, Terry and I kept reassuring them it was just all routine. They needed to find out how Matthew had died and we must let the authorities do their job.

'Why is this happening to us?' I sobbed one afternoon as I sat with Stephen on a bench in the garden. 'How could we have lost him? What are we going to say to Jade when she comes home?'

'I don't know, Ange,' he replied, as he put his arm around me. 'But everything will get sorted out. The police will find out what happened to Matthew. You're a great mum. You must never blame yourself.'

We fixed our thoughts on Monday when we expected Jade home and the results of a post-mortem. But the day came and went without Jade's return and it wasn't until late afternoon that Gill Dawson finally came to see us.

Our hearts sank when she told us the pathologist could not establish how Matthew had died. We knew it meant Jade would not be coming home.

'The result of the post-mortem is unascertained,' she told us as we sat looking blankly at her.

'What do you mean?' I asked.

'No cause of death has been found and so we need to do more tests. It will take some time,' Gill replied.

'But if you can't find anything why are you continuing with the tests?' said Terry. 'Nothing was found with Gemma and Jason so it must be a cot death again. When are you going to finish? Jade needs to be back home.'

We were desperate to see her, talk to her, touch her – it was now three long days since Matthew had died and we had had no contact with her. But it never occurred to us to challenge the police. Grief and a lifetime of following the rules made us silently submit to yet more waiting and we heavy-heartedly accepted that it would be at least another day before they finished their enquiries and Jade was returned to us.

It was about 10.30 a.m. the next day when the doorbell rang and

Claire and I peered out of the kitchen to see Gill Dawson and Rob Findlay. I was expecting them, but as they stepped into the house, my sister and I exchanged a quick glance – our eyebrows raised in surprise at Gill's outfit. She was wearing a navy dress with a long jacket over it, full make-up and her blonde shoulder-length hair was perfectly done. She looked strangely out of place in our little house.

'Angela, I need to talk to you, there is something I need to say,' said DS Findlay, as he motioned me towards the lounge where Terry was standing.

As I sat on the sofa, he crouched down on a footstool opposite me and Gill looked on from the other side of the room. I braced myself for what was coming next. Finally someone was going to give me a proper reason why one of my children had died – tell me that an infection, something in his system, a weakness he had been born with had killed Matthew and we could begin to grieve. After all these days in limbo, it was finally going to end and Jade would come home to comfort us with her bubbling, three-year-old presence. I took a deep breath and looked at Rob.

'As a result of our enquiries and because of the nature of the deaths of your children I am arresting you on suspicion of the murder of Gemma, Jason and Matthew Cannings,' he said, as he gently took my hand in his and a wail ripped open the silence.

I looked up blankly, the breath punched from my body, as Claire started screaming.

'You can't do this,' she shouted. 'You can't do this.'

I stared back at Rob Findlay. There was no triumph in his eyes, no glimmer of victory you might expect from a man who had just apprehended a mother suspected of the worst possible crime. Instead he looked at me softly as my whole body crumpled in dis-belief that I was being arrested. I started to cry as one emotion pierced my emptiness – anger.

How dare you? I wanted to scream. We've done everything you asked. How dare you come into my house and arrest me for the murder of my children? I loved my babies. I only ever loved them.

But I said nothing as I stood up and followed DS Findlay when he told me we needed to go to the station.

'What about me?' Terry asked.

'We don't need to talk to you about any criminal matter,' came the reply. 'But you'll need to come with us to meet the social worker who's been put in charge of Jade's case.'

Terry looked at the officers in horror. For us, ordinary people who'd worked, paid our taxes and never put a foot wrong, the words 'social services' were horrifying. We knew nothing about that world, it was for people who abused and neglected their children, didn't want them, not us.

'I did nothing wrong, Terry,' I said as I was led away and put into the back of an unmarked police car with Claire beside me. I was so shocked at what was happening and I knew he would feel the same. I just wanted to reassure him – to hear the words said out loud so that he would never doubt me.

As we sat in the car, Claire gripped one hand as Rob Findlay held the other – an oddly comforting gesture from the man who had just arrested me for murder. I sat silent – unable to take in what was happening.

After arriving at Salisbury police station, I was led in through a back door and up to a counter where an officer stood. Fear washed over me as I caught a glimpse of cells with bars on the door. Suddenly I realised where I was.

They must think you've done something wrong, a voice inside whispered.

How could they? my mind answered back. They could never think that. I've done nothing. It's just a mistake.

I was introduced to a friendly woman in her mid-twenties called Elaine Hattersley, a legal assistant at a local firm of solicitors called Pye-Smiths. She was going to sit in while the police questioned me.

'You need to tell me everything, Mrs Cannings,' she said. 'I need a full history of what has happened. You must tell me everything you can remember about your babies.'

'Please tell me what is going on?' I replied. 'Why is this happening to me?'

As we sat and talked a police doctor also arrived to see if I was well enough to be interviewed. I insisted I was able to continue. I wanted to tell everyone that I had not killed my children. How could I have been arrested for murder? Later I signed a form giving permission for our house to be searched. I had nothing to hide.

About an hour later I was taken into a different room, which looked as if it had been transported from a TV set. There was a frosted window high up on one wall and a table with a tape recorder on it in the middle of the room. Two CID officers sat grim-faced behind it. They were as different as chalk and cheese. One was tall with a bit of a tummy and jet-black curly hair, the other was short with thinning hair and a bald patch. Both looked in their mid-forties. The shorter one put a tape into the machine and the questions started.

'So did you have a happy childhood, Mrs Cannings? What was it like being in a family of four? Tell us about Claire and Andrew's health problems.'

'What were your teens like? Did you have boyfriends? Was there anyone you fancied? Who did you babysit for?'

'How are things with Terry? Did you get on with Stephen? What happened on the day you miscarried? You've been sterilised, haven't you?'

'Tell us about Gemma, Mrs Cannings, tell us about Jason, tell us about Matthew.'

I didn't know where the police had got all their information about me but their questions seemed to go on and on. Elaine had warned me they might seem harsh but even so I was surprised at just how many questions the officers were asking. Again and again they kept coming back to my medical history – appendicitis, a mouth rash, glandular fever and a broken wrist – they even asked me about a swollen toe I'd had fifteen years before. I couldn't remember all the details.

But, horrifying as it was, I felt as if I was on the outside looking in, watching myself in a TV drama. I told myself to pull myself together as I started to sob. All I needed to do was tell the truth and answer as fully as I could. By 6 p.m. I had gone through my whole life history – my childhood, my puberty, my relation-ships, the births and deaths of my three children.

It meant nothing. Days before I had lost my third child and everything else seemed meaningless. I answered blindly, stumbling back in my mind to all those years ago as I tried to answer the officers' questions, dredging up tiny details from those awful days up to a decade before which were a blank in parts. For more than four hours I sat and told the officers all I knew.

'All we ever wanted to know was why,' I told them. 'They were healthy babies and we had nothing to cling onto.'

When we had finished, the officers left the room before return-ing to say I was going to be released on police bail pending further enquiries. Like so many other things that day, the words washed over me – their significance lost in the chaos of my grief and utter confusion. But I bristled to attention when Gill Dawson walked into the room and said: 'You will be released on police bail because we haven't finished our investigations. That means you will have to fulfil certain conditions but you have a choice. Either you can go back with Terry to your family home and Jade will go into care, or you will leave this police station and live away from your family home with no direct contact with her. You will be able to see her on supervised visits only.'

I sat there stunned. Who was this woman to tell me I couldn't be with my husband and daughter? That someone was going to have to supervise me like a criminal when I wanted to see Jade?

I looked up.

'There is no way my daughter is going into care,' I told her. 'Jade needs to be with her daddy and I will do anything so that she can stay at home with him. Don't take her away. I'll leave.'

I was escorted back out to the counter and given a sheet telling me that I had to report to the police station again at the end of January. When all the paperwork was done, I was taken into a waiting room at the front of the station where Dad, Claire, Kevin, Andrew and John Walton were all waiting for me.

I have never seen a man of the cloth explode before but John started shouting at Rob Findlay as soon we entered the room.

'What on earth do you think you are doing with this woman?'

he demanded. 'Don't you think she's been through enough? She has just lost her third child and you have the nerve to bring her to this police station. I will be complaining to your chief. It is absolutely disgraceful.'

'I am sorry that this is distressing for you all but there are procedures we have to follow,' was all Findlay could reply.

But as we left the station, Findlay walked up to me and said, 'Whatever you do, Mrs Cannings, do not lose your contact with Jade. Whatever happens from now on please keep your contact with her going. It is very important.'

As he squeezed my hand, I felt angry inside. Why was he treating me so kindly?

'Don't worry,' said Dad, as we walked from the police station to Claire's flat which, ironically, was just at the end of the road. 'It will be all right, love. We'll get it sorted. They know what they're doing. You'll be all right. Don't worry, this is all a huge mistake.'

Later that evening, after everyone had talked and talked round their outrage in a useless attempt to still it, Terry came to see me.

'Are you all right, love?' he asked as he put his arms around me.

'How's Jade?' I replied.

'She's okay,' he said. 'They brought her back to me while I was at my mum's and she seems fine. Gill Dawson drove us home. She even stopped on the way to buy Jade some sweets.'

I listened in disbelief as Terry told me he had met a social worker from Wiltshire social services who had been put in charge of Jade's case. Social services were now officially involved in our daughter's life because a care order had been taken out due to the police investigation into me. Jade was considered in need of protection because I was a threat to her. Essentially she was now the property of the courts and Terry had been told in no uncertain terms that unless he agreed to share his parental rights with the powers that be, he would lose our daughter. I sat, unable to utter a word.

'There's something else,' said Terry quietly. 'They've gone through the whole house. They've taken Matthew's cot, gone through his bedroom, the wardrobes, taken his changing mat, the nursery box, his apnoea alarm. They've gone into the kitchen cupboards and taken Calpol and paracetamol tablets. They've even taken a Barclaycard statement away with them, and Jade's comforter.'

I was utterly bewildered.

'Why?' I whispered. 'They treated me as though I was a common criminal today, Terry. They looked at me as if I've done something. They think I'm a murderer.'

'No,' he replied. 'They can't think like that. It will be fine. We'll get it all sorted out. It's all just a huge mistake.'

But panic filled me as I looked at him and realised he wasn't convinced about what he was saying. My chest constricted as I looked into Terry's eyes and saw worry there for the first time. After he left I climbed into the bed in Claire's spare room – the first night I had ever spent away from my family and my home. It would be more than four years before I slept again under the same roof as my husband and daughter. Silently, I cried myself into a dreamless sleep.

CHAPTER FOUR

'We cannot allow you to be alone with your daughter, Mrs Cannings,' the social worker said tonelessly. 'You will be able to see her for two hours three times a week with a social worker present at all times, and you will not be allowed to provide any intimate care for Jade such as giving her a bath or putting her to bed.

'I must stress, Mrs Cannings, how important it is that you abide by these conditions. If not, we will have to review the situation.'

It was five days since Matthew's death and I was finally going to see Jade. But, as the real-life mechanics at the heart of at-risk registers and protection orders was coldly laid bare, I felt my world cave in for a second time since finding him.

I was only going to be able to see Jade for six short hours a week – and I was going to be watched every minute. I was not going to be there all the time to chat to her, wash her clothes, play with her, feed her, read her a story and put her to bed – be her mum. It was unbelievable. Until five days before I'd been a full-time mother with two children, doing what millions of women did every day – my life finally, gloriously, ordinary. Now strangers were telling me when and how I could see my daughter.

'Why are you doing this?' I whispered.

'There is an on-going investigation, Mrs Cannings, and Jade's safety must be ensured,' came the reply.

I felt utter disgust. Dirty. They thought I was a threat to my daughter and, if I hadn't been so shocked, I would have laughed at the sheer ridiculousness of it all.

A few hours later, a social worker called Marlene brought Jade to Claire's flat for our first visit together. I had not seen her since the day of Matthew's death and I held her tightly, breathing in her comforting smell and never wanting to let her go. But, aware that I must not pass on my sadness, I forced myself to act as naturally as possible.

Soon we were playing with a dolly as the social worker watched us. She was in her mid-twenties and nice enough but for that precious hour I could not forget her presence. As I watched the minutes count down, relief that I was finally with Jade jostled with the strain of trying to behave as normally as possible.

'What have you done today, darling? What did you do at pre-school?' I asked her as we played.

'I did some painting and then me and Daddy had ham sand-wiches,' she solemnly replied.

'And have you watched *Teletubbies* today?'

'Yes. Tinky Winky fell over.'

We fell silent for a minute before she looked at me and asked, 'Is Matthew really a star in the sky, Mummy?'

'Yes, darling,' I told her softly. 'He's looking down on you and he's watching over you.'

Later I climbed down the three flights of stairs leading from Claire's flat to the front door with Jade's small hand clutched in mine. She had greeted me excitedly when she arrived but fell quiet as I put her into the car with Marlene watching. I could see she was upset.

'Why aren't you coming with Daddy and me?' she asked as I did up the straps on her car booster seat.

'Mummy's got to stay at Aunty Claire's house because we've got to work,' I replied, tears making my throat feel thick. 'But I'll be back home very soon, darling.'

Terry and I didn't say a word to each other as I closed the door. Every part of me longed to go with them but I could only stand and watch as my husband and daughter drove off – and I was left alone.

*

Six days after Matthew's death we arrived at Salisbury Magistrates Court for a hearing regarding an emergency protection order for Jade. It was another type of care order and replaced the police protection order which had been put in place on the day of my arrest. Later would come an interim care order – a dizzying array of administrative officialdom to cover one basic fact: the loss of our parental rights to social services and ultimately the courts.

'It's all just routine,' said Tony Luscott, the social worker who had been put in charge of Jade's case. A pony-tailed man in his late forties, he smoked a roll-up as he casually explained the legal decisions that would render us powerless as parents.

Earlier that morning Terry and I had met Bill Bache, the solicitor from Pye-Smiths who was acting for us. He was a tall man with a shock of white hair and a laidback manner. With his clipped vowels and thoughtful speech, he seemed reassuringly in charge of the situation. His legal assistant Jacqui Cameron was a glamorous Irish lady who gave off a no-nonsense air. The two, I thought, made a good team.

Bill explained that all the details of the care order covering Jade would be decided in the family courts. I had never really heard of them before but he explained they dealt with everything legal to do with families such as divorces, custody arrangements and care orders on children looked after by social services. To protect children, their hearings were closed to everyone except lawyers, parents and the judge, which was why they were seldom written about in the newspapers. We were about to go to a family proceedings hearing overseen by a magistrate, but cases could also be transferred to the county court or even the High Court in London.

We were ushered into a room with a huge table in the centre. I was surprised. I had expected everything to take place in a courtroom proper but this looked like somewhere a business meeting would be held. But in truth I hardly knew what to expect. The only other time I'd been to Salisbury Magistrates Court was when I was fifteen and a St John's Ambulance volunteer on a stall at a Christmas bazaar in the Guildhall next door. Terry was a bit more clued up about it all because he sometimes spent his day off from the bakery wandering round the court listening to proceedings. He was fascinated by the law and enjoyed peeking into the lives laid bare by legal cases. Now ours was one of them.

The meeting got under way as strangers started discussing Jade, Terry and me in impersonal tones. I sat listening in disbelief at the opinions they had seemingly formed about me – and the measures needed to protect my daughter – without ever meeting me. As they discussed Jade and what was in her best interests, I just wanted to scream: I know what's in her best interests, I am her mother and she should be with me.

Their complete matter-of-fact attitude was what struck me most. As they carried on their low-key discussions in measured tones, the fact that I had lost a child just a week before did not seem to figure. As I started to cry, no one gave me even a glance of comfort. Everyone – including the women – looked at me with coldness and no compassion. I hadn't even been charged with anything yet, let alone anything proved, and yet I felt I was silently being accused. I could feel the anger in the air.

Suddenly revulsion dripped down my spine as I realised what they all believed – that I was a murderer. My heart hammered in my chest as I looked around the room and saw that everyone in there thought I was capable of killing my children. I pushed down the nausea that rose in my throat.

Ridiculous as it seems, even after I was arrested I had never allowed myself to properly acknowledge the awful thought that someone would really believe I had deliberately harmed my children. But as I sat there one thing was absolutely clear to me. The investigation might be ongoing, but here I had already been tried and convicted. Later, as Terry drove me home, I would ask him to stop the car before leaning out and being sick in the road while he silently watched.

For Terry the sheer mechanics of being thrust from a two-parent to essentially a one-parent family were hard. Suddenly he found himself caring alone full-time for our little girl. The first morning he woke up with her in our home he simply cried. He said he felt totally useless as he realised that a seventy-hour working week in the bakery meant he had no idea about the tiny details that made up Jade's world. Because of his work, Terry had always been the early riser and, while he knew about the routine at the end of the day, he had no idea what happened at the beginning of it. What breakfast cereal did Jade like? What coat did she wear in what weather? Did she have a bath or a wash or nothing at all?

But he didn't keep running back to me with questions because he knew he had to work things out with Jade and, even though she was only approaching four, our little girl was quick to guide her forty-five-year-old father. She had always been a very independent child, wanting to do things like pick out her clothes for pre-school, so she was soon helping him do things.

'It's all right, Daddy, I can do it,' she would tell him as he tried in vain to tie her blonde hair back tidily.

'I'm trying to be happy for her but it's just such an act, Ange,' he told me when we finally had some time alone together on the first Sunday after I had left home.

'I'm so worried she'll pick up on what's happening that I'm like Coco the bloody Clown with her most of the time although I'm sure that somewhere she knows what's going on.'

As I reassured Terry everything would be fine, I found it hard to put my own worries to the back of my mind. In the five days since my arrest I had become increasingly paranoid about what he thought. Usually, of course, we'd have talked it over, but our enforced separation meant I had no idea what he was thinking and part of me worried that he had good reason to doubt me – for a third time I had been alone when our baby died.

He looked at me. 'I've wracked my brains about anything I did that could have hurt Matthew,' he said. 'Was the milk I gave him when I was looking after him the night before we lost him too hot? Was the banana too chunky? I did the same with Gemma and Jason.' He looked up and into my eyes. 'Is there anything you think you could have done, Ange?'

There was a long pause as panic and disbelief washed over me.

I couldn't believe we were having this conversation and fear gripped my throat tight – now even Terry was questioning what had happened. I'd told him I hadn't done anything as I was led away after my arrest and I couldn't believe he was asking me again.

As I sat looking at him, I fixed onto the one thing I was anxious about. I had been worrying for weeks about Matthew because he was constantly dribbling – cheeks inflamed, I'd sometimes have to put a towel on his mattress because it was so wet – and I had started using teething gel after the health visitor had suggested it. I had worried about the amount he'd got through but she had reassured me everything was fine.

'Perhaps I put too much teething gel on,' I replied as I looked at Terry.

'Well, if that's all you have to worry about then I know you didn't do anything,' he said simply. 'It's up to the police to find out what happened.'

The following Wednesday we were invited to a child protection conference at Wiltshire County Council's social services department. I had been sent a letter telling me the meeting was being held because 'of concerns that will have been discussed with you by a member of the department' and that an accompanying leaflet would answer my queries.

I stared blankly at the piece of paper. There had never been even the slightest whisper of concern over my care of any of our children and it had come to this?

We arrived at the meeting to find sixteen people sitting ready to discuss our lives. In addition to Terry, Bill and me, the room seemed full of strangers. But as my eyes travelled round the circle of chairs, I was relieved to see some medical people who had actually known us for longer than twelve days.

They'll tell them how ridiculous this all is, I thought. They know this is all wrong. They've known us for ever, they've seen me with my babies and tried to explain to us why they died.

The chairman opened the meeting.

'We are here today to decide whether Jade should be put on the at-risk register under the category of physical harm,' he said.

The words cut straight through me. It was the first time I'd heard it said so plainly that I might attack my child.

Slowly the chairman asked each person in the room to speak and, after the social workers had had their say, I wanted to cheer when one medical professional we knew said in angry tones that he had not been consulted and was most concerned about the situation.

I was grateful for his words and felt confidence prick inside me – but it was soon crushed by the impersonal and passive declarations of others who knew me. They told the meeting in non-committal tones that there were no medical problems or concerns with Jade. No more, no less. I was shocked that not one person stood up for me and said 'Angela is a loving mum'. As we sat and listened to them speak in turn, I slowly realised that one by one they were abandoning us.

Then it was Terry's turn to speak.

'We've done everything possible to help everyone who's been picking over our lives,' he said. 'But despite that, Angela is only allowed to see Jade for six hours a week. It's just not enough. Not good enough. Jade is a happy and healthy little girl but she's missing her mum.'

When it came to my turn to speak, like so many meetings over the months and years to follow, my words were stifled by the threat of the police investigation hanging over me. Rendered dumb through fear of how my words could be used against me, all I could do was cry as I uttered the six words that summed up the situation.

'Jade wants to see her mum,' I said.

But I could only sit in silent horror as everyone – except the one angry medic – nodded when the chairman asked, 'And so is everyone in agreement that Jade's name should be placed on the at-risk register?'

Two weeks before some of those people had looked at us with sorry eyes when Matthew had been taken into hospital with breathing problems. They had comforted me when my children died, reassured me when terror rose up inside me that I had let my babies down. But now it seemed as if fear had made them dumb, that what-ifs and might-have-beens had overwhelmed common sense. I have never been able to understand how their attitude could change so easily – to treat me as a loving mother and then, within the space of a few days, agree that my child needed protection from me. I don't know if the police involvement had caused them to doubt me or if some had suspected me in the past, but I felt betrayed by the refusal of people who had known us for years, and never raised any concerns, to believe in us. No one spoke up for us. It was heartbreaking to see people who knew me and Jade, who had watched me with my babies, and who had held my hand after I lost my children, agree that my daughter was at risk.

Terry looked at them all.

'I don't know why you had this meeting,' he spat. 'You'd all made your minds up before you came here and you've all followed like little sheep. You're all sat together on a wooden bench with splinters up your arses.'

In the weeks that followed we settled into something approaching a routine as we kept telling ourselves that everything would be sorted out by 25 January, the date I was due to answer my bail. We focused on that day as the one that would release us from the nightmare engulfing our lives.

In the meantime I concentrated on being as much of a mother to Jade, during the designated hours of supervised contact, and a wife to Terry, in our snatched moments together, as I could be. On 1 December a new social services rota was drawn up which meant I was able to see Jade for two hours every weekday and on alternate Sundays. I'll never forget seeing the first one listing in black and white the hours I could spend with my child and which social worker would be keeping an eye on me. But the practicalities of the visits could prove highly complicated and access meetings were called off at short notice if a social worker went sick or was unavailable. Each time a huge row erupted as Terry got on the phone to social services to berate them for failing to honour the agreement that had been made and I would wonder in sickened disbelief how it had come to this.

'My wife only gets the chance to see her daughter a few times a week,' he would shout. 'Don't you think that somehow all you people could manage to see that she does?'

Initially, at least, Jade seemed to cope with the changes in her life in the seemingly easy way children do.

'Why aren't you staying here with Daddy and me?' she asked during one of my visits. After seeing her that first time in Claire's flat, I then visited her at home in the hope it would seem more natural.

'Because I need to go back to Aunty Claire's and work in the bakery at night-time,' I told her. 'During the day I go to sleep and when I wake up I'll come to see you and then I'll go back to the bakery with Aunty Claire to make cakes.'

She looked at me seriously.

'So when you have finished with Aunty Claire, you will be coming home to sleep with me?'

'I hope so, darling,' I replied.

It seemed so wrong to lie to Jade but what could we do? I told myself we had been forced into that position by other people and we had to give her some reason why I wasn't living at home. But deep down it felt wrong.

My visits were unpredictable. At times Jade would hardly seem to notice when I left, at others she would cry and cling to me, anxious for me to stay. Each time I left my heart broke just a little more, knowing that all any of us wanted was for me to stay.

Meanwhile Terry was becoming increasingly anxious about the police investigation. The child protection conference had scared him deeply and, as he had sat and watched people we had known for years agree to put Jade's name on the at-risk register, it seemed to him that a juggernaut had been set in motion against us we were powerless to stop. But he did not confide his fears in me.

He was also worried about money. After losing one house when he got divorced from his first wife, and buying our own home in 1991, he was concerned about having to sell another.

We had both been signed off on long-term sick leave from Tesco but Terry knew this couldn't last for ever. All we could do was look to the end of January as the time ordinary life would begin again.

I simply remained as frozen as I had been from the moment I had found Matthew. It is a clichéd expression but I was in complete denial. While thoughts of the suspicions hanging over me occasionally bubbled up to the surface, I buried them on a day-to-day level and refused to acknowledge – either to myself or others – what might be happening. Forbidden from grieving for my son, barred by officialdom from the natural processes of mourning – such as a burial – I shut down. Even today people ask me how I coped and the truthful answer is I don't know. It was almost as if I detached myself and focused on the most important things in life – visits with Jade, attending meetings with social workers, seeing Bill and Jacqui. I went through the mechanics of day-to-day existence, it was all just a blur to me. No matter how hard I tried to fit it all into my reality, I just could not take it in. It was like having a nightmare or watching a horror film – you're scared but there's a constant voice in the back of your head telling you it's not real.

Even now, it is hard to put into words what the loss of Matthew meant, but I can only say that it stripped me of my final reserves of hope. I do not want to underestimate the impact of Gemma and Jason's deaths, but when Matthew arrived we thought we had finally laid so much sadness to rest. Then within a matter of a few hours, everything we had built was destroyed, and some hidden, silent part of me finally shut down. I had sustained the loss of two children but Matthew's death, and everything it triggered, was just too much. I couldn't believe it had happened – even now I haven't fully accepted it. It made no sense and the only thing I could keep returning to was that I must have done something wrong. I was a woman, I was meant to give birth to and protect life, not see it drain away before me, and I felt certain that my mistakes had cost my children's lives. I lived life like a ghost – functioning on the outside but shut down within.

It was only at nights when my guard would finally be lowered. Questions rolled continuously round my head and I cried myself to sleep night after night.

Why did Matthew die? I thought. Why is this happening? Why are they doing this to me? Why can't we be together? Why did they take all those things from the house? What are they doing with Matthew?

But while there was no hope of any answers to the big questions, the everyday ones were in a way the most painful, because they represented all I was missing.

I wonder what Jade had for breakfast, I'd think as I got out of bed. I wonder if Terry remembered to polish her shoes. What are they doing this minute?

I began to dread going to bed, painfully aware of Claire and Kevin in bed together next door and aching for Terry. I would think back to all the nights we spent lying chatting until one of us would insist we got some sleep – never appreciating how precious that time was. But as I tried to switch off my mind, the doubts set in. To be accused of murdering your children turns your world upside down and I felt as if I was floating in an unknown universe like a spaceman cut adrift from his ship. At times, as I hovered between sleep and wakefulness, I thought to myself: If the police believe I've done something, then surely I must have? Irrational thoughts raced through my brain as a voice told me that maybe I had committed some awful act and forgotten it, blacked out the truth. But on the occasions when I doubted myself, another louder voice would shriek in my head, You did nothing, and I would shut down the thoughts. I was separated from my husband and daughter and all I could do was concentrate on them – I had to get through each day and exist, and then I would see them again. I could not afford to let myself fall apart.

At the beginning of December, Terry and I paid for an independent post-mortem to be carried out on Matthew. We were not happy with the 'unascertained' result of the police examination and were anxious to see if a second opinion could come up with a conclusive reason for Matthew's death. But a week later we were told once again that nothing had been found. We just couldn't understand why the police were still investigating. Like Gemma and Jason before him, no one could find a reason for Matthew's loss. His was another cot death – as mysterious as any of the other hundreds of babies who died each year for no apparent reason.

Relief flooded over us when we were told that his body could finally be released and we could start making funeral arrangements – the first proper step towards mourning our son we had been allowed to make. Neither Gemma, Jason nor Matthew had been baptised and so it was important to Terry and me that we had proper Christian funerals for them. I had never sought comfort for myself in church after their deaths because I felt too angry with God and was scared of how I might feel, but I wanted a proper goodbye for them.

John Walton, though, delivered some devastating news when he came to discuss the arrangements.

'I'd like to see Matthew one final time,' I told him. 'I just want to say goodbye.'

I'll never forget the words he used in response – hard, graphic words which haunt me still.

'Angela, I would advise you not to see Matthew,' John replied, obviously distraught. 'He looks as if he has been on a butcher's slab. They have done extensive tests on his body and I think you should have him cremated.'

It was as if someone had kicked me in the stomach and, like the day I was arrested, anger welled up in me. How dare they do this? Matthew didn't deserve this, he needed to be remembered, mourned and given back to us. No one had told us he would be treated in this way. He had been cut and tested and poked, and we, his parents, had lost the right to give our permission about what happened to his body. It is something that still haunts us today and in some ways I wish I had seen Matthew because an imagined image of his brutalised body continues to fill my mind.

In the end we took John's advice and opted for a cremation, to be held on 17 December, the same date as Jade's pre-school nativity. That day summed up all we were facing – the tug between honouring our grief for Matthew and our responsibility to make sure life went on for Jade.

I had been devastated the week before when Tony Luscott told me I would not be able to attend the nativity because it would mean unsupervised access to Jade. If she had been a baby I might somewhere have forced myself to accept some speck of reason in their logic. But was it really likely that a mother would murder her three babies, leave one unharmed and then, once under suspicion, attack her daughter in a room full of parents? The longer the situation continued the sicker I decided the minds of social services were. But eventually Tony agreed that I could go to see Jade – as long as he came too – and Mum, Brian, Andrew, Terry and I trooped off with him in tow.

I fought back tears as I watched Jade come into the hall carrying a card with the number seven and a picture of a swan. She was 'Seven Swans A-Swimming' for the 'Twelve Days of Christmas' and I was once again filled with the sense that she was a ray of hope in that dark time as I looked at her.

'You were wonderful, darling,' I said, as I took photos and tried to push everything else out of my mind and clutch onto that one tiny moment of happiness. Terry had dissolved into tears next to me but I forced myself to keep smiling for Jade, anxious for her not to see both of us upset.

But my strength evaporated the second we walked into Salisbury crematorium later that afternoon to find just nineteen people waiting to mourn our son. We'd been advised by the police to keep the service low-key in order to keep the press away and only our immediate family were there. But it struck me how empty it all seemed as soon as we walked in. The church in Winterbourne Gunner had been packed for Gemma and Jason's funerals but the mourners at Matthew's service could hardly fill the front two rows. He would only get a whisper of goodbye and I knew he deserved more.

Matthew's coffin was at the front of the crematorium with a Southampton football shirt and mascot draped over it. But other than that I remember little about the service, which lasted just fifteen minutes and was taken, once again, by John Walton. The fact that Matthew was in the coffin was the only thing that was real and the rest was a blur. I was on autopilot and all I can remember is a desperate desire to hold my baby boy and kiss him one last time. Tears streamed down my face as I stood at the front of the crematorium, trying to say goodbye to him but aware that deep down I simply couldn't accept he had gone.

As I left the service I noticed Gill Dawson and Graham Fisher seated at the back.

'What are they doing here?' Tina hissed as we looked at the floral tributes outside, while another family lined up to take their place on the seats we had left seconds before. 'This should be family only. They shouldn't be here. You shouldn't have let them come.'

'Terry wanted them to come, he wanted them to see what kind of family we are,' I sobbed. 'He wanted them to realise that I could never hurt one of my children.'

The letter dropped on the doormat four days before Christmas.

Agreement relating to arrangements for contact between Jade Cannings and her mother, Mrs Angela Cannings, on Saturday 25th December and Sunday 26th December 1999.
The aim of this agreement is to enable Jade to enjoy as normal a Christmas as possible given the necessary constraints relating to her contact with her mother. To this end, the Social Services Department has consulted with the police, with Mr and Mrs Cannings and with their respective extended families.
It has been agreed that:
1. There will be contact between Jade and her mother on 25th December 1999 between the hours of 6.30am and 7.30pm.

2. Mrs Cannings will be brought to and from the family home by her sister, Miss Claire Connolly.

3. Contact will take place at the family home save for a period between the hours of approximately 12 noon and 2pm when Jade, her parents and other members of her extended family, including her maternal grandmother Mrs Mary Barry will go to the Trafalgar Hotel, Salisbury, for Christmas lunch.

4. Between the hours of 6.30am and 2pm, Miss Claire Connolly will take on the role of 'supervisor'. This will mean that she has responsibility for ensuring that Jade is not left alone with her mother at any time, also that Mrs Cannings is not involved in any of Jade's intimate care.

5. Between the hours of 2pm and 7.30pm, Jade's paternal aunt Mrs Jenny Robinson will take on the role of 'supervisor' as described above at paragraph 4.

6. Jade's father will put her to bed at sometime between 7pm and 7.30pm. Mrs Cannings will not be involved in this.

It was the first of a series of unsupervised contact agreements, which gave us permission to spend time together alone as a family, and it had taken weeks to sort out. In the run-up to Christmas, Terry and I had kept asking about what would be happening, only to be told no one was available to supervise visits. When we suggested family members could do it, social services had finally agreed to apply for a court order allowing me to see Jade. Claire, my mum and Terry's sister had had to be police checked and the whole process had left me feeling exhausted. During every meeting I'd been told time and again that if I was allowed to see Jade without a social worker present I must not be alone with her, and here it was yet again in the agreement – the black and white expression of suspicion that sent a shudder through me. I highlighted points four and six in shocking pink marker before filing the document with the rest of the paperwork I was building up. Instead of social workers watching me on Christmas Day, my family was being given the job. I had felt sick when Tony Luscott came over to pick up the agreement with our signatures on it and shook my hand as he said goodbye. Last year I'd spent Christmas at home with Terry and Jade, pregnant with our fourth child, and now my relatives were being forced to 'guard' my daughter from me.

My alarm went off at 5.15 a.m. on Christmas morning and an hour later Claire and I were driving through the deserted streets of Salisbury in the pitch black. I couldn't believe I was driving to be let into my own home on Christmas morning, but when I saw Jade waiting for me with Terry at the front door I determined to make the most of the day.

Sod them, I thought to myself. There is no way they are going to win. In front of Jade, in front of Terry and in front of my family, today will be a normal day. I can be miserable when I get home later but I won't let them ruin today.

I walked up the path towards a beaming Jade, who was wiggling with excitement.

'Father Christmas ate the food I left out for him and his reindeer had the carrot,' she excitedly told me as I walked through the door.

First up was presents and, while Terry and I had not had the heart to buy each other anything, Jade was overcome with excitement when she ripped open the Barbie dressing table and duvet cover we had given her. My dad, Katherine and Andrew also arrived with more packages to unwrap. Then it was on to the Cannings tradition that has to be observed every Christmas morning – cold gammon on a plate with fresh bread 'dunkies' – as we watched Jade do one of her beloved dancing shows.

We'd decided to go out for lunch at a hotel because every minute of that day seemed precious, and I thought we'd made the right decision for the first few minutes after we arrived. There was happiness all around us. The tree was sparkling and the place was full of families with mummies and daddies and grandparents sitting together, everyone dressed up and happy, and for a few seconds I felt part of it.

But I was suddenly filled with a rush of jealousy as I realised we were not like everyone else. We were running Christmas Day according to rules set down on a piece of paper – playing a game of happy families when everyone else was doing it for real. Mum, Brian and Claire were all pretending so hard and, with bright smiles painted on their faces, did all they could to make it seem okay. But I knew it wasn't. It all felt totally wrong.

Soon Jade picked up on the unhappiness we were all trying so hard to smile away and started playing up. But I found it difficult to discipline her. The one thing I didn't want to be doing on Christmas Day was telling her off, being the bad mummy, and I was acutely aware of the clock ticking.

'She's upset,' I said to Terry after we'd rushed through our meal. 'Let's get her home where she'll be happy because I've got to go in a few hours. We don't want to waste any of the day.'

In the hours after we got home and because I was there for longer than usual Jade seemed to settle. Terry and I both noticed how her behaviour changed from erratic to calm that day when for that precious time it felt almost as if we were a normal family.

But of course all too soon I had to leave and Claire came to pick me up. Christmas Day stopped for us on the dot of 7.30 p.m. There was no final brandy for Terry and me as we sat on the sofa and looked at the tree, no smiling chats as we remembered Jade's face when she opened her presents. Instead cold hard reality hit us as I got into the car to leave.

'I don't know how much longer I can do this,' I sobbed, 'I'm exhausted.'

'You've got to hang on in there,' Claire told me, as she tried to drive the car and console me at the same time. 'You will get through this. I love you so much, Angie. I hate seeing this happening to you. But it will all end soon.'

Back at home Terry poured himself a brandy, pulled a chair into the hallway and sat staring at the front door, willing someone to knock on it and walk in to see him. No one did.

*

Much as we'd have liked the rest of the world to give up on the festivities as quickly as we did, Britain was thrust into millennium fever for the next week. Newspapers and television were full of excitement as people got ready to see in the twenty-first century. Terry and I decided not to do anything special – Jade had had to go and stay with Stephen, Kellie and the kids for the night and we stayed at home with a Chinese takeaway.

But just before midnight I felt we had to do something to see in the New Year. With all that was happening, it suddenly seemed important that we try to look forward and imagine a time when we would recover.

'Let's go up to the kids' room and watch the fireworks at the cathedral,' I said to Terry and he followed me upstairs.

As midnight struck and the sky lit up, all we could hear amid the cracks and bangs were cheers from people lining the streets. All around us people were having fun and suddenly I knew I had been stupid to think, even for a second, that there might be something for us to look forward to other than uncertainty. The house felt so empty without Jade and Matthew and I started to cry.

'What has happened to our lives, Ter?' I sobbed. 'How can it have come to this? Jade away and no Matthew? I don't think I can cope with it much longer.'

Terry turned to face me.

'We've got two choices here, Ange,' he quietly replied. 'Either we go under or we survive. If we go under then they've beaten us and so there's nothing else we can do – we've just got to survive.'

CHAPTER FIVE

I'm always filled with sadness when I look back and remember our innocent faith that life would return to normal on 25 January 2000 – the date I was due to answer my police bail. We were so naïve, so trusting that common sense would prevail and the onslaught of social workers, care orders, court hearings and police investigations against us would be stopped. But the day came and went with the police saying they needed more time to complete the medical investigations and I was rebailed to February. When the police finished looking at Matthew's death, charges would either be brought or the case dropped.

I was bitterly disappointed by the delay and increasingly felt that instead of investigating, the police were actively trying to prove me guilty. The feeling was sparked by their attitude to information my father gave me a few weeks after Matthew's death. He had rung one day to tell me he'd discovered that a second cousin on the Irish side of my family had lost two babies to cot death. The couple had gone on to have a daughter and a son who had both had breathing problems and been closely monitored into childhood.

'Angela,' my dad said gravely over the phone, 'it must be a genetic problem.'

It was a bolt from the blue. Terry and I had never been told there might be a hereditary element to cot deaths. But the news also gave me a scrap of comfort because it was something else to think about other than blaming myself. The lack of explanation for the loss of my children continued to torment me and at last there was a glimmer of a reason – however faint – for their deaths.

Terry told Gill Dawson everything and she assured him it would be investigated. But after a visit to Ireland in January, the message came back that the police didn't feel the information would help my case. I just couldn't understand why they were dismissing a potential genetic factor linking Gemma, Jason and Matthew's deaths, and felt they were shoving the possibility under the carpet because it didn't fit with their view of things.

As time went on my relationship with the police became an uneasy truce and I saw Gill only occasionally. Terry, as the 'victim' of a crime, had far more dealings with her. She went to see him nearly every day and kept him updated with what was happening and he also spoke to Graham Fisher occasionally.

But while Gill might have been friendly towards Terry, I felt under investigation whenever she came to see me. She was supposed to be a liaison officer, nothing more, but ever since the day she had accompanied me to see Matthew's body, I had felt she was trying to extract information from me. I tolerated her visits until one night when she came to Claire's flat and the situation reached breaking point. Claire had distrusted her from the moment she took us to see Matthew's body and, as Gill stood and talked to me in the kitchen, she came in breathing fire.

'Why are you here?' she demanded. 'Actually, don't bother telling me, I know, just here for a chat. You know, you're treating us like mushrooms – keeping us in the dark and feeding us on shit – and I'm sick of it.'

Gill left hurriedly and I never saw her as much after that.

The lack of contact I had with the police allowed me to sustain the cosy bubble of denial I had blown around myself, but there were still times when even I could not ignore the investigation. The first weekend of January 2000 was one such occasion. Some of the property that had been taken from our house when it was searched on the day of my arrest was returned, enshrouded in a large brown bag with 'Police Property Forensic Samples' stamped on the side. Inside were five videos, a couple of photo albums, receipts and even a screwed-up envelope with a verse written on it that Claire and I had chosen for Matthew's death announcement in the local newspaper. The mundane detritus of an ordinary life made extraordinary by a police sample bag. I felt sick as I sorted through everything – the concrete symbols of the violation of our family – and wondered what else the police had touched.

The weeks stretched into months as meeting after meeting was held and medical expert after medical expert was asked their opinion. By the end of January, more than two hundred people had been interviewed. Friends, family, neighbours, even people I went to school with, all were approached and asked to add their brushstroke to the picture of our life the police were building up. I kept asking myself when it would all end.

Four long months after losing Matthew, I returned to Salisbury police station to answer bail again and be re-interviewed. I felt nervous but also hopeful it would finally mean the end of the investigation and my return home. As far as I knew, none of the medical investigations had found anything, and so what possible reason could there be for carrying this charade on?

It was just before 2 p.m. on 8 March when I was taken into an interview room by the two CID officers who'd questioned me when I was arrested. Again they sat grim-faced as the seal was taken off the tape and again I heard the snap of the recording machine as it was put inside and the wheels started to softly whirr.

'So, Angela,' they spat. 'We need to go over a few things again in the light of what we've found out since we last spoke to you.'

I couldn't believe we were here again, going over the same old ground. I'd told everything again and again to police, social workers, lawyers and doctors and here I was running through the same story. But I willed myself to stay calm as the interview got under way.

They went back to the day of Jason's breathing problems. How had I reacted to finding him? Where was I when his apnoea alarm went off? Then they moved on to the day of his death. Jason was cold when I'd found him, which meant he had been dead for some time. But he should have been warm because apnoea alarms sound within seconds of a baby stopping breathing. Could I explain that?

'No, I can't,' I told them. 'I'm sorry. I just heard the alarm and went into him. I'm just telling you what happened.'

But I should have heard the alarm go off if I was in the flat, they told me. Shouldn't I have been more vigilant? Hadn't I heard the alarm start?

Unlike the day of my arrest, their questioning seemed very specific and as the minutes ticked by fear took a tighter hold of me. It was obvious the officers were not there just to tie up a few loose ends. But, as hard as I tried to decode the meaning behind what they were saying, I simply could not understand what they were trying to get to. Then came the bombshell.

'You see, Angela, iron deposits have been found in Jason's lungs, which is extremely unusual in SIDS. And we have consulted with experts who say that it points to upper airways obstruction – or suffocation. Can you explain that?'

'No,' I whispered, as I started to cry. 'I'm sorry but I can't.'

I felt shocked, sickened, as my mind raced. To hear a police officer say they had some kind of evidence against me was devastating. How could they? I had done nothing wrong. I just couldn't take in what they were saying.

'Three experts agree, Angela,' they said. 'We've got to go on what they're telling us.'

'I did not do anything,' I kept repeating. 'I did not harm my babies. All I ever wanted was to have children with Terry – that is all I wanted to do and I don't know why this has happened. I've never done anything.'

I didn't know what to say. I couldn't understand how anyone could believe my children had been smothered. But even as I tried to take in what they had said, the officers flipped on to something else. Time and again they mentioned upper airway obstruction, asphyxia, suffocation, before moving on to another part of the story – leading me to the point of no return only to shy away from it, leaving me dangling over the precipice but unable to get back onto safe ground.

I sat unable to believe that they thought I had suffocated my child. It was unimaginable, horrible. Panic started to rise in me.

'What are they doing? Why are they saying I have killed my babies?' I said tearfully to Elaine, the legal assistant who had sat in during my first police interviews, during a break in questioning.

'They are here to do a job,' she replied. 'They are CID officers and this is what they do.'

'But I didn't do anything,' I whispered.

'Don't worry. Just carry on. You're doing really well.'

As the hours went on, the officers pumped more and more questions at me.

Why didn't I carry Jason with me when I went to answer the door to Gloria Peacock on the day of his breathing problems? Why had I appeared calm? Why hadn't I used the resuscitation techniques I'd been taught each time I found one of my babies? Why had I phoned the doctor instead of an ambulance when I found Jade struggling? How could Matthew's alarm have been going off on the day of his breathing problems when I'd said he was being sick and he was therefore moving so it should have cut out? Why had I written in my diary about feeling depressed the day before Gemma's death?

'I did not do anything,' I kept repeating as question after question was fired at me. 'I loved my babies. I'm just telling you what happened.'

It was so hard to remember every thought I'd had, every action I'd taken, on those awful days.

'I just panicked when I found them. I tried to remember what I'd been taught but for some reason just couldn't seem to deal with it. Everything went out of my head.

'I don't know if I heard the alarms start or not. I just heard them.

'I wasn't calm when I found Jason. I could not believe it was happening again. I was in shock.

'I phoned the doctor when I found Jade because she was only in the next street – nearer than an ambulance.

'I just wanted Terry with me when I found Matthew. I'd always been alone.'

It seemed to me the officers sneered at every word as they pumped questions at me. Again and again, they took me in loops around the days of my children's deaths, always leading back to the same thing – the experts said my babies had been suffocated.

'I cannot believe it,' I whispered, as tears welled up inside me and my voice became weaker. 'I never did anything to my children. I loved them.'

'Well, we can only go on what we're being told,' they said to me, aggression straining their voices.

'But I haven't done anything. I loved my children.'

I must have said it a hundred times as we sat there.

'I'm just telling you what happened, what I remember,' I kept repeating as they asked question after question about those dreadful days so long ago. 'So much of it is a blank. I don't know what other people are like if they've been in the situation but I just could not deal with it. I panicked.'

I didn't try to fill in the holes, explain what I couldn't. I just kept telling them what had happened, that I hadn't harmed my children, the truth.

But as the afternoon wore on I felt that my lack of 'cooperation' was making those officers angry, and after all those months of jumping to everyone else's tune, I finally realised no one was on my side. The police were not here to iron things out, to find out why Matthew had died and give Terry and me some long-awaited peace. To me, these officers seemed determined to hear me admit that I had killed my children – and I was not going to be beaten by them.

For all those months leading up to sitting in that room, I had stumbled through the days and refused to acknowledge what was happening. But as I realised what I was facing, I finally found my fight.

'Have you made all this up?' they said for a final time at about 5.30 p.m.

'I haven't done anything to harm my babies,' I replied yet again. 'I did not do anything to harm them. I did not do anything.'

With that they scraped back their chairs and walked out of the room before returning a few minutes later.

'We have taken advice and this case will now be taken to the Crown Prosecution Service who will decide whether to proceed. You can go now.'

I stumbled out of the police station – drained, shocked and sickened by what had just happened in the interview room. I was met by Terry, who had gone up to the police station with Stephen and Terry Chambers to see Gill Dawson.

'You look dreadful, Ange,' he exclaimed when he saw my grey face. 'Are you all right?'

'It was hell in there – it was horrible,' I replied. 'They think I killed Gemma, Jason and Matthew. I didn't think I would be coming out of there. Terry, I might go to prison for this. They say they've got evidence against me. If I'm locked up then I don't want you and Jade to be part of my life. I don't want the two of you to have to visit me.'

Terry said nothing – simply turning to hug me before leading me away.

The faith he showed in me that day is something I have only recently understood.

'I've got some bad news for you, Terry,' Gill Dawson had told him while I was being interviewed. 'We've got some evidence to suggest that Angela did smother your babies.'

'What is it?' he replied.

'There were small spots of blood on Jason's lung, which indicate he was smothered.'

Terry was silent and, for the first and only time during that whole investigation, he doubted me. Adrenalin rushed into his brain as his age-old conditioning clicked into gear – if the police had found evidence then it must mean I had done something.

But then he stopped himself and remembered he knew me better than anyone else in the world. He had watched me nurture our children, seen me stumble through life after losing them – and he knew I had done nothing wrong. From that day on Terry read everything he could about my case – including hundreds of pages of medical reports. Nothing ever again made him doubt me.

'No,' he said, as he looked at her. 'She hasn't done anything. I know she hasn't. You've got nothing.'

Over the next two months, I finally woke up and realised things were not simply going to go away. But my newfound realism meant there were also new fears to confront. For instance, sending the papers to the CPS scared me, because I knew strangers in a faraway office would look coldly at my case and decide whether or not to charge me with murder. Even during the worst of times you create a series of fixed points around yourself as a way of making something so overwhelming seem manageable. However much I disliked their presence in my life, the investigation by Salisbury police officers had a human face in the guise of Gill Dawson, Graham Fisher and Rob Findlay, and I believed that by knowing me as a person they would be persuaded I was not a murderer. Now, though, people I had never met were putting a coolly analytical gaze over the information the police had given them – was there a realistic chance that I would be convicted or not? Simple as that. It scared me deeply.

As reality hit, I realised just how important Bill was going to be because he was the one fighting for my freedom. My meetings with him had started in the cordial way those with strangers do – me, hiding my upset and a little in awe of Bill's learned, softly spoken tones, and him, professional and matter-of-fact. But after a couple of meetings he turned to me and said something that would shift the basis of our relationship for ever.

'From what I've seen and what I've heard I can tell you now that I don't believe you have done anything,' he said assuredly.

Bill's faith in me made mine in him complete. Before Matthew's death, I had only ever met a solicitor when we bought our house, and didn't understand the legal system and its complexities. But as I got to know Bill, I grew to trust him and he became my friend. When every other system of authority and power seemed to have turned against us, the fact that Bill – as a legal expert – was on my side was something I had to hold onto. And it wasn't just about him believing in me, I could also see that he was as frustrated as I was with the ridiculous beast that was social services. He had a daughter about Jade's age and I think the case became incredibly personal for him as he fought to right the wrong he believed had been done to us.

His assistant Jacqui was equally devoted to my case. Where Bill spoke slowly and diplomatically, she was refreshingly outspoken in her disgust at what was happening. Organised and with an encyclopaedic knowledge of dates, times and people, she was the perfect foil for Bill and they wrote letters of complaint to social services about their never-ending bureaucracy, put angry pen to paper when the police kept rebailing me, soothed away my worry during long conversations and even gave me the odd hug after particularly bad meetings. Bill and Jacqui fought every step of the way for me. Here were two people who were not part of my family but believed in me without prompting. Bill was a calm, constant presence, Jacqui a fiery one, and they seemed gripped by the injustice that had engulfed us.

On 10 May 2000 I returned to Salisbury police station where an officer behind a counter matter-of-factly charged me with the murder of Gemma, Jason and Matthew. After all the delays and questions, I had of course been preparing myself for this, but still could not quite believe it was coming so nightmarishly true.

In a small side room, an officer pressed my finger into the cool moistness of an ink pad before guiding it to a nearby sheet of blotting card. As each finger was pressed in turn onto the pad, my vision blurred as tears streamed down my face. It was as if someone had put a knife into me and I could only shallow-breathe to try and ease the sharp pain of distress.

'Step away from the table and hold this board up,' the woman officer said blandly and gestured me to the corner of the room.

Wordlessly I picked it up as a camera flash popped blindingly

77

and shafts of white light were fragmented in the tears that filled my eyes. Finally I sat in a chair as the officer bent down to take DNA swabs from my mouth.

I found those ten short minutes utterly humiliating. Earlier, as the words 'You are charged with . . .' were said at the strip-lit front desk, I felt stripped of every remaining shred of dignity. I knew I was now carrying the burden of a label that would never leave me.

Until that day, however thin the thread of hope been stretched, I had always thought life would somehow return to normal – despite the scars months of separation had etched on us. But being charged made me realise just how much I had been lying to myself – whatever happened, things were never going to be normal again. I had been charged with murdering my children and it horrified me.

I was now subject to bail conditions – to live at Claire's flat, have no unsupervised contact with Jade, surrender my passpost and report to Salisbury police station twice a week. I could be fined or imprisoned if I failed to comply. But it was the formalisation of the suspicion which had hung over me that was the worst thing. Now everyone would know what before only the police had suspected. I felt so ashamed.

A week later the first hearing about my case was held at Salisbury Magistrates Court. It heralded the start of the amazingly complex legal administrative process that awaited me. The wheels of justice grind slow and I was about to enter a world of rules, pomp and ceremony I had never even glimpsed before.

Earlier that morning, I had been put into an unmarked police car and taken to the outskirts of Salisbury in preparation for the hearing.

'We are going to take you to a secret location,' an officer had told me. 'Because of the seriousness of the charges against you and the level of press interest, we feel you need to be protected.'

We drove to a car park in an outlying suburb of Salisbury where a police van with blacked-out windows was waiting.

'Keep your head down,' I was told as I climbed into the back and saw a pale blue blanket lying on a seat.

Me with my mum and dad.

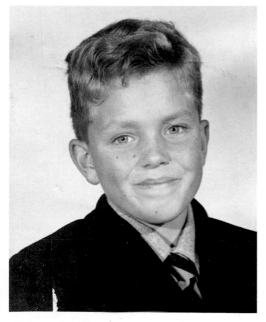

Terry when he was at secondary modern school.

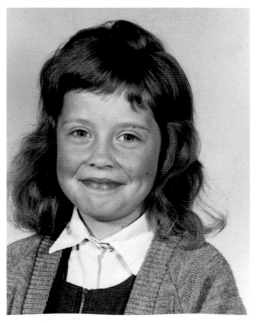

Me when I was at Catholic junior school.

Terry and me during the early days of our courtship.

Terry and I got married on 21 March 1987. It was a lovely day even though there was snow on the ground.

Here I am with Stephen, so pleased to be his stepmum.

Gemma was born on 14 August 1989. Here we are, proud parents with our first child.

Jason was born on 25 April 1991. I am happy to be a mum again, but I am also filled with anxiety.

OUR
LITTLE CHILDREN
GEMMA CANNINGS
BORN 14·8·1989
FELL ASLEEP 14·11·1989
JASON CANNINGS
BORN 25·4·1991
FELL ASLEEP 13·6·1991
Goodnight God bless

The gravestone marking the resting place of our babies Gemma and Jason.

Jade was born on 15 January 1996, but it was a fearful time for Terry and me when she was admitted to hospital with breathing problems.

Celebrating Jade's first birthday. This was an important milestone for us as a family, and the icing on the cake was that Jade was given the all clear from the hospital.

Matthew was born
on 5 July 1999.
His arrival made
our family complete
and life was good
again.

Jade with her little
brother. A treasured
photograph of my
two children together.

OUR
LITTLE CHILDREN
GEMMA CANNINGS
BORN 14.8.1989
FELL ASLEEP 14.11.1989
JASON CANNINGS
BORN 25.4.1991
FELL ASLEEP 13.6.1991
MATTHEW CANNINGS
BORN 5.7.1999
FELL ASLEEP 12.11.1999
Good night, God bless

Life dealt us another devastating and cruel blow when four-month-old Matthew
joined his sister and brother.

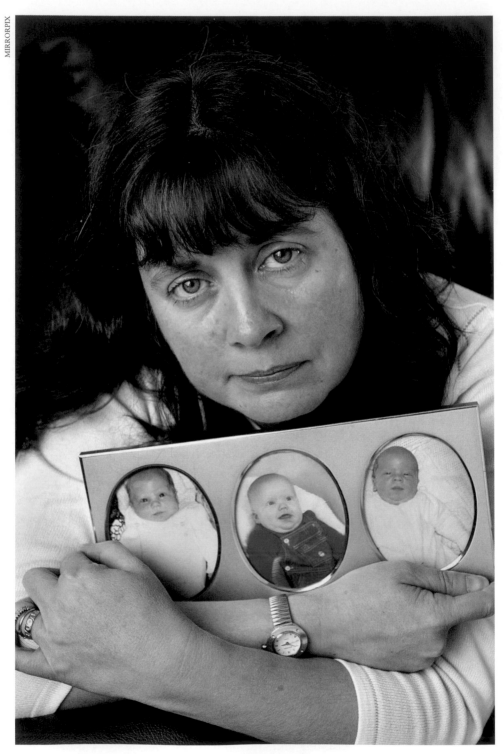

No need for words.

'When we get into the centre of Salisbury, please put that blanket over your head. The press will do anything to get a picture of you so we'll back the van as close as possible to the door of the court and then lead you inside.'

As we set off, I could see a police motorbike in front, siren blaring through a gap in the windscreen.

What are they doing? I thought to myself. They're ruddy bonkers.

I almost had to stop myself laughing as an officer's voice crackled 'We're clear, we're clear' in deadly serious tones through the police radio. It all seemed so macho.

This is hardly going to keep things low-key is it? I couldn't help thinking as cars pulled into the side of the road and pedestrians stared. I felt almost embarrassed by all the attention and couldn't help wondering why they were making all this fuss. It was only me in that van – no one dangerous.

But any sense of comedy disappeared as we arrived in the centre of Salisbury and the van was surrounded by market-goers who stared intently as we drove by.

They think there's a criminal in here, I thought as I hid under the blanket.

Suddenly hands began to thump on the windows and I froze with fear with the thought that people were trying to get in. Panicked, I peeked out from under the blanket and saw flashes dully lighting up the blackened glass.

'Just photographers,' a voice said and I pushed my head down again as the van drove through a cordon.

The searing sound of metal scraping against concrete filled my ears as the driver – intent on denying the press their prized picture – hit the side of the van on a wall as we drew up within inches of the court door. As we stopped, hands pulled me up and I was bundled out of the van and into the court. It seemed eerily quiet after the pandemonium we'd just passed through.

Inside I met Bill, Jacqui and Terry and, as the minutes ticked by while we waited to go into court, I kept stifling the panic that rose wrenchingly through me and into my throat.

But later, as the court hushed before the hearing began, I could no longer control it. I was sitting in a slightly raised dock with a bar surrounding it and a bench at the back. As I waited I had to keep pushing my feet into the floor to steady myself because my tights were slipping against the bench's shiny seat. Below and to the front of me I could see my family, the magistrate to my right, and on benches opposite my family, a lot of people with pens poised above notebooks – journalists I presumed.

A feeling of utter loneliness overwhelmed me as the charges were read out. Sitting there with a bar to pen me in, I realised for the first time that while I might have shared the experience of losing Gemma, Jason and Matthew and being separated from Jade to a greater or lesser extent with many people, this was one thing I would have to do alone. No one could share this murder charge with me, protect me from its brutal accusation and lift me up when I wanted to give in. Instead, I was going to have to face it on my own. As I looked at all the people I loved sitting metres away from me, I had never felt so distant from them.

I remember answering 'Yes' when someone asked me if I was Angela Cannings but the rest of the hearing passed in a blur. I couldn't take in the fact that I was standing in a dock, in a court room and I had been charged with murder.

'All rise,' a voice boomed as the room shuffled to its feet and the magistrate walked out only minutes after he'd walked in.

A few hours later I was back at Claire's watching myself plastered across the television news – the mother charged with murder, the lowest of the low. Switch it off, this isn't happening, this isn't true, my mind screamed. But as the newsreader intoned that a Salisbury mother, Angela Cannings, had been charged with the murder of her three children, I knew this was no bad dream. It was awful reality. My face was in newspapers and on television screens, and I felt filled with shame both for myself and everyone who was close to me. I imagined the whispers on the street, the stares at work my family and friends would have to contend with. Now the whole world knew I had been accused of the worst crime a mother could be and everyone around me would be affected.

Another thing struck me about those first reports – there was no mention of Jade.

Two weeks after Matthew's death, an injunction had been granted restricting mention of her in press reports. Terry had requested something was done when journalists started banging on our front door as word of the case spread and Jade had answered the door to a couple of them. Terry had also been watched as he left the house and become increasingly unhappy with the attention. John Pook, the social services manager in overall charge of our case, had agreed with him and the injunction had been granted.

But while it is normal that children involved in criminal proceedings are not identified, my case was unusual because over time, with different hearings and different orders imposed by judges, the terms of the injunction meant Jade's very existence could not be mentioned. Instead of press reports containing the fact that I had a daughter but not naming her, Jade was never written about. She was the living denial of my so-called murderous instinct and the general public had no idea she even existed.

For them, Angela Cannings had given birth to three babies and had lost three babies – and I was convicted in many minds because of that one fact. What so many people never knew was that I had a daughter whose healthy, happy childhood ran completely counter to the suspicion that I was a cold-blooded murderer. Jade became my invisible child – another chink of light snuffed out on that dark road towards facing my accusers in court.

CHAPTER SIX

Jade started to cry as she climbed the stairs to bed. I stood on the bottom step, torn between going to comfort my daughter and aware of the social worker's ever-present gaze.

'What's the matter, darling?' I asked as she hesitated on a step.

'I want Matthew to come back and be with us,' she said in gulps. 'I am crying because I am sad about Matthew.'

'Come here, Jadey,' I replied, and she shuffled down the stairs and into my arms. 'Daddy and I are sad about him too. We cry sometimes that he isn't here with us. But we know he's in heaven and looking down on us to make sure we are all right. So while you can't see him, he's with you because he's looking after you.'

'Is he, Mummy?' said Jade, as she looked at me with tears staining her cheeks. 'I want it to be you, Daddy and me and nobody else. I don't like your friends from the bakery here. When are you coming home?'

'It won't be long now,' I said. 'I've just got to work a bit longer but I'll be with you soon.'

I fell silent as Jade turned and made her way up to bed where Terry would tuck her in. It was the summer of 2000 and the stress of the previous eight months was beginning to cause cracks in my family that I doubted would ever be mended.

As hard as we tried to keep our upset from Jade, who'd turned four that January, we knew she was picking up on our sadness. Children may not be able to put into words the currents of

82

emotion running through their lives, but they are intuitive in a way that adults forget they too once were.

We were a family living our life with an eye on the clock every second we were together. It was like having a long-distance love affair and trying to cram every bit of happiness into tiny snatches of time. Instead of flowing with the natural currents of family life – be it a good day, bad day or plain boring day – we were constantly trying to relate to each other in artificially short bursts.

The biggest chasm it had opened up between us was our inability to grieve properly for Matthew. Separated, Terry and I weren't able to draw on each other as we had after we'd lost Gemma and Jason, and all Jade knew was that her parents smiled brightly from the moment her brother disappeared from her life. I knew it was confusing for her but I had no idea how to solve the problem. My time with her was so limited that I tried to make every moment a happy one – something no parent can reasonably expect. But my relationship with Jade lacked what other parents have – time – as I tried cramming being her mother into a few short hours a week.

Initially, she behaved well whenever she saw me, but as the months went on she would vent her confusion on me. A difficult visit – when she was moody with me or clingy when I had to leave – always left me feeling upset.

If time was one thing ruling our lives, social workers were the other. We did not know it then, but it would be two and a half long years from the day of Matthew's death to my trial, and during that time some ten social workers would supervise my visits. Most of them were reasonable, but in truth you can never really feel anything but resentment towards someone there to ensure you don't harm your child.

The overwhelming feeling Terry and I had about the situation with social services was the utter absurdity of the logic that governed it. Everything started from the point that I was a mother suspected of killing her three babies who had to be supervised every hour she was with her living child. But when a contact agreement was drawn up for time alone on Christmas and Boxing Days – when there weren't any social workers available – a piece

83

of paper was magically expected to stop me attacking Jade? The family who had surrounded me throughout the years I had 'murdered' three children were now going to stop me harming her? There were inconsistencies at the heart of the way we were treated, which Terry and I kept pointing out but everyone else ignored.

One of our greatest sources of frustration was Jade's guardian ad litem, Ellen Paterson-Russell, the person appointed by the court because of the interim care order covering Jade to represent her legal interests. We were told she was the most powerful person of all those involved in our daughter's care because she could bar us from contact with her if she felt it necessary. But she never gave us any indication of what she was thinking. During court hearings and social services meetings, she simply sat silently observing.

Over time the social workers became more relaxed about their supervision of my time with Jade – particularly once they'd got to know me – and I would disappear with her to play with no one in hot pursuit. I am not complaining that I got to have those brief moments alone with my daughter but there seemed to be a constant tension running through the situation. On one hand I was a suspected murderer, but on the other my deathly impulses would be magically stopped once a social worker was within 20 metres or I had a contact agreement in my hand.

'This is a bloody joke,' Terry would exclaim to whoever was supervising the visit when Jade and I had been gone a while. 'I don't know what they're doing so how do you?'

The social worker would simply smile and carry on watching television or reading a book.

Tony Luscott, our key worker, was the one person who didn't allow the rules to be bent. He would hover at the bottom of the stairs if Jade and I went up to play – obviously unsure whether he should follow or not. But if we were gone for more than a few minutes, he would casually appear just to ensure our game of hairdressers or schools hadn't taken a darker turn.

Of all the social workers we dealt with, he seemed the most suspicious of me. If Jade went out to play, he would often draw our conversation back to the investigation and inferences about how 'unusual' my case was because I had lost three babies. Increasingly I felt that he agreed with the police about what I was and, like many other officials involved in our case, could not accept that I was allowed to spend time with my daughter. It annoyed me – he wasn't there to judge me.

I wasn't the only one who found the situation intolerable. Jade too was protective about our time together. One memorable day she kept insisting she wanted to have a bath and I glimpsed the determined streak that would help my child survive.

I knew it was against the 'intimate care' rules, but they were difficult to follow when I was faced with my daughter innocently asking me to give her a bath. The cold confines of legal documents are worlds away from real family life.

'Come on, Mummy, let's go upstairs,' Jade said, as I hovered, torn between being 'good' or being a mum.

Sod it, I thought. I'm not going to be the one to stand here and say no. If Tony wants to stop us then he's going to have to do it himself.

We went upstairs and ran a bath. Conscious of breaking the rules, I left the door slightly ajar, but Jade closed it firmly shut before stepping into the water. I knew Tony would be absolutely seething.

'You're not allowed to do this, Angela,' he shouted up from downstairs. 'You know the rules.'

Jade wants her mum to give her a bath and I'm bloody well going to, I thought to myself as I watched her splash around. I didn't answer Tony, pushing down my humiliation at being treated like a naughty schoolgirl, and guilt that Terry might be made to pay for my behaviour.

A few months later, another social worker replaced Tony in charge of our case. But I still sometimes think about him now and wonder where he's ended up. Of all the people involved in our story, he is one of the few I would like to confront. The way in which he seemed to follow rules frustrates me still and I long to ask him why he appeared to close his mind to every concrete fact about our family that stared him in the face.

As the weeks turned into months and we began to approach a year of being apart, Terry and I knew we would have to explain the situation to Jade more fully. She was asking more and more questions about Mummy's friends from the bakery who always accompanied me on visits, and it saddened me to see her stripped of her unsuspicious innocence.

It sickened me to imagine how I would explain to her what people thought I had done. It was – and still is – one of the hardest things I have had to do, as I explained to my little girl that people thought I had hurt her brothers and sister. But I knew I had to say something and, just before Jade started at Wyndham Park Infants School in September 2000, I sat her down.

'There are some people who think that Mummy did something to Gemma, Jason and Matthew,' I told her. 'And they won't let me stay at home because they think I might do something to you. That's why I'm not living with you at the moment, Jade, but I will be home soon, I hope, and I love you every minute I'm away.'

'But, Mummy,' she said solemnly, 'you wouldn't hurt me because you're my mummy and you love me and you loved Gemma, Jason and Matthew. You didn't hurt them, did you?'

'No, darling, I didn't.'

From that day on, Jade called the social workers and police the 'horrible people'. Terry and I had been very conscious of not influencing her because we didn't want to add to her feelings of insecurity, but Jade came up with her own words to describe the people who had destroyed her world.

A few weeks later I walked with my heart in my mouth and Jade's hand in mine up to her new classroom. It should have been one of the most memorably happy milestones in her life but for me it was a devastating day. I'd wanted an early visit that morning to help her get ready but there was no social worker available and instead I'd met her at the school gates.

'Will they have colouring and puzzles, Mummy?' she asked as we trotted up the path in the sunshine.

'I hope so, honey,' I replied, as Terry videoed us and I looked enviously at the other mothers walking their children towards the school. I longed for the normality of their ordinary day. No social worker watching at the school gates, no knowing looks as I deposited Jade in her new class and, above all, an end to the exhausting effort of pushing down my feelings when all I wanted to do was stand amid the everyday chaos and weep.

As the months went by, it became increasingly clear the investigation was having very different effects on Terry and me. While I grappled with the lack of time with Jade, Terry was spending every waking hour with her. Where I felt lonely because I spent hours on my own during the day when everyone was at work, he felt isolated in the evenings.

From being a man who worked upwards of sixty hours a week and managed a busy department, he was now at home full-time with a young child and realised just how difficult being a single parent can be.

'I found her today staring in the mirror and saying she wanted you,' Terry said anxiously one night on the phone. 'I just don't know what to do with her.'

'Reassure her,' I told him. 'She's just feeling anxious. She's as confused as we are and doesn't know what's happening.'

'But when I went up to her, she hit me, Ange, I mean really gave me a whack,' he replied.

I was shocked. Jade had never been an aggressive child and it worried me that she had started reacting in this way.

'Well, you've got to make her realise she can't do that, Terry. You mustn't allow her to. Explain to her that she can't hit Daddy.'

'But I just can't bring myself to tell her off,' he replied. 'She's upset enough after all she's been through and I don't want to make it worse.'

Terry had always been soft with Jade. Even before all this started, he'd let her fall asleep with him watching television on the nights when I was at work. But I found those conversations heartbreaking. I was stuck on the end of the phone, rendered completely useless as a mother by distance, while he was struggling alone.

There were other things too – I knew he had lost any kind of routine at home and he and Jade were living haphazardly. Terry had always had someone to look after him domestically and, to be honest, thought shirts magically appeared ironed and food spontaneously appeared on plates. He struggled to cope on a practical level and meals were no longer at set times, with Jade often snacking rather than eating properly, or I would turn up for a visit on a cold day to find her dressed in something summery. The house wasn't as clean as it once had been and bedtimes had fallen by the wayside – Jade and Terry would watch television until 9 p.m. or so and then he would take her upstairs to settle her – often falling asleep with her because she didn't want him to leave.

But I never blamed Terry for the things he found difficult – he was after all in a situation most men would find impossible – and we seldom argued about it. If the odd flash of annoyance rose in me when Jade told me she'd had chocolate biscuits for breakfast, I was careful not to show Terry because I knew he was dealing with all that was happening as best he could. I convinced myself it would have been unreasonable to lash out at him when things weren't done as I would necessarily have wanted. He was the one there 24/7. With so much else going on, I did not fight minor battles about his disorganisation in the face of the war to keep my family together.

I also knew he was the one taking the emotional brunt of Jade's reaction. He was the one who held her hands when she struck out in frustration or dried her tears when I left. He did anything he could to distract her and the two spent hours wandering round electrical shops or watching trains at Salisbury station because amid bright lights and loud noises Jade would temporarily forget.

In February 2000 we had been forced to sell our house in Waterloo Road after Terry gave up work to look after Jade. We felt she needed full-time attention from the one full-time parent she had left and giving up our wages meant we couldn't keep up with the mortgage and insurance payments of about £500 a month. With everything that was happening Terry did not want the extra pressure of trying to find the money each month, and he also wanted to leave our home – feeling its every corner had been invaded by police.

My husband and daughter were declared officially homeless and moved into housing association accommodation in an area where children urinated on the street and music blared all night. It was another big change for them.

Terry and I had also gone onto benefits for the first time in our lives and it affected him deeply. He was one of the old-school for whom working and providing for his family were what was expected of him as a man. We had always worked, we had always paid our way and it was soul-destroying for Terry to be dependent on the state. We were also forced to cash in all the savings plans and insurances we'd put money into and gradually things became more and more tight.

But I think Terry could have coped if the consequences of the investigation had been limited to his becoming a 'mum' and a downturn in our finances. What really destroyed him was the fact that within hours of his son dying, he lost control over his life. Until then he had been the head of our household and master of his own destiny but the start of the police investigation signalled the end of that.

For the two and a half long years before my trial, Terry lived his life at the beck and call of social services, police and lawyers. It destroyed his identity as a man, ate away inside him – and I could only watch it happen. Every safe point he'd had to fix onto – his job, his home, his wife, his children, his finances, his status in society, his belief in the police, legal system and medical profession – disappeared almost overnight and it wreaked havoc in his mind. We'd worked hard to keep united after losing two children, but Matthew's death took us into different territory altogether.

'You know, Ange, they did it to Sally Clark and they're doing it to you,' he would say every so often.

I knew, of course, that Sally Clark had been jailed after being convicted of murdering her two babies days before Matthew died because I'd read about the case in the local paper – she had been brought up in Salisbury and her conviction had made big news. But it never struck me for a second that I could be in the same boat. There were things written about her in the papers that made mine a completely different case from hers, I thought to myself. But from the moment the police came into our lives, Terry feared I would be found guilty and kept warning me I was going to be treated in the same way she had been.

'They're digging and digging and they're not finding anything but it hasn't stopped the investigation,' he would say to me. 'Can't you see what they're doing, Ange? They're not trying to get at the truth. They want to find something against you.'

But while being charged had woken my fight, I still believed common sense would win out. I had no comprehension of the fear that was paralysing Terry. I was – and would be for months to come – living in denial and refused to believe I could ever be convicted. I had done nothing. I had told the truth.

Of course, I went to meetings with Bill and Jacqui, answered my bail and attended occasional court hearings, but it all seemed so separate from me. I was aware that expert after expert was giving their opinion on what had happened to Matthew and that the case was becoming increasingly complex. But as we moved towards 2001, I would not allow myself to think about it – Terry and Jade were my priority.

For the first six months after I left home, Jade was looked after every weekend by Jenny and I would go back to the house to spend time alone with Terry. In some ways I relished every hour as I fulfilled my mother's role, though the voices of my lost children haunted me as I cleaned, washed and ironed. I was always anxious to leave my mark on our home and made little gestures like leaving Jade's clothes laid out on the bed to show her I still existed. But I was also intensely aware of play-acting my role as a mother, and felt angry at my own pathetic gratitude that I was being given a chance to do it. Events had reduced me to a ghost mum who was forced to make her presence felt in meaningless touches on the house she had to leave. I hated doing it.

I cried an ocean of tears in that first year and, as well as the sleeping tablets I had been taking since Matthew's death, I was prescribed antidepressants – something I'd never taken regularly before, despite grieving for two children. I would spend hours gearing myself up to leave Claire's flat and put on a cheery mask

90

for the world. I never wanted to upset Jade by crying, or give social services the satisfaction, so my guard only came down when I got back to the flat. I cried myself to sleep every single night, and also turned to my sister in my worst moments.

'I just feel so desperate at what they're putting us through,' I wept as we sat together in the evening. 'Why are they doing this to us? I just don't understand why it is all taking so long.'

'They're bastards,' Claire would reply. 'But they'll see in the end there's nothing going on. You've got to hold on.'

'But it's so intrusive,' I sobbed. 'They've taken over my life, I can't grieve for Matthew and I don't know how long I can cope with this.'

'We're all here for you, Ange. You're not alone.'

After all those years of looking after Claire when we were children, she now became my strongest support. I was very aware of how much our situation was affecting her life and did my best to help out. During the long hours when I was alone, I did the housework and cooked the odd meal, forcing myself to root my 'temporary' existence around the concrete things in it, like my daily visits with Jade and weekends with Terry. I saw him most days when Jade was at school but all we did was talk about the investigation. Otherwise, with everyone at work, I would spend hours sitting in parks or in front of Salisbury cathedral with the same question that had haunted me since the first day running through my mind: Why?

I also did the occasional night of babysitting for friends and spent time with Mum and Brian, Stephen and Kellie, Dad and Katherine, Tina, Andrew, Ally, Steve Grant, Steve Crouch and their families. But I knew people had their lives to lead. Time moved on. I had seen less of Mum since her marriage to Brian but was happy it had given her a new lease of life, Tina was married, Andrew was busy with his life and Stephen and Kellie had had two more children – Brandon in 1998 and Shayleigh in 2000. The following year Shauna-Esme was born. My dad and Katherine also had a son, Joshua, in 2000. I couldn't expect everyone else's life to go on hold because ours was.

Slowly, I retreated into myself and lost the fun-loving personality I'd been known for. Increasingly I found myself simply staring into space, numbed by what was happening to us. Where once I had been a busy person, I wound down like a toy as I tried to push down the sadness that filled me.

Keeping silent put a huge strain on me and there were times when I longed to howl at the injustice of it all during a social services meeting or when I met a police officer. I'm sure there are many parents who, if in the situation we were in, think they would argue and fight every step of the way. But we are all different and I had been brought up to respect systems of authority and it was hard to dismantle years of thinking. I was also petrified of antagonising anyone and making the situation worse. Like Terry, I felt we could never give social services any kind of reason – however slight – to take Jade and feared arguing back might provide them with that. And so I forced myself to keep playing their game and trust in Bill to point out its absurdities.

But I paid a high price for the self-control I exercised. I became abnormal, an actress who played a role before switching it off and playing another. I had to steel myself to be strong and gradually I froze bit by bit inside.

Terry too learned to play roles and after sixteen years of friendship and love it was this I think that made us begin to slowly drift apart.

'I don't know how much longer I can cope with this,' he would say.

Now, months after he had buoyed me up at the beginning of the investigation, it was my turn to quietly reply, 'It's survive or go under, Terry,' as I was filled with sadness when I looked at him.

'You're my soulmate, Angela, and you being taken away from me is like another death. I feel like I'm living a double life being cheery for Jade all the time and crying alone when she's asleep and when I'm with you I just can't do it. It's so hard. I can't do anything to help you. It's all been taken out of my hands and there's nothing I can do.'

'We'll get through it,' I told him. 'We'll be together again. It can't go on and on because someone will realise how ridiculous it all is. You've got to remember that, Terry – it will end.'

We always tried to make the most of our time alone and, in the beginning, our love life was a source of great comfort and reassurance to me. We had always enjoyed a healthy sex life and at the beginning of our separation it was still there. It was less passionate, less regular, but we still drew physical comfort from each other.

But when Terry decided it was too much for Jenny to look after Jade every weekend – after all, she had a family of her own – we had to instigate a rota system. Five families were police-checked – Mum and Brian, Terry and Gill Chambers, Dad and Katherine, Stephen and Kellie and Claire and Kevin – so that they could look after Jade. But it was a nightmare juggling everyone's demands. It felt as if we were going cap in hand asking people to swap and change and fill in spots that others couldn't do because they had things arranged. As a mum, it deeply upset me that some people didn't seem to want to give up their time to look after my daughter, while others were only too happy to have her.

Gradually Jade picked up on all the difficulties and, while there were times with Jenny when she would play up or refuse to eat, she became more and more resistant to going away to other people. Her distress at our separation was heightened by feeling that people didn't want her and we had to tell her lie after lie to get her to go. It created real problems between Terry and me as we argued over whoever had caused a problem and how to handle it. And so, in the end, the rota system broke down and we snatched a few hours or the odd night together whenever possible. But you can't be a couple with no real time alone.

During the summer of 2000 I watched helplessly as Terry became increasingly depressed. Fear was another emotion he struggled with. From the moment social services came into our lives, it was made clear that if we put a foot wrong we could lose Jade. We also knew suspicion hung over Terry about whether he'd been involved in the 'abuse' of our children. Anxiety about losing Jade began to control him and, as our relationship weakened, he became more and more focused on her.

At times it was almost more than we could bear to follow the rules set down for us. For instance, I would always be picked up and dropped off for visits by a social worker, and no one ever seemed to do random checks to make sure we weren't together at other times. The temptation to turn straight round as I opened the front door into Claire's flat was always overwhelming. But Terry and I knew we mustn't put a foot wrong.

'I'm off into town with Jade,' he would phone up to say – making sure I didn't go in and accidentally bump into them, which would break the supervision rule. Or he'd watch every drop he drank on an evening with Jade at a friend's house because he knew he could never have a few too many and stay over. Anyone who cared for Jade had to be police-checked and Terry couldn't stay overnight with a friend who hadn't been. It meant he never relaxed properly – either he was at home surrounded by all he had lost or he was out visiting friends aware that he had to get back home – and Terry started to distance himself from many people in his life.

There were bright spots amid all the officialdom – Chris Howard Jones from Victim Support provided Terry with invaluable friendship. He phoned her every day and nothing was too much for her. Chris did a million things for my family – like getting a refund on the money we'd put down before Matthew died on a family holiday for the four of us, to helping Terry find a new home and finding Jade a Brownie pack to join. She was brilliant and we will be forever grateful. But mostly Terry felt that everyone in a position of authority over him was against him, and things were made worse by the attitude of the social workers who constantly seemed to drop tiny pebbles of threat into his mind.

'You know you really shouldn't leave pills lying around,' they'd say gesturing to a bottle of paracetamol on top of the fridge, invariably on a Friday, which meant Terry spent all weekend worrying over what might happen.

'It's unbearable,' he'd say. 'I know it sounds strange but the fear of losing Jade is beginning to seem worse than losing Gemma, Jason and Matthew. We lost them and we have tried to cope with it. That's one thing. But to lose the one child we have left would be too much.'

94

For more than two years, Terry felt bowed by the constant threat of our daughter being taken into care. It ground him down. So great was his fear of losing Jade that he always kept £400 in cash tucked away somewhere so that if the social workers came in the front door he could be out the back. However tight things were he never touched that money because he felt it was the one thing that could save him if he heard a knock at the door – enough money to spirit our daughter away and keep her with him. But there was never the need because month after month we played it exactly by the book so that they wouldn't have a reason to come for Jade.

To cope with it all, Terry began to drink more and more at home. Until Matthew died, we had been weekend drinkers – a bottle of wine with a takeaway and a couple more on big celebrations. But he turned to the bottle to try and quell his demons and, during the quiet night-times when sleep eluded him, he downed more and more booze in an effort to block things out.

I knew his drinking had increased – although the social workers of course didn't – but I never realised how bad things had become. By the end of the summer he couldn't face a day without drink and regularly knocked back four lagers and quarter of a bottle of brandy every night.

By this time it was only Jade who kept him going. She was his focus in all the chaos and I wonder if he would be here now without her. She was the one bright point of reference as he descended deeper and deeper into the darkness of despair.

The first few lines of the contact agreement echoed in my head as I sat looking into the mirror. 'The aim of this agreement is to enable Jade to enjoy a family day out on the occasion of her aunt's wedding on Saturday 4th November 2000 at which she will be a bridesmaid', it had read.

What a joke, I thought to myself, angry that yet another memorable day for our family had been reduced to a seven-point social services agreement. But I forced myself to quell the feeling as I smiled at the hairdresser who was pinning my usually unkempt hair into a glamorous 'up do'. Claire, Tina and two other brides-maids sat in nearby chairs chatting and laughing excitedly about the day ahead.

It was organised chaos. Claire was marrying Kevin at St John's Church in Lower Bemerton and my family were decking out the Castle Street social club in the centre of town for the reception. What Claire didn't know was that there was a huge panic on – with just hours to go the tables weren't yet set up properly and most of the decorations still had to be put up.

'Is everything okay?' Claire had asked me when I arrived to be transformed into her matron of honour.

'Oh yes,' I lied, as an image of Kevin and his best man franti-cally blowing up balloons popped into my head. 'All under control. It looks fantastic. You won't recognise the place.'

I knew it would be another bittersweet day for me. I was so pleased to see Claire walking down the aisle and couldn't wait to see Jade in her bridesmaid's dress, but, as ever, some fundamental part of me felt excluded from the happiness. Yet again I would be an actress playing a role leaving the real me hidden somewhere deep inside.

'Mum, don't forget you've got to take Jade in a separate car from me to the church so you should leave first. We're not allowed to go together,' I shouted, as I slipped Jade's dress over her head after we'd got back to Claire's flat.

'It's a load of rubbish,' my mum replied as she walked in. 'Completely ridiculous. I'm going to tell a social worker what I think when I next see one.'

I fought back tears as we gazed at Jade. Her dress had a blue satin top with a white ballerina skirt and she wore a headband decorated in blue and white flowers.

'Do I look like a princess, Mummy?' she asked, as she looked down at herself excitedly.

'Yes, you really do, darling,' I whispered.

Just before 2 p.m. we met Terry outside the church. I knew the day was going to be hard for him. The depression that had been a shadow on his shoulder for months had finally engulfed him a few weeks before. It was one of our rare weekends together and

I was surprised on the Saturday night when Terry had dissolved into tears because he couldn't get a duvet cover on.

'I just can't do it, Ange. I just can't do it,' he had kept repeating as he crumpled to the floor.

I'd had no idea what to do. Crippled by fear about what was happening to my strong, independent protector, I crouched down and put my arms around him. It scared me to see Terry slowly disintegrate and realise there were now gaps in our once rock-solid relationship. I just couldn't seem to find the right words to convince him to seek treatment. He was locked in a world I couldn't find the way into and to see him cry over a duvet cover made me want to scream in fear.

But he'd refused to talk about it that night and instead had gone to bed in silence. The next morning, though, I had come downstairs to find him incoherently weeping like a child, curled up on the living-room floor like a wounded animal.

'I can't bear it,' he had sobbed. 'I just can't bear it any more, Ange. All I can think about is how to stop this pain.'

As Terry pleaded to be sent to a psychiatric unit, I phoned a doctor who arrived, gave him Valium and told me he was suffering an acute reaction to strain. Two days later, after a mental health assessment, he was put on two types of antidepressants, and nurses from the Salisbury community mental health team started daily visits, which became his lifeline. Terry knew he would lose Jade for certain if he didn't hold himself together and he had forced himself to carry on.

But as we stood outside the church, it was as if all the light had gone from inside him. He looked blank, expressionless, and I knew he didn't want to be there.

'C'mon, Terry,' I said. 'We've got to make the most of the day. It's Claire's big day and we've got to at least try to be happy.'

'Leave it,' he replied. 'I'm here, aren't I? I know you can but I'm sick of putting on a front. I just can't deal with this. I can't play happy families. It's almost a year to the day that Matthew died and I can't live this charade any more.'

He walked off to have a cigarette as my dad came up to me.

'Are you okay, love?' he asked.

'Not really,' I replied. 'But we've got to keep smiling, Dad. There's nothing else we can do.'

I was painfully aware Terry and I had swapped roles. While I had initially been locked in a cosy world of shock and denial, he had been the strong one. But month after month of coping had sapped his emotional reserves and now I was the one determined not to be beaten. My fierce refusal to let my family fall apart almost scared me at times, but I loved them more than anything in the world and wasn't going to let them go. Gradually I had assumed the role of the 'strong one'.

One photo taken in the soft sunshine of that afternoon as we stood outside the church unmasked the unhappiness all three of us felt. It is a group picture and Terry stands at the back, his brows knitted and a blank attempt of a smile on his face, while I am at the front next to the bride and groom with a frozen look in my eyes. Jade nestles slightly into my side, sadness and confusion etched on her childish features. As everyone else smiled, the camera momentarily dismantled our sadness and captured it for ever.

But the day was also about celebrating for Claire and, like so many other occasions, I pulled myself together, forgot for a few brief hours and concentrated on the happiness of the people I loved. As the afternoon passed, Jade's confidence grew amid the hum of chatter and peals of laughter at the reception and, by the time we had finished our meal, she was walking from table to table introducing herself.

About 9 p.m. I began to feel anxious again. According to the rules of the contact agreement, Jade had to leave with Jenny in an hour and I wondered how we would ever persuade her to go. She was on a high and I knew she would be distraught when we told her she had to leave. In a normal situation, we would have been able to take her home and hush her reluctance, but we couldn't, and I knew she would hate to leave Terry and me when she was having such fun.

Just before ten I walked into the hall where the music was blaring and gathered her into my arms. 'Come on, darling,' I said. 'Aunty Jenny is here to pick you up and you've got to go home with her now.'

Immediately she started struggling to break free, writhing against me in a desperate attempt to get away. I tightened my grip around her, and fought back tears as I carried her out. 'I want to stay here with you,' she screamed. 'I want Daddy. Don't make me go, Mummy.'

I stumbled towards Jenny who grabbed Jade from my arms before turning and running into the darkness. All I could hear were Jade's screams echoing in the black night as I stood looking into it.

'Terry's gone,' I heard someone say as I tried to stop myself sobbing.

I said a hurried goodbye to Claire and ran out of the hall. It was a freezing night but I slipped off my shoes anyway as I started to run – I couldn't get to Terry fast enough.

I found him sobbing in the car and slipped wordlessly into the seat beside him. Neither of us spoke as I drove home.

But while Terry was overwhelmed by despair, only one feeling filled me – anger.

You bastards, my mind screamed. What gives you the right to do this to us?

CHAPTER SEVEN

At the beginning of 2001 Bill and Jacqui glimpsed their first – and vital – chance to get the case against me dropped. My committal hearing was being held in January and they were hopeful they would finally be able to stop the juggernaut that was advancing on me. A judge or stipendiary magistrate decides if there is sufficient evidence to transfer a case from the magistrates to the crown court for trial at a committal hearing. Both sides outline their arguments before the court and it is then decided if the case will be transferred – or thrown out.

Fourteen months on from Matthew's death, Bill and Jacqui were still as mystified as ever why the police thought they had a case against me.

'I've often met clients who say they have no idea why they have been arrested,' Bill once told me. 'And then you get the papers and read them and there is some nugget of information which shows why they were and you can see what lies behind the police interest. But in your case, Angela, I simply cannot see it. There has never been any suggestion that you have harmed any of your children before, there is nothing unusual in your background, there have never been any problems with Jade and you said nothing in your police interviews.'

Like Terry, Bill had scoured the papers sent to him by the CPS for any concrete evidence – however slight. But despite searching through ten ring binders stuffed with documents, he could find nothing that went any way to proving I had harmed my children. It was all speculation – a question of how events were viewed rather than facts, gaps in my memory that time and shock could explain, expert opinion about possible causes for my children's deaths rather than concrete conclusions.

Michael Mansfield QC was the barrister who had taken on my case, a famous lawyer who had been involved in a string of high-profile cases including the Guildford Four, and the murders of Jill Dando and of Stephen Lawrence. He took the unusual step of appearing at Salisbury Magistrates Court for the committal hearing – not the usual place you'll find such an eminent legal mind.

The prosecution's case was essentially circumstantial – that I was always alone when one of my children had breathing problems or died, that extensive tests had failed to discover any medical reasons for the events and that experts believed they were characteristic of smothering. The prosecution also pointed to supposed lies I had told about the apnoea alarms. It was obvious the police believed I had never used them at all. I'd told officers that I didn't know if I'd heard them start or not, but engineers said they would have been clearly audible. I'd also said my babies were cold when I found them lifeless. Apparently the alarms would have alerted me seconds after they stopped breathing, and therefore they would have still been warm. I couldn't explain away their suspicion, I could only tell the truth. I had used the alarms and that is what had happened.

'I still can't understand where they think they've got proof of murder,' said Bill. 'They sent me the papers and I turned the pages with my heart in my mouth waiting to find something that could sink us, but I never found it.'

My defence team were bold in their submissions to the court. They argued that it wasn't a question of whether I had committed murder or not – but if a crime had been committed at all. There was no conclusive evidence that my babies' deaths were unnatural and certainly no proof I had been the one to harm them. There was no body with a gunshot, no evidence of motive and no confession, simply what the prosecution said was a suspicious sequence of events, 'unnatural' behaviour from me and physical evidence that could only suggest – and not prove – smothering.

'The only reason Angela Cannings finds herself before the courts arises from the combined circumstances of there being as many as three deaths in her family without any specific cause being found,' my defence submission read. 'The possibility that they arose from some natural cause which medical science in its present state of development is simply unable to identify is one that must be allowed.'

But while the judge listened patiently and threw out the murder charge relating to Gemma because of a lack of evidence, she wouldn't agree to halt the case altogether and committed it for trial at the crown court. I was devastated.

Weeks later we agreed to make a documentary about my case with the BBC. Programme makers had approached us soon after I was charged – keen to make a film about a woman like Sally Clark who had lost babies and was on trial for murder. We had thought long and hard about taking part and were concerned about putting our life on show. But we finally agreed because we felt it would at least give us the chance to keep a record of events and put our side of the story forward when things ended. We started working with the programme producers; Terry was given a video camera to record his feelings, and they visited me from time to time. Jade was not involved in any way at all but none the less the whole thing caused lots of problems with Wiltshire County Council because they were jittery about possible breaches of the injunction covering her. But we were determined to go ahead.

As the months passed, I convinced myself that someone would have to listen at some point and the whole ridiculous case against me would fall apart. What I could never have imagined back then was that however loudly my legal team shouted that there was no case to answer, however many arguments they put forward that the trial should be stopped, it was going to go ahead come what may. As one eminent legal mind involved in my case mistakenly said: 'There are four dead children and someone has to be brought to book.' This attitude ran through every authority we came into contact with – police, the legal profession and the world of medicine – because in cases like mine the British justice system had been turned on its head. Instead of the prosecution having to prove guilt beyond reasonable doubt, mothers were being asked to prove their innocence. Where women were once treated with kindness, the attitude had shifted by the time Matthew died. By then many in the medical profession believed that two or more babies simply did not die naturally in one family. Professor Emery was one of the first doctors to alert the medical world to the fact that some deaths described as SIDS were in fact the result of abuse and the two could be hard to tell apart. But where most reasonable doctors accepted that of course some babies were killed, but the vast majority died of natural causes, others began to see murder everywhere. As the years passed this 'think dirty' school of thought had become increasingly powerful, first within the paediatric profession, and then within the courts.

Bill knew the case against me hung on the evidence of three medical experts – one of whom was Professor Sir Roy Meadow, a fearsome adversary to have. One of the country's most eminent paediatricians and a leading expert on child abuse, he had been giving evidence in criminal and family court cases for years. He was known for pioneering work on Munchausen's Syndrome by Proxy which drove some mothers to harm their children in a bid to gain attention for themselves. He also supported an American pathologist's theory known as the rule of three. In a book Professor Meadow had edited called *The ABC of Child Abuse*, he described it as 'a crude aphorism but a sensible working rule'. It has since come to be known in the UK as Meadow's Law – one sudden infant death is a tragedy, two is suspicious and three is murder until proved otherwise.

Professor Meadow was one of the most influential doctors of his kind and his evidence, if not his face, was known to millions. He was the man who had told Sally Clark's trial that the likelihood of two SIDS in a family like hers was one in 73 million. As far as the general public knew, the chances of winning the lottery were greater than losing two babies to cot death.

When Bill discovered Professor Meadow was working for the prosecution, he phoned Sally Clark's father, Frank Lockyer. Bill had known Frank for years because Frank lived in Salisbury, and he put him in touch with John Batt, a solicitor and close family friend who had worked on Sally's legal team. Their conversation made Bill realise just how big the mountain was that we had to climb.

He realised it was going to be almost impossible to 'prove' my innocence because we would never be able to 'prove' how my children died. The very term 'cot death' means that no one knows how a baby has died. It is not a diagnosis but a description applied when known causes have been ruled out. All that is certain is that some babies inexplicably stop breathing. It is a phenomenon stretching back to the judgement of King Solomon, but modern medicine has yet to explain it. Advances have been made – such as the discovery that putting babies on their backs lowers death rates – but SIDS essentially remains a mystery. No one could possibly know how my babies had died – and while an expert might believe they had been smothered, there was no test we could use in my defence to prove they had not been.

Bill decided that the more he could do to say the deaths were inexplicable, that no one knew exactly how my children had died, that there was no evidence they had been murdered – let alone by me – the better. He started to explore as many avenues as possible to suggest other causes, from genetics to environmental factors. As long as we created reasonable doubt over the murder charges, I would walk free.

I knew nothing of all this. Bill didn't want to add to my worries and I had little comprehension of the difficulties he was facing. But he also knew he must prepare me for facing my accusers in court.

'Professor Meadow is a very respected doctor and is seen as a champion against child abuse,' Bill said as we sat discussing the case. 'He is going to appear against you for the prosecution as he did in the Sally Clark case.'

'But we lost three babies and she lost two,' Terry replied. 'How are we going to defend Angela when Sally lost?'

'Well, we will go out and find experts who will counteract what those for the prosecution are going to say,' Bill told us. 'And if we can show that what Professor Meadow's evidence amounts to at most is his belief that Angela might – only might – have harmed the children, then that is good enough for the court. There are ways of combating everything he will say.'

Bill and Jacqui believed genetics were one of the key ways to do this. They had been to Ireland to see my cousins and asked me to draw up a family tree. Bill had also started working with Professor Michael Patton, a consultant in clinical genetics at St George's Hospital medical school in London. He worked with families in which there were inherited genetic disorders or disabilities and asked if I could extend the family tree right back to my great-grandmother's time. But I wasn't able to – we just didn't have the information. When Terry, Bill and I went up to London to see Professor Patton, he told us of his strong suspicion that a genetic problem in our family was missing generations, and he took our blood to test.

We also went down to Southampton to have ECG tests done to check for heart abnormalities – an exhausting process because we had to get the family court to agree to let Jade go.

As the months passed I still clung onto the hope that someone, somehow would see the light, and so did my defence team. In the future we would be offered ways to avoid a murder trial – such as the suggestion that I plead guilty to manslaughter or infanticide – but we refused. I had done nothing wrong. I would never admit guilt for something I hadn't done, however big the gamble. We all agreed that we would get the charges thrown out or see me walk free from court.

My legal team made two further submissions at my trial asking to have the case stopped but they were rejected. The legal profession's deafness to our pleas still amazes and angers me. I was trapped from the moment Matthew took his last breath.

I blinked in the bright afternoon light and looked at the social worker asleep in our garden. She was supposed to be there to supervise my daily visit with Jade but had dropped off about three-quarters of an hour ago.

'Do you want a drink?' I shouted to Jade.

'No,' she called back as she carried on playing with her friends.

I looked anxiously at my watch. It was 5.15 p.m. and I would have to be gone in quarter of an hour. Jade knew, of course – all too used to living her life by the clock, she had been the first child in her class to tell the time – but she didn't follow me as I opened the front door and walked inside alone.

I sat down with a sigh. It was summer 2001 – almost two years since Matthew's death – and I was desperately fighting to hold onto the threads of my relationship with my daughter. I still saw her six times a week and on the occasional family day when a contact agreement was issued. But a silenced part of me knew I was fast becoming a mother in name only. Jade had blossomed from a toddler into an independent five year old and I knew I was losing the battle to keep our relationship intact.

Whereas in the months after Matthew's death she had kept asking when I was coming home and crying when I left, she now seemed to have accepted the fact that I wasn't around. I would arrive for a visit and she would be gone within minutes, only coming back to say a quick goodbye. As time went on she also became less and less affectionate towards me. A brief kiss hello and goodbye were all I could expect and I longed to cuddle her properly.

'Would you like me to sort out your hair, Jadey?' I would ask when she arrived home scruffy after the school day.

'No thank you, Mummy,' she usually replied. 'I can do that myself.'

It cut me to the quick to see her growing self-sufficiency. She dressed herself, did her hair, hoovered the carpet and fed the dog. I kept telling myself that forcing her to spend time with me to make myself feel better would only be selfish because a clinging mother wouldn't do her any good. But in truth I found her distance heartbreaking. To lose my living child was almost more than I could bear.

I longed for everything to stop, for someone to look up and say 'We have made a huge mistake.' I felt almost teased by my daily visits, a tiny bit of time to try and reconnect to what I had once been before I was whisked away again.

Our separation was worse because our situation was always

'temporary'. Unlike traumatic events like a death or a divorce, which are concrete happenings, there was no fixed point on the horizon for us to tell Jade about and we could never tell her when I was coming home. After two years of living in limbo she now treated me more like a visiting relative than her mother.

'I just can't believe they think Jade isn't being affected by all this,' Terry said to John Pook, the social services manager, one day.

Weeks before, Jade had been assessed by a psychiatrist at our request because we were so worried about the stress she was under. But the report had come back saying she wasn't unduly affected.

'Mmm,' John replied in a non-committal way, as he sat nursing a cup of tea.

John might have been a social services big-wig but he was the one person who had always approached our case with common sense. From the start he had treated us as a family rather than a case study and his humanity was plain.

'We waited months for that and then they say everything's a-okay when it's not,' said Terry. 'Can't they see what's happening between Jade and Angela? Do they really think it's normal for a little girl to be like a stranger with her mum? It's ridiculous. We asked for help nearly two years ago and we've got to wait until October for her to start play therapy – twenty-three months after Matthew died. And all the time I keep worrying that one day they'll say, "That's it," and take her from us.'

'You know I'll do all I can to keep Jade with you,' John replied, his voice low.

I looked at him with relief. We knew there were many people who believed Jade should have been taken into care – that the suspicions about me and the support Terry had shown me meant we shouldn't be anywhere near our daughter. But, thanks to John, we had been able to keep her and we knew it hadn't been easy for him.

'I've been in this job twenty-eight years and I am being laughed at,' he'd told Terry one day when they were talking about his belief that we should be allowed to be a family.

But whatever professional difficulties he faced, John always treated us with fairness and compassion – and for that we will always be grateful.

Time had also wreaked its havoc on Terry. In the year since I'd found him weeping on the carpet he had never again expressed the suicidal desperation of that day. But he was living like a zombie – able to slip into the roles of happy daddy, smiling daddy and funny daddy with ease but doing everything else on autopilot. The only thing fixed in his mind was keeping hold of Jade and he orbited his life around her. If she wanted to stay in the playground for a go on the monkey bars he would stand silently for an hour while she did; if she wanted to go and look in shop windows he would agree. It was all a way of filling up time. Terry still longed for adult company. He saw Stephen and Kellie, his parents, Steve Crouch, Steve Grant and Terry Chambers regularly, and of course me, but he still spent hour after hour alone and always had to say goodbye to whoever came to visit him. Loneliness would grip him as he shut the door and went back into the lounge to pour himself another brandy.

He also found spending time with Jade and me increasingly difficult. It was too painful a reminder of what was happening to his family. Where once he had sat in on visits, Terry now went for a drive and listened to Meat Loaf at top volume to drown out the thoughts racing through his mind. He'd leave the house at 3.31 p.m., a minute after I arrived, and return at 5.29 p.m. to see me leave.

'Can't you at least try to stay, Terry?' I asked angrily one day when I'd made another meal he hadn't turned up to eat with us. 'Do you really think Jade won't notice if every time I walk through the door you go out of it? That I cook a meal and you don't turn up? I can't do everything on my own.'

'I just can't take the social workers any more, Ange,' he replied. 'I don't want to sit and eat a meal with them looking on. I know they've got it great here. They've said enough times we're the most normal family they've ever dealt with. But I just can't stand being with them any more.'

'Well how on earth do you think I feel?' I exploded. 'There's someone watching every minute I spend with my little girl and you leave because you can't handle it?'

'Exactly, Ange,' he shouted back. 'I spend every minute alone with Jade and I need a break from her. Your visits are the only chance I get to take a break, to let go of her. Is it so wrong that I want a bit of time on my own?'

I turned away. No longer sure of who was right and who was wrong.

Later, when Jade finally fell asleep, Terry spent hours lighting bonfires of rubbish and staring into the flames – losing himself in his own world. The loss of control over his life continued to haunt him and thoughts of Gemma and Jason filled his mind.

'It was so different, Angela,' he would say. 'We decided on the funeral arrangements, when we went back to work, everything. But with Matthew we never had that chance. I feel we've let him down.'

'Terry, we couldn't have done anything differently,' I told him, knowing the explanation wouldn't calm his hurt because it didn't rid me of mine.

'But it's so wrong,' he replied. 'What they're doing to us is torture. They've ripped the heart out of this family, Angela.'

The first year we were apart was mostly about getting to grips with how we were being treated and the timetables we had to run to – social services and legal meetings, family court hearings every eight weeks to renew the interim care order. But during that second year we almost stopped feeling because we were both exhausted by living in limbo.

There were times when I would lie in bed wondering how much longer I could cope with it. I had been referred to see a psychologist in December 2000 and after six months of seeing her every two to three weeks she had warned about the long-term stress I was under. Soon social services would comment that I was acting out of character with Jade – shutting the door after going upstairs with her and washing her hair. After so long I was finding it hard to follow the rules and, at times, could not stop myself from breaking them, in whatever tiny ways.

I had long ago lost any shred of faith in the authorities and was filled with an almost overwhelming sense of shame about what was happening to me. I was a local Salisbury girl and had grown up in a respectable family who knew all sorts of people in the town. But I now stood accused of the worst crime a mother could be. Like the day I was taken to the magistrates court in the police van, I felt strangely embarrassed every time I saw something in the newspapers about the Salisbury mother charged with murdering her children. And because I was unable to speak out and defend myself, I knew the general public would form their own opinions of me and, for some, a label had been fixed to me that I would take to my grave no matter what the court decided.

In the beginning I would go into town alone and force myself to hold my head up high but that stopped after I was charged for fear people might lash out at me. My feelings, though, were mostly paranoid. I might have got the odd look but by and large the people of Salisbury treated me well. Instead of being spat at in the street, many expressed their sadness at what was happening – in particular some of Mum's lifelong friends – and there were also near strangers who went that extra mile to reassure me. I remember one particular day when a girl whose face I vaguely recognised ran up to me in town. I couldn't remember for the life of me where I knew her from.

'Angela, I worked with you at Milford House nursing home before you had Jade,' she said breathlessly. 'Do you remember? You did a few shifts to earn some extra money? I just wanted to say that I've heard what is happening and if there is anything I can do to help please don't hesitate. There are lots of people who support you.'

She reached out and squeezed my arm as she spoke and I have never forgotten that moment of kindness because it showed me, however briefly, that the whole world didn't think I was a monster.

It wasn't just Terry, Jade and I who suffered. Our parents had lost another grandchild, our siblings a nephew, Stephen his half-brother, and two years on they continued to helplessly watch the suffering of the people they loved. There were times when words failed them and, while no one tried to brush things under the carpet, they just didn't know what to say or do to make things better for us. They too were exhausted – the situation just went on and on and it is difficult to keep talking, to keep going in circles of 'why', to keep giving a shoulder to cry on when things never change. After fifteen months living with Claire and Kevin it was obvious they needed some space and I had moved to my mum and Brian's flat in February 2001, where I now slept on a blow-up bed in the living room. Just as Claire had done before, it was now my mum's turn to wipe away my tears and reassure me on the nights when it all became too much. Emotionally and practically our story affected many more people than the three at its heart. The people around us were shocked that we had lost another child and horrified at what the police and social services were doing to us.

Terry had started to let go of me as a wife from the moment I was charged and, as the autumn of the following year approached, our relationship became increasingly distant.

The reason? His belief that I was going to be convicted. There had been several court hearings as my case slowly moved through the system, the postponement of two trial dates, the rejection of an application to the Court of Appeal to hear the two murder charges separately and hundreds of pages of medical reports from experts telling us why they thought Matthew and Jason had died. But while I still believed common sense would out because I had done nothing wrong, Terry took a different view of the situation – Sally Clark had been convicted.

He felt he had to prepare for life without me and, although I didn't know it at the time, began to resent me. I was a constant reminder of what had once been so good and he slowly withdrew in an effort to prepare himself to lose me for many years – meaning he would be in his sixties, and Jade in her twenties, when I was finally released.

The intimacy had drained out of our relationship on every level. Physically our love life had dwindled soon after those first few months of weekends together and it made me sad. We had enjoyed a long and loving relationship and I felt as if my role as a woman had been put on hold. But it was the emotional aspects of his withdrawal which were the most upsetting.

Terry, once so talkative and funny, became off-hand with me and avoided contact. If I went to hug him, he froze, and if I tried to ask him what was happening, he told me he was dealing with things the best he could. After Jade started school we saw each other during the day but, as with her, it wasn't enough time in which to relax and go with the flow. Instead the court case and situation with social services dominated our conversation and we sat drinking cups of tea and smoking cigarettes instead of doing the things couples do – a bit of DIY, the supermarket shopping, planning a holiday, having a row.

Sometimes I was gripped by a desire to be close to Terry again – both emotionally and physically – because after seventeen years together I felt very lonely without him. I had always looked up to him because he was that bit older than me and it was strange that gradually our roles had reversed. But I honestly never felt angry or frustrated with him. I felt like I was fighting for my life. I wasn't going to do anything like argue with or condemn him because it would only push us further apart. I was also so tired much of the time that I couldn't even think and as long as he was around I felt I could cope. Jade was the one area where niggles could surface because it was hard being patient when she announced she'd eaten crisps for breakfast. I also longed to at least have the chance to spend time with her that Terry had.

As for me, two years after losing Matthew I continued to be frozen inside – grief, anger and outrage all locked down within me as I simply focused on each day as it came. Afraid to look back – or forward – for fear of being overwhelmed by my feelings, I concentrated on Terry and Jade rather than myself. Numbness still filled me and I didn't allow myself to let go of the control I had exercised for so long. I was too afraid that if I fell apart the fragile remnants of my life would also collapse, that I would lose absolutely everything I had left, and so I made myself stay together.

I know Terry found my control frustrating at times. He would want to talk and talk about the case but sometimes I just couldn't.

'Why don't you ring Bill and ask if we can have a weekly update on what's happening?' he'd ask if we hadn't heard anything for a while.

'Oh, there's no need, he'll be in touch when there's something to say,' I would listlessly reply.

'But, Ange, you really need to know what's going on. It's important, the trial won't be long now and you need to know what's happening. You are fighting for your life and you just don't seem to care. Look at us. We've hardly got anything to say to each other any more. You might be able to shut yourself off but I want to talk about it.'

Where Terry withdrew from me but remained interested in the case, I withdrew from the case and was only interested in my family. I still couldn't take on board exactly what was happening, acknowledge the awfulness of it all, and it was only when we got the trial date of February 2002 that it began to sink in.

Four months before I was due in court we went on a rare day out with Terry and Gill Chambers and I realised just how far Terry and I had drifted. The BBC documentary producers, who we had been working with throughout the year, had suggested they take us to Lingfield Park race course in Surrey for the day to film. I was looking forward to it, hopeful Terry would enjoy it because racing was one of the few things he had kept an interest in since we had lost Matthew.

But from the minute we arrived he made it obvious he didn't want to be there. He'd get a winner and instead of celebrating would look glum; we'd be at the railings cheering and he'd be silent.

'We've got this one day, Terry,' I told him impatiently as anger pricked inside me. 'Just one day to enjoy ourselves, so let's just shut it off. Terry and Gill have made the effort to be here and it would be nice if you could at least pretend. I just want to feel normal for a few hours. That's all. It's not too much to ask, is it?'

But Terry just wouldn't cheer up and I spent the day trying in vain to compensate.

As we were leaving I brushed past Mick Channon, a former Southampton football player turned horse trainer – for Terry the ultimate sporting hero – and saw a chance to finally put a smile on his face. I looked at Gill.

'I can't believe it,' I said breathlessly. 'Should I get his autograph? Do you think I should go and get it? I don't know if I'm brave enough. Terry would love it though. The Saints and horse racing rolled into one – his ideal man.'

Gill laughed. 'Go on,' she said. 'He won't mind. It won't take a minute.'

Desperate to put a smile on Terry's face and sure that he would love the autograph, I took a deep breath and ran up to Mick Channon. Seconds later I ran back to Gill with the prized signature in my hand.

'I can't believe I just did that!' I laughed as I looked for Terry who was up ahead. 'There he is. I'm just going to give it to him. He'll be so excited.'

I rushed up to Terry and thrust the piece of paper into his hand with a rush of pleasure – eager to see his face break into its familiar smile for the first time in weeks. He looked down.

'Right,' he said and carried on walking.

It was as if someone had kicked me in the stomach and I stood confused, unsure of what to do. I felt stupid, ridiculous, humiliated. I had run up to Terry like a little girl and he had dismissed me. What was happening to us? Where was the man who had protected me, comforted me, laughed with me and dreamed with me for all those years? There was nothing I could say as Gill took my arm.

'Come on, let's go,' she said. 'It's been a long day. Don't take any notice, Angie. He's just in a bad mood.'

But I knew it was no mood. A mood is a passing emotion which soon changes but Terry had in many ways permanently left our relationship and, whatever I did, he wasn't coming back to me.

'I can't believe there's just a month to go,' I told Terry as we sat having a coffee while Jade was at school. 'But at least it will mean it's finally over. When we get into court the jury will be able to see I did nothing wrong. They're ordinary people like us.'

'I'm not so sure, Angela,' Terry quietly replied. 'I think it's about eighty/twenty.'

I looked at him. He'd always been pessimistic about my chances but in the months leading up to my trial had begun to talk quite openly about his belief that things wouldn't go well for me.

'What do you mean?' I asked.

'I think you will be convicted,' came the response and, yet again, I died a little more inside.

'Well, if you think that then what's the jury going to think?' I asked angrily. 'How on earth can I be convicted when I've done nothing wrong?'

'Ange, you know I believe in you but from the moment Matthew died I've been trying to find a reason why and everything I've read from the prosecution shows the system is against you. I've been to the hearings, I've listened to what's being said and it's obvious that the defence could serve up a five-course meal and not win but the prosecution only has to produce a boiled egg and the judge agrees. Bill can't prove you're innocent, the prosecution can't prove you're guilty but you'll get convicted because you were on your own and because of the attitude we've seen from day one. They think three children don't die for no reason – and they don't. But the difference between me and them is that they think you did it.

'I'm sorry, Ange. I know I'm hard but it's the truth and I've got to tell you the way I see it.'

I stared at him in disbelief. I felt let down, disrespected and abandoned by the man I had loved for all those years.

How can he be so cruel? I thought to myself as I bit my lip and doubt filled me for the first time whether our relationship would ever recover.

As the days counted down, Terry and I knew we would have to talk to Jade about what was happening, and we did so, just after her sixth birthday.

'It's been a very long time now that people have been looking at whether I hurt Gemma, Jason and Matthew,' I told her. 'But now the people in the big building are going to decide whether I've done anything. If they decide I have then I will have to go to another big building, and if they don't I will come home.'

'Will I see you then, Mummy?' she asked.

'Well, it won't take just one day to decide, darling. It will take a little while and because of that I will only see you at weekends instead of every day. But I'll be thinking of you all the time I'm there and when I see you at the weekend you can tell me all about what's been happening at school and with Daddy.'

I was distraught that I wouldn't be seeing Jade every day during the trial – my visits with her were my lifeline and I wondered how I'd cope without them. But I knew I would be leaving to get to court at about 8.30 a.m. and not getting back until after 6 p.m. and there was no way social services would cover a visit each evening.

I also knew I wasn't going to see much of Terry during the trial because, after much discussion, we had decided he would stay at home to look after Jade. We felt it would be less disruptive for her. She'd had enough to put up with and pushing her from pillar to post with friends and relatives during a trial lasting several weeks would do her no good. There had even been the suggestion that she go into care and there was no way Terry and I were going to give social services an inch after coming this far.

My family, though, made it clear that they felt Terry was letting me down and one night my mum confronted me when I got back to her house.

'Why can't Terry be there with you?' she asked angrily. 'He needs to be by your side. You need your husband there. It's important.'

'Mum, we don't know how long this will last and if it does last a long time then Jade really doesn't need the disruption,' I replied.

'But someone else could look after her.'

'What are you talking about?' I snapped. 'Don't you think we've been through enough? We both agree it would be best if Terry stays at home with Jade. I know if I wanted him to be there he would, but I just want to do the right thing for her.'

My mum fell silent as I made it clear I wasn't going to carry on the discussion but I knew she wasn't convinced.

Apart from deciding what was going to happen to Jade, I resisted all attempts to prepare me for the trial, and it was Claire who forced me to go shopping for a suit to wear in court.

'You've got to show them what kind of family you're from and you've got to look dignified,' she exclaimed. 'We are a respectable family and you've got to look respectable.'

But even as I bought new clothes to face the jury in I didn't allow thoughts of prison to enter my head. I knew I would never be able to deal with what lay ahead if I started to consider the possibility that I might be convicted.

It was on one of my final visits with Jade that I was thrown a lifeline of hope by John Pook.

Even with the trial looming, Terry and I were still concerned about what might happen with social services when it ended because an acquittal for me didn't mean I would be innocent in their eyes. We knew we might still face a fight to get the interim care order lifted and Jade's name taken off the child protection register. Criminal courts might work on reasonable doubt but family courts adhere to the principle of the balance of probabilities and don't have to listen if a jury acquits a defendant – not guilty in a crown court doesn't mean you can't be treated like a criminal in a family court.

But I will never forget the moment that John turned to me as he dropped me off at my mum's.

'Angela,' he said, 'I wanted to tell you that if you come through this trial, if everything is positive, then there will be no more involvement from us.'

I looked at him in disbelief. Here was a man with years of social services experience, who worked for the organisation that had treated me with such suspicion, and he believed in me. If he did, then surely the jury would? I started to cry.

CHAPTER EIGHT

'Don't look up,' said Bill, as we hurried towards Winchester Crown Court. 'There are lots of press. Lots of cameras. Just look forward.'

Flanked by Bill and Jacqui, I fixed my eyes on the wide concrete expanse that lay between us and the huge modern building we were heading for – we only had to cross it and we would be inside the court, away from the prying lenses of the press. But, even as I tried to stare ahead, my gaze slid right towards a high brick wall where cameras jostled for space. Photographers might not be allowed inside the confines of the court but they were determined to get a picture of me arriving and, with flashes popping blindingly, my ears were filled with the gun-like sound of closing shutters. As the cameras gobbled up my frozen expression, my throat constricted and a rush of mouth-watering adrenalin swept over me.

It was 19 February 2002 and finally, twenty-seven long months after losing Matthew, my trial was beginning. In the run-up to that day, I had felt almost relieved that something was happening, that Terry, Jade and I would soon be free of the uncertainty that had kept us trapped for so long. But all that was forgotten as the rasping metallic click of the cameras serenaded me into the court building and I felt pure, cold fear cut through me.

*

An hour later I stood beside a security guard in a cold corridor at the back of court number three. Banging noises and muffled sounds echoed up from the stairs behind us, while in front of me was a door leading to the court. As the minutes ticked slowly by, I felt panic build inside me and forced myself to think back to the previous day when Terry had driven me away from the house for a few final precious minutes together.

'Ange,' he said as he turned to me. 'There's something I need to say. I'm sorry about how nasty and distant I've been. I know I've been hell. But I wanted to tell you that I admire you for the fact that you've fought for us. You've done everything possible to keep the mother-daughter relationship going with Jade and I take my hat off to you because I couldn't have done it. Whatever they say, I know you're a top-drawer mum. Not just with Jade but with Gemma, Jason and Matthew too. And even though I won't be with you at the trial, I'll be thinking of you every minute of the day. I love you and I always will do. We'll get through this and when we do we'll be better than ever.'

'I'm so scared,' I whispered as the tears rolled down my cheeks and Terry took my hand before hugging me. 'I wish this wasn't happening to us.'

We'd been separated, tested to the limits and, after all those months of drifting further and further apart, Terry was reaching out to me. As I stood waiting to go into court, I thought back to what he had said. Terry and Jade, they're what matter, nothing else, I kept telling myself as I tried to breathe down the fear that constricted my throat. Whatever they say about me in there, they are what is important. Only them.

As the security guard led me into the court I looked up to see a bare-looking modern room. I steadied myself in the front of the dock and saw Michael Mansfield and his junior counsel Jo Briggs to my left on benches running parallel to the dock. I'd met Mr Mansfield a few times in the run-up to the trial and instead of the stiff, snooty type I'd expected, had found a very human man who seemed genuinely worried about the effects the investigation had had on our family. I had also warmed to Jo. Energetic and bright, I could almost picture her out on demos waving a placard, and I

119

could see she, as the mother of a young son, was incensed about what was happening to us. Behind them sat Bill and Jacqui, surrounded by files.

To the right of my legal team sat the prosecution headed by Paul Dunkels QC, who was quite possibly the tallest man I had ever seen. His huge frame soon earned him the nickname of the Giant among my family, and Dunkels (I'm afraid I could never bring myself to address him as Mr) also had a junior counsel. Behind them I could see Rob Findlay and Gill Dawson; to my right on benches running horizontally down the side of the court sat the press, and to my left was the empty jury box.

I felt so alone as I looked around the courtroom for the first time and realised I could not see any familiar faces. My legal team had their backs to me, my relatives and friends were perched invisibly up in the public gallery above me, which looked down over the court. So many people were there to witness my public humiliation, and yet I could not see a single pair of friendly eyes. I felt desperately lonely.

A knock sounded and the court shifted to its feet at the words 'All rise'. Hush descended as everyone bowed their heads in response to the entrance of Mrs Justice Hallett.

Sitting straight across from me at a bench looking down over the room, she was far removed from the old man I had anticipated. She had blonde hair and immaculate make-up, looked as if she was in her late forties and, engulfed in a red cloak and wearing a wig, reminded me of the priests of my childhood. I was surprised. She was so different from what I had expected and yet, when the proceedings got underway, it was not so different from what I'd seen on television. The wigs, the bowing, the standing and sitting, the low commands from the court clerks, the journalists' deferential addresses about the reporting restrictions covering Jade to the judge who sat on high above us all. It amazed me that in 2002 I was fighting for my life in what seemed an almost medieval setting – complete with a strict hierarchy and rules – and that my fate lay in so many other people's hands.

*

A rush of nervous adrenalin washed over me when, after the jury had been sworn in, Dunkels stood up to open the prosecution. Even though I had been primed to expect it, the sheer venom in his voice took my breath away. Unfurling himself from the prosecution bench, everything about him bristled with disgust – his voice, his body language, the look in his eyes – he seemed almost sickened to be in the same room as me.

'For a mother to attack her own child in this way is, of course, against nurture and instinct,' Dunkels boomed in clipped tones across the courtroom. 'But the prosecution say that the evidence will demonstrate that that is what Angela Cannings has done to these, her two babies.'

I could only watch as he spat his terrible accusations at me and, just as it had on the day of my police interview, panic started to rise in me as I listened. I sat transfixed by what he was saying, shocked that the accusation that had only ever been uttered in a police interview room was now being proclaimed to the world.

Dunkels told the jury it was no coincidence I was always alone when my babies died or suffered breathing problems – now called acute life-threatening events or ALTEs. Jason, Jade and Matthew had all had them, he said, but no one had ever been with me – be it Terry, a neighbour, a friend, a relative or a doctor – when my children struggled for breath, because I was the one who had attacked them.

Again the details of my babies' lives were trotted out like an accusation – the bleeding found on Jason's lungs after slides from the original post-mortem were reviewed, Jade's ALTE and the extensive tests run on Matthew's heart after he was born, which had found nothing out of the ordinary. Then there was my behaviour, which suggested guilt – my supposedly sloppy use of the apnoea alarms, such as the time when I'd had a conversation with a neighbour and left Matthew at home for a couple of minutes – it meant I knew the alarms were useless because I was the one causing the problems. Then there was Gloria Peacock's memory of me retching in the bathroom as she resuscitated Jason on the day of his ALTE, and the fact that I had phoned Terry instead of an ambulance when I found Matthew for the final time.

As I listened to Dunkels lay out his case I saw that everything which had happened over the preceding thirteen years was going to be twisted into a blackened picture of my life. It was like being in a hall of mirrors at the circus and seeing a hideously contorted reproduction of yourself – you know it's you but the representation is so twisted you can hardly recognise yourself. I felt sick with dread as I realised what was going to happen.

Mr Mansfield will put it right, I told myself as we filed silently out of court at the end of the first day and I tried to gulp down my fear. The jury will hear from my character witnesses, Terry, Stephen, my dad, my mum – they'll realise I could never have done this.

Over the next few days I could only watch as the prosecution called nurses, paediatricians, midwives, paramedics, anaesthetists, A&E consultants – all the professionals who'd been involved in my children's births and deaths – into the witness box. Most of them looked uncomfortable as they stood and explained how they had been involved in my children's care. Some had treated my children, others had run tests to find out if they suffered from any kind of illness or disorder, which had all turned up nothing.

But it was the people I knew who hurt the most when they added their piece – however tiny – into the jigsaw the prosecution was building up against me. Gloria Peacock was followed by a neighbour Jane Aldous and Roland Revell, my dad's best friend and ambulance partner of more than twenty years. I knew none had an axe to grind, they were obliged to tell the court about what they knew, and that people like Roland in particular, who had known me since I was a child, felt awkward about appearing for the prosecution. But still I could not help feeling irrationally hurt as they gave evidence against me.

I soon realised I might struggle to make sense of the dense technical and scientific evidence. More than a dozen medical experts would eventually give evidence during an eight-week trial – each with decades of experience in their field, each speaking a language of huge scientific complexity. I wondered how the jury would cope as I started jotting things down in a notepad which, at the end of each day when Bill, Jacqui, Mr Mansfield, Jo and I gathered in a small side room to talk over the evidence, I would bring out to have my questions answered.

As the days passed, I began to create a routine for myself – something familiar to cling to in all that was so strange. My handbag contained the same things every day – a good-luck card Jade had made me, my cigarettes, phone, purse and the notebook – and round my neck I wore a shamrock necklace Claire had bought me. There were other routines too – the home-made sandwiches the catering staff let us eat in the canteen after we realised it would cost us an arm and a leg to buy lunch every day, and the court usher who gave me two cushions to sit on each morning after I told her how uncomfortable the bench in the dock was. I was genuinely touched by those gestures of kindness. Mum and Brian attended every day of the trial – driving me home each night to their flat – and other family came as often as they could. My dad was there a lot, Claire came as often as she could and Andrew and Tina also attended. Other friends – including Steve Crouch, Terry and Gill, Gill's parents, John Walton, his wife Sandy, and Ally – also came. I was also touched when people who needn't have made the effort also lent their support – my old store manager at Tesco and the psychologist I had seen both came to wish me well.

I began to realise the courtroom was like a stage and I was playing just a minor part as justice was performed. I was a bit player in this drama of legal minds and I was forced to sit in silence as the jury listened intently, the judge sat impassively and the reporters wrote furiously in their notebooks.

But the overwhelming feeling as I sat in the dock and listened to the prosecution build their case remained one of disbelief. Sometimes I almost thought I would have to pinch myself to make sure it wasn't simply an awful dream I had accidentally woken up in. However much I got used to the everyday mechanics of the trial – the standing and sitting, endless legal argument, trying not to squirm with discomfort during hour after hour in the dock – it didn't stop the feeling of horror that I was at the centre of this grotesque charade.

There were times, of course, when I couldn't stop my tears. I remember vividly day seven of the trial when tapes of my 999 calls were played. I couldn't stop myself from crying as I sat in that cold courtroom and strangers listened to my sobbing pleas for help. It just seemed so unreal that I, Angela Cannings, Terry's wife, Jade's mum, Mary and Steve's daughter, was sitting listening to my words being replayed for public consumption. I felt so humiliated.

But mostly I forced myself to stay strong on the outside – just as I had during my separation from Terry and Jade. I feared I would be overwhelmed by sorrow if I let even a fraction of it show and I forced myself to wear a mask of cool calm every day when I walked into that courtroom.

With a growing sense of horror, it also began to dawn on me how the prosecution was building its case. Before I went into that courtroom I had naïvely believed that facts were facts, truth was truth and medicine was black and white. But as I sat there day after day I discovered there were no such absolutes – it was all a question of presentation. Again and again, something that had seemed so innocent was twisted and contorted against me. Conversations with neighbours, my family, things I'd said to the police during the hazy interview days after Matthew died, decisions we'd made as we lost not one, not two, but three children and tried to find a way through such extraordinary circumstances.

For instance, when Dr Barnes took the stand against me, however neutrally he tried to explain the involvement he had had with our family, Dunkels seemed to shine the worst possible light on his evidence. When talking about coming to see Terry and me on the day of Matthew's death, the paediatrician told the court he had considered the possibility that I had killed my children and, moments after the word 'filicide' being uttered, Dunkels brought his evidence to a close. Under cross-examination, the kindly paediatrician explained that although the loss of three children had inevitably aroused suspicion, he had never had concerns about Terry and me. But I couldn't help feeling that in the cut and thrust of the courtroom, it was the prosecution's unspoken accusation that always hung heaviest in the air – people don't remember good news, they latch onto the bad.

But however devastated I was to see Dr Barnes give evidence against me, it wasn't until paediatric pathologist Professor Peter Berry took the stand that the full horror of what was happening became clear. He was a retired consultant from Bristol who had carried out a post-mortem on Matthew, as well as reviewing those on Jason and Gemma.

The court had previously heard from Dr Christine Scott, the Salisbury pathologist who had concluded that both Gemma and Jason had died of SIDS. She'd also said that Professor Emery, the eminent paediatric pathologist who had sadly died since visiting Terry and me, had reviewed her findings and agreed Gemma's and Jason's were natural deaths.

But Professor Berry had discovered the one piece of physical evidence the prosecution believed they had against me. He told the court he had found evidence of bleeding on Jason's lungs in the form of siderophages. These are scavenger cells that eat up foreign bodies, and their presence in Jason's lungs suggested he had had blood in them before he died. Professor Berry told the court they were only a warning sign of smothering – not a diagnosis – because there were many natural reasons why a child could bleed and siderophages be present.

But it seemed to me the pathologist made it clear how he thought they had come to be present in Jason.

Professor Berry told the court: 'There are many conditions, most of them quite rare and obvious at post-mortem examination, why a child might have bled into their lungs. They might have severe congenital heart disease with obstruction of the circulation in the lungs, they might have a local disease lesion in the lungs, such as abnormal blood vessels that burst, they might have had a very severe attack of pneumonia causing bleeding. But in Jason's case there was no such natural cause apparent.'

Later Professor Berry would say his post-mortem examination of Matthew had not found a cause for his death. But because of the histories of my babies – the ALTEs and their deaths – he thought both Jason and Matthew's deaths had the features of 'imposed upper airways obstruction' or smothering.

'It doesn't prove anything,' said Claire later. 'Just because something suggests smothering, it doesn't prove it, and apart from that he found absolutely nothing.'

'But surely it must sound bad to the jury?' I anxiously asked, terrified that yet again they wouldn't remember the question marks, only the seeming certainty of the word 'smothering'.

'There wasn't a mark on your babies, Angela – not a bruise, not a scratch, not a cut, nothing,' Claire replied. 'And they'll never get anyone in that witness box to say you were a bad mum. The jury will soon forget it when you put your side of the story. It means nothing.'

The next day my fears intensified. Professor Berry kept stressing that certain features of my sons' deaths had only 'triggered suspicion' but seemed to reject every suggestion that would dull the impact of what he said – from the suggestion of one defence expert that low levels of siderophages in Jason's lungs were the result of blood he inhaled at birth, to the assertion of another that their significance was 'questionable'.

He also gave evidence about the minute examinations he had made of Matthew's body in the hunt for evidence of smothering – such as bleeding around the nose or mouth, tiny pinpoint haemorrhages in the face and eyes, pressure marks and previous evidence of abuse such as fractures or brain damage. None were found, yet even my baby's face had been dissected in a fruitless hunt for clues.

It was then, I think, hearing the coldly impersonal language of medical investigation applied to my beautiful son, that I finally cut off from what was happening. Until then I had tried to engage as fully as I could with what was being said in court – however legally or medically complex. But as the cold hard facts about the investigations made on Matthew and Jason's bodies started to emerge, I took myself out of that courtroom. It was as if I left my body and hovered somewhere above – distanced, safe, separate from that unimaginable description of the havoc wreaked on my son's body in the name of a police investigation.

As I listened to Professor Berry's evidence, John Walton's words kept flooding back to me from the day they had released Matthew's body – he had used the word 'butchered' and only now did I realise just what it meant. As the voices in the courtroom receded to the back of my mind, I told myself to block it all out.

Remember the happy times with him, I whispered in my head. Remember going to the beach in Weymouth for the eclipse and sitting with Jacqueline and her kids on the beach. Me, Terry, Jade and Matthew.

Remember when Jade helped feed him. She'd sit on the sofa holding the end of the bottle and when we finished we'd put Matthew down on his changing mat and she would help change his nappy.

Remember his smiles and gurgles when I put him under the play arch and Jade crawled under with him.

Remember him smiling as Jade splashed him in the bath and later how she would help put on his powder before we put him clean and fresh into his all-in-one.

Remember walking with them in the buggy with Jade at the front and Matthew at the back as she proudly told people he was her brother.

As this expert detailed the destruction of my son's body, I forced myself to remember my beautiful, happy baby. My family. Whatever happened in that courtroom, I told myself they couldn't rob me of my memories. Of course, I would soon find out I was wrong. Even the most precious things can only withstand so much suspicion before they become tainted by it for ever.

At the end of days like that I would return to my mum's house to discuss things over a glass of wine. We had never been everyday drinkers but during the trial I relished the quick release that alcohol brought.

'What did the Giant think he was up to today?' Mum would spit.

'Who does he think he is?' Brian would say, bristling with

indignation at whatever had been twisted against me that day. 'He's never even met you.'

At times we would angrily pick apart the day and at others scream with almost hysterical laughter – because in all the gloom there was of course the odd bit of light.

'I'm taking Mr Mansfield in some hot-cross buns tomorrow,' Claire announced one night.

'What are you doing that for?' I asked, looking at her questioningly.

'Because he's lovely,' she said, as her eyes lit up at the thought of the charismatic barrister. 'I told him I was a baker and asked him if he wanted to try some and he said he did. He told me he'd put them in his wig box and eat them on the train home. I might even take him a Mars bar too.'

Claire wasn't the only one Mr Mansfield had charmed and even at the end of the worst days he could still make me laugh when we came out of the court. He also made sure he spoke to my family and on one memorable occasion even allowed Brian to try on his wig. In addition to Bill and Jacqui, I became quite close to him and Jo as the weeks passed. One day we all toasted Jacqui's fiftieth birthday with champagne drunk out of plastic cups as we gathered to talk at the end of the day.

Each evening I would phone Terry to fill him in on what had happened – sometimes going into detail, at others almost resenting the fact I had gone through it all once that day and now had to relive it. I ached to be with him and Jade and I missed them desperately as the days of the trial turned into weeks. Until then, however unsatisfactory it had been, I had at least seen Terry almost every day and had time with Jade. But during the trial I saw Jade for a four-hour visit each Saturday and Sunday and was going through the most daunting experience of my life without Terry. I felt increasingly emotionally and physically drained. On some nights when Claire popped round or Ally came over there was a small angry part of me that didn't want to see them. I wanted Terry and, however kind my family and friends were, at times I felt almost annoyed that they were with me and he wasn't.

128

Each night when the talking was done, I would settle down to sleep on the blow-up bed in my mum's living room and replay the day's events yet again in my head. But as much as I tried to distance myself, to tell myself that everyone was only doing their job, I couldn't be that impersonal. My life was at stake and it cut me to the core that Jason and Matthew were being paraded around the courtroom via paper and words. It was as if our whole family life had been stripped for inspection and it was all about tests, reports and medical experts. All I could think as I lay there searching for sleep was that I had carried our babies, fed them, nurtured them, grieved for them and been accused of their murder and the trial seemed like the final kick in the teeth. They weren't court exhibits or physical shells, they were individuals, my sons, and every ounce of my maternal protectiveness screamed against what was happening to them in that courtroom. It seemed such an insult to them and it sickened me.

But every morning when I walked back into court I would force myself to switch off from all that. Once again I feared that if I gave into it, I would fall apart, and so I fixed my features into a mask of calm and stared ahead. At times I found the evidence so complex, so dense, so medically involved that it was hard to follow; at other times, dare I say it, it was boring, but I always forced myself to start listening again, desperate to make sense of what was happening to me.

'I call Professor Sir Roy Meadow,' Dunkels boomed across the courtroom on the second Friday of the trial.

After all the months of imagining, I was surprised by how normal Professor Meadow looked. Instead of the cartoon baddie I had expected, he was a slight man in his sixties, with greying hair and glasses – yet another oldish doctor. But I was soon overwhelmed as the emeritus professor of paediatrics and child health at the University of Leeds reeled off his qualifications and detailed his twenty-five years of interest in child-protection work, including an involvement with a hundred families in which children had died of smothering. He was certainly an experienced and a well-educated foe.

129

Professor Meadow's time in the box that first day was cut short by the end of proceedings, but even during his limited appearance he spoke with authority and confidence. He told the court that after reviewing medical notes he believed Jason and Jade had probably been smothered and it became clear that their medical history, and the breathing problems they'd suffered, had persuaded him of that fact.

When asked about Jason's death a week after his ALTE, Professor Meadow replied, 'The fact that a previous child had died in the family is relevant because that combination of circumstances, that sort of story, is one that is very typical of a child who had died as a result of smothering.'

And of Jade's breathing problems, he said, 'In the context of the family as a whole it is of importance because one of the reasons for such an event as this is smothering.'

As I sat in the dock, I realised that as far as Professor Meadow was concerned, I was going to be damned because of a past I'd had no control over.

The following week he went back into the box and, when asked about Matthew, told the court: 'It was a terrible tragedy first of all and an awful tragedy and very unusual – the third death in the family, that's a rare event, very rare.'

But despite the 'tragedy', Professor Meadow seemed suspicious of the real reason for this 'rare' event.

'The investigations and pathologists did not find a reason for him dying,' he told the court. 'For me, the unusual feature is death so soon after being seen well, the fact that there had been previous deaths in the family and the fact that he had had an episode of some sort only nine days before he died . . . those features are ones that are found really quite commonly in children who have been smothered by their mothers.'

As I sat listening to Professor Meadow speak in his soft but firm tones I was incredulous. How could a pattern of events convict me? How was it the pattern revealed that mothers – and not fathers – smothered their children? How could it be that I had smothered Jason and Matthew and attacked Jade but not killed her? How did that fit into his pattern?

Rage rose inside me as I listened to his almost apologetic tones and all I wanted to do was scream: How can you know all this? No one who knows me has ever said it. There's never been a single hint that I might be abusive. How can you say I murdered my babies when everyone else says they don't know how they died? You've never even met me, spoken to me, you don't know me at all and yet you say I am capable of killing my children?

But I forced myself to listen as the paediatrician finished his evidence by saying that he had considered other possibilities.

'I don't find a likely diagnosis of a naturally known condition,' he told the court. 'One then goes on to say, well, it is possible it is a condition that is not yet understood by doctors or described by them? – and that must always be a possibility. But nevertheless as a doctor of children I'm saying these features are those of smothering.'

My anger did not subside when Mr Mansfield started his cross-examination. Stunned, I sat in the dock as it became clear Professor Meadow had been called in by the police within days of Matthew's death. They'd spent months telling me they were keeping an open mind and yet they'd had this child-abuse expert advising them within days. It made a mockery of everything they had told me.

I could only listen in disbelief as he said that large sections of his case paperwork had been shredded when he'd retired. I bristled with fury that he could come into court and seemingly talk in anecdotes.

Later I would sit confusedly as Professor Meadow told the court he hadn't actually talked to anyone who knew me or my children – health visitors, our GP, Dr Barnes, Professor Emery, no one. He'd seemingly decided I was a murderer thanks to a paper exercise and hadn't spoken to the people who'd cared for us through all those years and never reported any concerns.

Professor Meadow was certainly impressive in the witness box – gently authoritative and steely at the same time, he determinedly rejected any other explanation for my children's breathing problems and deaths – that Jade, for example, had not been smothered but suffered a severe bout of gastroenteritis, which had affected her breathing. I felt the ground fall from beneath me with the realisation that he was utterly convinced he was telling the truth. While no one would be able to give a definitive reason for my babies' deaths in my defence, Professor Meadow was giving one for the prosecution. How would the jury ever dare not to believe such an eminent doctor?

I remember one exchange late in the day which made me shudder. Mr Mansfield yet again insisted that looking at the whole picture – me, our family, the lack of injuries on Jason and Matthew, the features consistent with cot death – it was a real possibility that my children could have died from natural, but as yet unknown, causes.

'I think the problem with that statement Mr Mansfield is saying because the family are normal, child abuse doesn't happen,' Professor Meadow replied. 'It is absolutely right to say that child abuse and smothering are more common in certain families but nevertheless most abuse, most smothering happens in families who on ordinary meeting seem normal and caring and that is so, and most of the mothers who smother children, when you meet them, are normal. The second point is to start talking about the features of SIDS. SIDS means that you don't know why the baby has died. It means that an unnatural cause such as smothering wasn't found, and nor was a natural cause, so that in any group of SIDS babies there are some who have been smothered.'

I was trapped. If I appeared normal, I could be a child abuser; if my babies were thought to have died of cot death, I could have smothered them. There might not be any actual proof against me but Professor Meadow had created a world of smoke and mirrors from which I could not escape.

He finished his evidence and the judge told him that another court in London was waiting for him. Who would he be giving evidence against next?

Two days later Dr Martin Ward Platt took the stand. I knew he was my other main accuser. He looked in his late forties and his only distinguishing feature I can remember was an enormous nose. A consultant paediatrician from Newcastle, Dr Ward Platt reminded me of an actor on stage who addressed the jury as if they were his personal audience. But where Professor Meadow had seemed almost apologetic, Dr Ward Platt was emphatic.

'My considered opinion on this, as I have stated before, is that having looked at the other possibilities, having considered the clinical situations, and if I may say so, also taking into account the whole situation – by which I mean, not just Jason but the death of Matthew and the acute life-threatening episode in Jade – it is my opinion that they were caused deliberately and in this case by smothering,' he told the court in no uncertain terms as he was asked about Jason's ALTE and death.

He even said he felt 'question marks' hung over Gemma's death. The charges against me relating to her death had been dropped but it seemed that in this courtroom, I would be tried in the shadows for her death.

Much of Dr Ward Platt's evidence centred on the tests that proved both Jason and Jade's bodies had undergone highly stressful events when they had their ALTEs. But he too dismissed any other explanation for both those and my children's deaths. Again and again history was used to condemn me, not facts, as Dr Ward Platt talked about the pattern in my children's medical histories.

He also dismissed the possible genetic cause for my children's deaths. Before the trial we had built up a full picture of what had happened in my Irish family. Patrick McDermott, my second cousin, had had seven children – two of whom had died of cot death, two of whom had had problems. One surviving baby girl had been treated with caffeine for nine months because of concerns over how deeply she slept, another baby boy had had to be resuscitated when he stopped breathing.

But Dr Ward Platt said that although the children shared some genes with mine, they were genetically distant.

He told the court: 'In between the McDermott children and the Cannings children we have a large number of people who have a common ancestry . . . in excess of fifty people who share some genetic characteristics. 'If we are to suppose that there is a female genetic link, one that exists for many of these people with the common ancestry, one that has not expressed itself in over fifty people in the family but has suddenly come out in Gemma, Jason, Jade and Matthew, Dermott, Orla, Fiona and Owen, we are looking at a situation that is extraordinarily unlikely.'

In contrast to Professor Meadow, Dr Ward Platt gave his evidence aggressively. If he had had the chance to shriek 'She's a murderer' across the court, I felt he would have done and, as Mr Mansfield cross-examined him, I felt the fight narrow to a personal one between Dr Ward Platt and me.

Until those experts appeared against me, I had clung to the hope that common sense would win. But fear filled me as not one, not two, but three experienced doctors all talked about my babies' deaths in terms of smothering. It felt almost surreal – like having a conversation with a stranger who appears normal but keeps telling you the sky is pink and refuses to listen however hard you try to tell them it's blue. As the conversation goes on and on, you begin to think you're the one with the problem, and I felt like that as I sat in the dock.

For so long I had at first believed and then hoped I would never be convicted. I knew I had done nothing wrong and to say otherwise flew in the face of the truth – something I had been brought up to believe in. But after listening to those experts, the tiny nugget of faith in the system that remained buried deep inside me finally dislodged itself. For the first time, I sensed I might be convicted. I knew I would never be able to explain my children's deaths, while three eminent doctors had all given evidence that centred on one thing – smothering.

CHAPTER NINE

'Angela Cannings is not in a position to explain what science is completely incapable of explaining. But she is in a position to tell you her own story. Members of the jury and with my lady's permission, I call Angela Cannings to give her evidence.'

I could feel a hundred eyes upon me as I walked into the witness box. It reminded me of the day I went to see Matthew's body when Gill Dawson had studied my every reaction. I felt paranoid that every look, word and expression would be studied for clues by the jury of eight women and four men and, as I placed my hand on the Bible to swear to tell the truth, I looked up into the public gallery. Peering down anxiously at me were my family – for the first time in that long, lonely trial I could see the faces of the people I loved and I gulped a dry throat as I sat down.

I looked at the jury, as I had done many times during the trial, and wondered what they made of it all, how they felt about my life being in their hands. Earlier Jo had told them none of the experts involved in the case could tell them conclusively what had happened to my babies because no one knew why some children died quite suddenly – and naturally – in infancy. She said if the key to cot death was ever going to be found, it was unlikely to be a single cause but a number of different ones. Experts were going to explain to the jury about a number of factors thought to be linked to SIDS. For instance, genetic conditions like Long QT, a potentially fatal problem with the pumping chambers of the heart; vaso-vagal shutdown of the nervous system, a rare physiological response which occurs when a baby vomits and the vagal nerve stops the child breathing to protect it from inhaling vomit and slows the heart beat – sometimes fatally. Or breakdowns in immunity which meant some babies were incapable of dealing with everyday bugs which then produced toxins in the body.

I pushed down my nerves as Jo started by asking about our life in the run-up to the trial before moving onto Matthew's birth and death and Jade's hospital admission. Then she requested that a home video of me with Jason was played to the court.

I could not stop my tears as I watched the grainy film and saw Terry and me long before this nightmare had started. There before me on the screen were our carefree and happy selves. Young, plump and free of the worry that had drained our features over the past two years, we laughed and smiled with Jason. It felt surreal to see the colourful, moving footage of our life reduced to a courtroom exhibit. I had to stem a howl when it showed me breastfeeding him – my nakedness and most private moments with my son served up for public consumption.

Surely you can see that I couldn't have done what they say? I thought to myself as I looked at the jury who stared impassively at my weeping face. You've seen me suckle my child. You've seen him in my arms – what more proof do you need that I could never have harmed him?

The next day I returned to the witness box to be guided through my evidence by Jo once again and to tell the jury about Gemma and Jason's lives and deaths, the times I had found my children struggling for breath or lifeless in their cots, the decision to try again for another baby. Finally she asked me how I felt.

'I do not understand how or why or what I have done, as I have said over and over again, what I have done to deserve this sadness,' I told the court. 'There were times when we lost Gemma and Jason that I even thought that perhaps I shouldn't be with Terry, that I should be on my own because I felt – I just felt that I was a failure.'

'Do you regret trying again, having Matthew?' she asked.

'Absolutely not,' I replied. 'If I hadn't been sterilised I would have tried again.'

Jo stepped back to her seat and I took a deep breath as Dunkels approached me. He started by firing question after question at me about my friends, family, children, Terry's work commitments and whether anyone was ever with me during any of the ALTEs or deaths.

'There was an occasion with Matthew, one night when we were all in bed and the alarm sounded in the night. I rushed in to him and it was actually a false alarm – we checked Matthew and it was a false alarm and it was a low battery indicator.'

'Right,' Dunkels replied. 'And I think that Terry went out and got replacement batteries?'

'Yes.'

'What straight away?'

'First thing the next morning.'

'He didn't go to an all-night garage or something like that?'

'No.'

'First thing the next morning, right,' he replied. 'A false alarm, in that sense apart, never ever happened when Terry was there.'

As I went to speak, Dunkels looked up to the judge.

'Would that be a convenient moment?'

The court adjourned with the accusation hanging in the air that I knew we didn't need batteries urgently because I was the one making my babies ill, I was always alone with them. I sat in the dock, wanting to explain but unable to say a word. We'd only waited to get them because after all that had happened Terry and I were desperate to try and instil some sense of normality in our family life. Jumping out of bed in the middle of the night to hunt down batteries would have seemed too nervous. There were many times like that during the witness box – when I desperately wanted to explain but couldn't.

The next few hours were some of the longest I have ever known. Mr Mansfield had warned me that I should keep calm and answer as fully as I could, but as the time went on I felt increasingly terrified. Sitting in the witness box, I was intensely aware that all eyes were on me – the jury, the judge, the lawyers, the press, my family, the public – and after more than two years of waiting to finally defend myself, to convince them all that I had done nothing wrong, I felt crippled by fear.

As the cross-examination got under way, I was taken back to the police interview room – to the looping, swooping lines of questions designed to catch me out as I tried to stop myself being led down the dark alleyway of insinuation – and panic rose in me as Dunkels asked again and again about being alone with my babies when they fell ill.

Well of course I was, I wanted to scream. I was a mum at home alone with my baby most of the day, of course I was on my own.

Once again I found it impossible to remember all the tiny details he asked about and I became increasingly agitated as Dunkels highlighted inconsistencies between medical notes, my police interviews and what I was now saying in the witness box.

For instance I told the court I'd heard the walkie-talkie for the apnoea alarm sound as I hung out the washing in the garden on the day of Jason's ALTE. But I'd told the police I hadn't had it with me. Under pressure, four days after Matthew's death, I simply hadn't remembered.

'Did you fling the window open and say, "Gloria! Quick!",' Dunkels said as he questioned me about the health visitor's arrival after I'd rushed inside.

'No, I didn't do that because as soon as I saw her I ran to the door.'

'Right. Well how long did you have to wait at the door whilst Gloria shut up her car, having got together what she wanted and made her way up the path into the downstairs lobby and then up the staircase?'

'I don't remember. I remember that I didn't have to wait very long.'

'It didn't seem very long?'

'No.'

'And where was Jason whilst you were waiting?'

'Jason was on the bed.'

'Why didn't you have him with you?'

'Because I was in a state. I had left him on the bed and I had gone to the door to get Gloria to come in.'

'It is not very far from the front bedroom to the door to your flat but wasn't your instinct to pick up Jason and take him with you?'

'No.'

'Or to just fling the door open?'

'And?'

'And rush back to Jason?'

'Yes.'

'And shout to Gloria from there?'

'Yes.'

'Yes? But that is not what you did, is it?'

'Sorry, not what I?'

'It is not what you did – just fling your front door open and rush back to Jason so that you could shout to Gloria to hurry up?'

'No, I didn't, no. I opened the door and Gloria came up the stairs and I brought her to Jason, who was on the bed.'

'When did you remember that you had heard the apnoea alarm start over the walkie-talkie when you were in the back garden?'

'When I was actually out in the garden.'

'You have already made some reference to it but you will know that what you have said to us today is different to what you said to the police when they asked you about this in November 1999?'

'Yes.'

'Yes.'

It seemed to go on for ever as Dunkels kept returning to detail after detail – whether I had taken the door off the latch as I ran inside on the day of Jason's ALTE, which button I had used to turn off the apnoea alarm, whether I had heard it start or not on the day of his death as I sat in the kitchen. I'd told the police I hadn't but I didn't know if I had or not. I'd just heard an alarm sounding, become aware of the noise, but I felt I couldn't be that hesitant in front of the jury and so I was definitive.

'I heard it start so my reaction was to deal with it. So I heard it start even though I might have stated that I didn't hear it start.'

'Well you did tell the police that you didn't hear it start?' Dunkels spat.

'Yes I did.'

As I was asked about detail after detail of those hazy days, I searched desperately through my mind to answer the questions. But I simply couldn't remember because then, as now, so much of what happened was a blur. All I can say now is that as fear rose in me I started pulling hazy recollections out of my mind to answer questions – inconsistently. I so desperately wanted to explain everything as I sat in that witness box and I know I made mistakes. I just wonder how anyone could be expected to remember every tiny detail of events that were so long ago and dominated by crippling grief, loss and shock, details such as whether I had opened the top bedroom window four inches or three on a summer day eleven years before.

But as the questioning continued, fear gave way to anger. After more than two years of social workers, police, lawyers and doctors, something snapped as Dunkels went on and on – whether I'd turned the apnoea alarm off before running upstairs on the day of Matthew's death, what attempts at resuscitation I'd made, why I'd left him in the house when I went to talk to a neighbour. But I simply couldn't answer all his questions. Angrily I said: 'I would like it to be known that before Matthew had his episode I had built up enough confidence with him and Jade and I would like to make the point that yes, I did leave him in the house on his own. The front door was open but I was conscious that he was in the house and what I was trying to do was I was trying to live as normal a life as possible. After everything that had happened, I just wanted to try and be normal.'

I desperately tried to explain as much as I could but nothing seemed to make a difference. I made mistakes in that witness box and I suspect that they, coupled with my anger, went against me in the jury's minds. They expected a docile, weeping mother in that box but, after years of never saying boo to anyone for fear of losing Jade, I finally let anger overwhelm me. It was, I felt, better than letting out the despair that threatened to explode in an uncontrollable scream across the courtroom.

I was terrified but I forced myself not to break down and the cold impression this gave to the jury was worsened by the fact

140

that my face, still frozen by Bell's Palsy, added to my emotionless look. The court had already heard how 'calm' I had been whenever my babies died and I seemed so again in the witness box. In truth I was far from calm – I had simply learned through bitter experience how to numb myself emotionally and I did so again during my trial. To survive it, I believed that I had to hold everything inside.

'When you were on your own with those three babies, did something drive you to attack them?' Dunkels asked at the end of what seemed the longest day of my life.

'No.'

'To place a hand, pillow, blanket, something, over the nose and mouth so as to obstruct the breathing of the baby concerned?'

'No, no.'

'With Jason on the fourth of June 1991, did you want to create a situation to confront the health visitor with?'

'No.'

'With Matthew on the twelfth of November 1999, did you want to create a situation to confront Terry with?'

'No.'

'So they would see what it was like?'

'No.'

'Did you find it difficult on your own, in your home with your baby?'

'No.'

'Never?'

'No.'

'Did you resent Terry's absence from the home for work, or any other reason?'

'No.'

'Did you want attention?'

'No.'

'You see, we suggest that you attacked each of these three babies – Jason, Jade and Matthew – on the days that they were taken ill and to hospital and on the days that Jason and Matthew died. That is what happened, isn't it?'

'No.'

'Something you did on your own, at times when no one else was in the house?'

'No.'

'And at the moment you carried out the act, something you did intending to cause your baby at least really serious bodily harm?'

'No.'

'Though when the full impact of the consequences were brought home to you immediately afterwards, no doubt you quickly regretted it?'

'Absolutely not – I did nothing.'

Dunkels stepped back and I slumped down exhausted into my seat. After two days in the witness box, my chance to explain was over.

It wasn't a medical expert or a member of my family who was first called to give evidence for my defence but Susie, a mother of two. She had lost two sons to cot death and I'll never forget watching her walk into the witness box – the first woman I had ever seen who had shared my experience. I felt filled with gratitude that Susie had taken the brave step of appearing in court.

An awful feeling of déjà vu washed over me as she told the court she couldn't remember many of the events on the day her sixteen-week-old son Aaron died of cot death in 1986.

'It was just total panic,' she said.

And again, my stomach sank when Susie told the court what a doctor had said to her after her son's death.

'He explained to me that they usually couldn't find a reason for these deaths, and it was like an umbrella and that there wasn't just one particular cause for each cot death, there could be numerous causes,' Susie said. 'I was told that it was highly unlikely it would happen again.'

But, as in my case, the medics were wrong and fourteen months later the unimaginable had happened again when her four-week-old son Taylor failed to wake after a lunchtime nap.

'I walked up the stairs and I knew, just this awful feeling that just – I just knew something wasn't right. It was just so very still

142

and quiet in the house. I didn't have a television or radio or anything like that.'

Susie went on, 'I walked into the bedroom and his cot was at the bottom of our bed. And I just knew before I went to the cot and remember thinking, Oh, not again . . . And I just knew and I picked him up and I knew it was too late . . . And I just picked him up and cuddled him and I sat on the bed and I thought – I really didn't know what to do because I knew that if I called anybody they would come and take him away.'

Susie paused as she struggled to control her grief before telling the court that she had phoned 999 and her husband before adding, 'I wanted him there. And I can't remember. I think I might have rung the doctor, I don't know. It just all keeps coming back in little bits every now and again. It's like a nightmare when you wake up and you remember some bits and you don't remember others. And after that really it is, you know, very much of a blur.'

The court was hushed as Jo asked Susie if she had tried to resuscitate her son.

'I knew it was too late,' she said. 'I just knew. I mean, I had been taught how to resuscitate – I knew how to do it – but I just knew it was just too late . . . I knew I couldn't do anything for him.'

She added, 'You have not got a reason, when there isn't any reason. You keep blaming yourself because you think, Was he ill and I missed it? Was there something that I was doing wrong? Why would a perfectly healthy baby go to sleep and then not wake up again? And you don't get any closure, and I still haven't got any closure fifteen years later.'

Later Susie told the court about an incident days after the birth of her surviving daughter when she thought the baby had stopped breathing as she fed her in hospital.

'All the time, instead of resuscitating her, I was trying to take her all-in-one off and I didn't quite know why I was trying to take her all-in-one off. I mean, I don't know what good I thought that would do. As it happened, because I pressed the panic button, the nurses came in, picked her up and she was fine . . . I knew what to do, I knew how to resuscitate and I just, even to this day, it was just sheer, I just . . . All logic and reason went out of the window. I was absolutely panic-stricken.'

As Susie spoke, I felt filled with compassion for her. We had never met each other, never spoken to each other, and yet we had shared a similar sorrow and the words she used to describe it echoed mine. Surely the jury needed no more evidence than that of another mother? I wasn't deliberately inconsistent, reluctant to answer the question or lying – like Susie, I found it impossible to remember everything that had happened and our experiences put us beyond the realms of 'normal' reactions. We were simply mothers who had lost our children and we each had a unique reaction to an almost unique event.

Over the next five days, it was almost more than I could bear to see my family and friends go through the ordeal of sitting in the witness box. Terry, my parents, Terry Chambers, Stephen, John Walton, Claire and Brian, all gave evidence for the defence and I felt so sad to see them all, desperately nervous about what they were there to do and anxious to help me as much as they could. Tears often got the better of me as I sat and listened.

I'll never forget seeing Stephen tell the court that Terry and I had made him a better person and describe me as his 'mum', or hearing the certainty in Terry's voice when he answered 'absolutely' when asked if he still loved me, or watching my dad's hands shake as he gave evidence. I wanted to leap out of the dock as Dunkels cast a familiarly dark shadow over my father's description of a conversation we'd had when he offered to talk me through resuscitation techniques but I'd told him that I'd been shown by a doctor.

'So she never asked you, as it were, for extra coaching?' he sneered.

'No,' my dad replied.

'Now. You have been in the ambulance service for?'

'For about twenty-eight years, I think, something like that.'

'Since she was about nine or ten years old?'

'Yes.'

'Yes. Thank you, Mr Connolly.'

Again, my 'disinterest' in reviving my lifeless children hung heavy in the air. They'd even tried to twist my father's words against me.

In the days that followed, expert medical witnesses also gave evidence for me. There was Dr Ian Rushton, a consultant paediatric and perinatal pathologist at Birmingham Women's Hospital with twenty-nine years' university lecturing experience, who said the number of siderophages found in Jason's lungs was only slightly higher than those seen in a small number of cot deaths. He told the court they could have been triggered when he inhaled blood during the caesarean to deliver him or during resuscitation attempts on the day of his ALTE.

Dr Rushton also seemed to express unhappiness at a 'set of rules being laid down' when it came to cot deaths.

'In a family with a history of this type, current dogma is that an unnatural cause has been established unless it is possible to demonstrate an alternative natural explanation for these events,' the court heard.

When Justice Hallett asked about his use of the word 'dogma', the doctor replied, 'I was using it in the sense of a set of rules being laid down which we now follow but which some of us feel are over-restrictive and we follow them because they are there but we are not entirely happy.'

Jean Golding, a professor of paediatric and perinatal epidemiology at the University of Bristol, who had first been instructed by the Crown before studying the case and deciding to give evidence for the defence, made a similar point. 'I think, to put it in context, there is a fashion nowadays that if you have more than one sudden infant death the next one must have been killed deliberately and that is something that people within the paediatric profession have taken on board without sufficient evidence. Certainly, obviously, there are cases where it happens, but in the vast majority there is no evidence of that.'

About the claims that smothering could be the cause of unexpected deaths, she told the court, 'I agree it is theoretically possible. There are a few cases where it appears to have hap-

145

pened. But it is by no means clear that the claims that so many families where more than one sudden infant death has occurred are due to smothering. The results haven't been subjected to what I would call an appropriate statistical analysis. They are mostly a hunch that the paediatrician or whoever is looking at it might have, but it is not based on any scientific foundation.'

Later Professor Golding was asked if she agreed that Professor Meadow had done more research into the area than most.

'I would refute that,' she told the court. 'I would say that he has collected cases that he claims are due to smothering and it is more like stamp collecting than doing a proper scientific study.'

Other experts appeared to give the court possible reasons why my babies had died. Professor Peter Milla, director of the Department of Gastroenterology of Great Ormond Street Hospital, told the court Jade had exhibited the symptoms of gastroenteritis on the day of her hospitalisation and she had in fact suffered a circulatory collapse – not breathing problems; Ian Hutchinson, a professor of Immunology at Manchester University, said Matthew had had less than 10 per cent of a crucial antibody, which would have left him susceptible to infections – particularly of the lung; and Dr David Drucker, who researched microbiological causes for SIDS at Manchester University, said relatively harmless organisms would be dangerous to a baby without proper immunity.

Dr Paul Johnson, a consultant clinical physiologist and neonatologist at the John Radcliffe Hospital in Oxford, gave detailed evidence about vaso-vagal attacks; Dr John Morgan, a cardiac specialist from Southampton General Hospital, said that although he could not diagnose Jade and Matthew with Long QT, he was highly suspicious they had it; and Professor Anthony Maden, a forensic psychiatrist at Imperial College who had examined me, said he had found no evidence of any psychiatric disorder. He told the court women who did not have a motive to kill their children were usually suffering from one.

The genetic evidence was also presented when Professor Patton took the stand to talk about my family and the McDermotts.

'I think this is a very striking family tree in that we have got a rare condition occurring in two parts of an extended family and I think there are two possible explanations for that. One is autosomal dominant inheritance, that's where a condition is passed from generation to generation, and that can have variable penetrance, meaning that some of those who have the gene abnormality may not fully express it and may not manifest it. That might be a way of linking the McDermotts and the Cannings.

'The other possible mechanism of inheritance would be autosomal recessive inheritance. In this case it would imply that both Mr and Mrs McDermott would be carriers but, because it is a recessive condition, they wouldn't manifest the problem. But if they both pass on an abnormal gene that can lead to the expression of a recessive disorder. That's another potential explanation – that both Mr McDermott and Angela Cannings have married a carrier. That can, of course, happen, and would explain why a recessive disorder comes out on two occasions within an extended family.'

Professor Patton also told the court there were many genetic conditions which had a low penetrance in families – which would explain why no one else had been affected as we and the McDermotts had been.

Under cross-examination, Dunkels asked the medic if any of the tests he had done on my blood sample had shown up a genetic abnormality. They had not.

'There is a lot in genetics we don't have analysis for,' the doctor told the court. 'We have not identified all the genes.'

But, unlike the repeated allusion to smothering on the prosecution's side, I was all too aware that none of my defence experts could give a single, definitive reason for my babies' deaths – they could only suggest countless possibilities. The loss of Jason and Matthew was ultimately a mystery none could solve. But some conceded under cross-examination that unnatural death was on the list of possibilities – it couldn't be ruled out because no other cause had been found.

But that doesn't mean it's a fact, I thought to myself. I can't get convicted for a possibility.

As the trial moved into its fifth week, it seemed to me that for every doubt raised by a prosecution expert, there was an answer from someone who appeared for the defence. It amazed me that all these experts, with their degrees and years of experience, could not agree on how my children died and yet I was sitting charged with murder. Everything was a question of interpretation in a case like mine, and even where there was physical evidence, such as the siderophages, no one could agree on how significant it was – to one expert it meant I was a killer while to another it was meaningless. I clung to the hope this would convince the jury I was not a murderer. They couldn't convict me simply because of numbers, statistics and patterns. Innocent until proven guilty, beyond reasonable doubt – that was what British justice was all about.

After a two-week break for Easter, closing speeches and the judge's summing up, the case finally closed on Friday, 12 April. Just one weekend lay between me and Monday morning when the jury would finally be sent out. It was all coming to an end.

It was Saturday night – the day after the case had closed – and Terry and I had gone to a local pub for some food but I hadn't been able to eat a thing. After two and a half years, the end was in sight and I had no idea what was going to happen. Part of me wanted to savour the time with Terry because I knew it might be our last, but I also felt he wasn't really with me any more. Fear was my only emotion as I pushed my food around the plate. When would the jury be back? What would they be thinking? Were they losing themselves in Saturday-night television, oblivious to my fate, or already weighing up their decision?

'Do you want a drink?' Terry asked as we returned home from the pub and walked into our lounge.

I knew I should reach out to him, try to explain my inability to lose myself in the moment, but instead I could only snap: 'Is that your answer to everything?'

He turned and looked at me, fury written across his face. 'If you're going to be like that, then just go back to your mum's,' he shouted, as I turned and slammed out of the front door back into the night.

Furious, I hesitated as I wondered what to do before turning and walking to the corner shop where I bought a couple of bottles of wine.

Minutes later the silence loomed large as I walked back into the house.

'If you think I'm going to give up on you now then you've got another think coming,' I said. 'Let's enjoy this evening. Please, please be here for me.'

I looked at Terry, willing him to come through for me, and with those words something did shift between us. I don't know what it was – desperation, a sense of duty, the stirring of our battered and bruised love – but it was as if the years since Matthew died had slipped silently away. Just as we had in the past, Terry and I uncorked the wine and listened to music as we drank. Slowly, as the alcohol eased into our system and the music lulled us into peace, we started to talk again – to really talk as we had done for so many years before our lives were engulfed. We talked about the past, the times we'd had, the laughs, the fun, the togetherness, and somehow Terry and I became what we were until the morning of Matthew's death. For that brief time we were natural together once more and stopped worrying about Jade, social workers and police. We went back in a time warp to being happy together and, for the first time since the trial began, I allowed myself to cry in front of him.

'I love you so much,' I told him. 'And I'm just so scared.'

He said nothing as his tears began to flow with mine and we turned up one of our favourite songs to full volume. Called 'The Future Ain't What It Used To Be' by Jim Steinman, it seemed to sum up everything we felt.

I never knew so many bad times could follow me so mercilessly, the female vocalist sung out.

> *It's almost surreal all the pain that I feel, the future ain't*
>   *what it used to be.*
> *It doesn't matter what they're thinking, it doesn't matter*
>   *what they're thinking of me.*
> *It's always so cold, I'm too young to be old, the future*
>   *ain't what it used to be.*

*Were there ever any stars in the sky? Did the sun ever shine
    so bright?*
*Do you have any dreams I could borrow? Just to get me
    through the lonely night.*
*Is there anything left to hold onto when the river's washed
    it all away?*
*Is there anyone left to hold on to? Is there anything left I
    can say?*

We must have played it twenty times that night, clinging onto the
words which said everything we couldn't, and, when we had
finally had our fill, I turned and left the room.

I walked upstairs and sat in front of the bedroom mirror before
turning to my make-up bag and, for the first time in such a long
time, made myself up and tried to recreate the woman – and
wife – I had been before Matthew died. Minutes later I walked
back into the lounge where Terry was sitting waiting. Wordlessly,
he turned to me. Nothing else needed to be said.

We clung onto those last moments together, the familiarity of
each other's skin and the comfort we drew from each other. But as
we lay in bed later I was filled with guilt. Surely we would be punished for such pleasure? As fear crept back into my mind, I knew
that the brief release from the present had disappeared as quickly
as it had arrived.

The following day I saw Jade and, as it had with her father, the
awful sense that this was the final time hung heavy on me. It is
impossible to put into words what I felt as I wrapped her in my
arms knowing that I might soon be parted from her but being
unable to prepare her for not seeing me again because I didn't
know what was going to happen.

'Have they finished in the big building yet?' she asked me.

'No, darling,' I replied. 'They still have to do a bit more
talking.'

She was so young, so vulnerable, just six years old, and every
instinct inside me railed against the thought that I might have to
leave Jade. I should be there to protect her, and I knew that soon
I might not be able to. I held on and on to her as we stood in the

doorway to say goodbye, my heart bursting with love for her and the unbearable ache that always filled me whenever I thought of the harm that was being done to her.

All I could see as I drove away with the social worker was Jade's tiny figure standing in the doorway with Terry, tears running down her cheeks. Inside I wondered if somewhere she sensed that this goodbye was different from all those we had said before.

It was just after 2 p.m. on Tuesday when we heard the court tannoy sound. I was waiting with family members – including Mum, Brian, Claire, Tina, Andrew, Dad, Jacqueline, Gill and her parents. Jo Briggs had tried to while away the time by showing us card tricks but I was nervous and subdued – unable to forget for a second that my fate was being decided by twelve strangers somewhere in that building. Terry was not with us. He'd told me he had to stay at home because of how upset Jade was by everything and part of me understood. But I also knew he was scared and I felt let down that I was on my own once again.

'Would all those involved in the case of Cannings return to court three,' it intoned.

Fear swept cold across me as I walked into the dock. I thought of Terry at home with Stephen waiting for news from the police, of Jade at school oblivious to what was happening, of my family and friends who were sitting above in the public gallery, of my lost children, Gemma, Jason and Matthew. Finally, after all this time, I had reached my day of judgement.

I watched as the forewoman of the jury got to her feet.

'Have you reached a verdict?' the clerk of the court asked her.

'Yes,' the woman replied.

'Please stand, Mrs Cannings.'

I held my breath as I got to my feet.

'In relation to count one – the charge of the murder of Jason Cannings – have you reached a verdict on which you are all agreed?'

'Yes.'

'How do you find the defendant – guilty or not guilty?'

151

'Guilty.'

I heard a gasp from the public gallery above me.

'In relation to count two – the charge of the murder of Matthew Cannings – have you reached a verdict on which you are all agreed?'

'Yes.'

'How do you find the defendant – guilty or not guilty?'

'Guilty.'

Everything went completely still, time was suspended in a hushed moment of disbelief before I heard a roaring in my ears.

'No, no, no,' I moaned as I snatched my breath in a gasp and felt my whole body crumble as I sank to my knees. I felt as if I had been shot. Staggering on my feet, the dock officer moved forward to help me stay upright as upstairs in the public gallery I heard crying and shouting as the judge called for silence.

Guilty, my mind screamed. Guilty.

'You've got to stand,' I heard, as someone steadied me on my feet.

My mind was blank. I felt disorientated, breathless, terrified. I had never dared to prepare myself for this moment and it was worse than anything I could have imagined. Even now I can find no words to describe it. Horror, revulsion, fear, panic, disbelief . . . nothing can do justice to those first few seconds in the dock after I was convicted of murdering my sons.

Dimly, I was aware of the judge speaking, but I couldn't see anything through my tears or hear anything other than rushing in my ears.

Now, of course, I know what Justice Hallett said as she sentenced me to life in prison – extraordinary words to come from the unemotional confines of the judge's bench.

'There was no medical evidence before the court that suggested there was anything wrong with you when you killed your children,' she said. 'I have no doubt that for a woman like you to have committed these terrible acts of suffocating your own babies there must have been something seriously wrong with you. All the evidence indicates you wanted the children and, apart from these terrible incidents, you cherished them. So in my layman's view, it is no coincidence that these events took place within weeks of your giving birth. It can, in my view, be the only explanation for why someone like you could have committed these acts when you have such a loving and supportive family.'

She added, 'As you know I have no alternative but to impose sentences of life imprisonment on you. This in my judgement is a classic kind of injustice that can be caused by mandatory sentencing. It's not my decision when you will be released, but I intend to make it known in my remarks that, in my own view, you will never be a threat to anyone in the future.'

But I didn't hear any of what she said – the allusion to postnatal depression and her thinly disguised sorrow at the life sentence she was forced to pass on me. Her sentencing remarks caused a sensation among legal watchers but the only word that rang in my ears was 'life'. It shrieked around my brain and I tried to focus on what was happening through the tears that had blinded my vision.

'Take her down,' I heard Justice Hallett say as I felt a tug on my arm.

I knew I should move but couldn't. It was as if my brain had been disconnected from my body and my feet rooted to the spot. I fell against whoever it was as they guided me out of the dock and, as I was led into the corridor behind the court, I realised I was being taken towards the stairs leading downwards, which I had seen before but never descended.

This can't be happening, I told myself. Guilty? Guilty?

As I was stumbling down those steps towards the cells, Bill stood outside the court and told waiting journalists that my conviction was reminiscent of a witchcraft trial.

'It is the kind of logic that says that when a child dies and an explanation cannot be found, it is therefore murder,' he said. 'What we are saying here is that when a mother is alone with her child and that child dies and that smothering that child cannot be ruled out, then that is what happened.'

He added, 'I am not alone in having my faith in the jury system shaken by the outcome of this trial.'

Even those who had built the case against me were unable to

153

offer any explanation as to why I had killed my children.

'I have no idea at all about the motive – only one person knows the answer to that question,' said a detective chief inspector from Wiltshire police.

But I knew nothing of this as the guard guided me down those winding steps. The only thing hammering through my shocked brain was that I was going to spend the rest of my life in prison.

She said I had to stay there for the rest of my life, I thought to myself as we descended the stairs and I heard sobs, not knowing if they were mine or someone else's.

When I look back at that trial and see the experts at logger-heads with each other I feel so frustrated that it even continued. It was, as Bill said, like a witchcraft trial – no evidence, no motive, no crime even – and how could it have happened in a British court-room? Even now it is one of the hardest things to under-stand. I don't blame the jury for what they did but I blame the system – the lawyers, the judges, the CPS, the police, the medical experts. If there are culprits in this it is them.

I was taken down into another corridor where Jacqui was waiting for me before we were shown into a cubicle where a woman secu-rity guard told me to empty out my bag. Stunned and unable to move, I sobbed uncontrollably as Jacqui tried to talk to me.

'I can't believe it,' I kept repeating, almost to myself. 'I can't believe it.'

'Neither can I,' Jacqui said softly.

I looked up at her, aware that soon she'd have to leave me.

'Don't leave me. Please don't leave me.'

'We'll never leave you, Angela,' she told me. 'We've no inten-tion of forgetting you. We will do everything we can to get you out. We'll fight all the way for you.'

'Please help me, please get me out of here,' I sobbed. 'Please don't let them do this to me. Please get me home.'

'We will do everything we can,' Jo Briggs, who had arrived just after Jacqui, said gently as they turned to leave.

If I had felt alone in the dock, I cannot find a word for the feeling that overwhelmed me as Jacqui and Jo left. There was nothing anyone could do to help me any more. This was it, the verdict had been given and I was utterly on my own. I sat unable to take it all in. Why had they ignored me when I told them I was innocent? Why had they done this to me?

How are Terry and Jade going to cope? I thought to myself. Who is going to look after them? What is going to happen to them?

I sobbed and sobbed, a river of tears that would not dry up for days to come, until I was taken into a room screened off by glass. Mum, my cousin Jacqueline and Claire soon came in and all we could do was cry as we stared at each other.

All the life and colour drained out of her face, Mum pleaded with me from the other side of the glass. 'Hang on, Angela.'

'Please, please look after Terry and Jade, Mum, because I can't be with them now,' I whispered back.

'Don't worry about them. I'll make sure they are looked after and I'll give up working if needs be to look after them.'

'Please, please, Mum. Look after them because Jade needs looking after and so does Terry. I can't be there and I don't know how long this will go on for.'

As we sat in front of the screen, I reached out and put my hands onto the glass as my family mirrored my fingers with theirs on the other side. I felt it lie cold beneath my touch.

Why can't I be the other side of that glass? Why can't someone tell me this is a bad dream and let me go home? I thought to myself as we sobbed our hearts out.

'Please don't give up, Ange,' Claire wept as she looked at me. 'We'll get you out of here. We will.'

But as she cried on the other side of the glass, I could only reply, 'What can you do? They've done this to me. I'll never be able to come out.'

'Yes you will, yes you will,' she told me. 'We are going to fight this. Please be strong.'

Terror and loneliness battled inside my stomach – like the sudden rush of fear you have when you realise you are lost as a child. I vividly remembered getting separated from my family when I was about eight on a trip to a summer fair in Salisbury's

Victoria Park. That moment when you turn round expecting to see the people you know and realise they are not there, that you are all alone. But as a child I went into the pavilion, asked for help and it was given – my mum soon arrived. Now, as an adult, I knew no one could help me. I would never find my way back to the people I loved.

Later, after what seemed like an eternity of waiting, a handcuff – cold and clasping – was attached to my wrist and I was taken into a courtyard where a prison van waited. I felt as if my legs might collapse as I was guided into the back of it and locked into a steel cubicle – tiny, tomb-like. I felt utterly trapped as my knees knocked the sides and I hunched down on the seat to stop myself from sliding about. I heard the click of the lock before we started to move and, as instructed, held a newspaper up to the cubicle's tiny window to block the camera flashes as, once again, the press tried to hunt down their quarry. No longer just a suspect, I was now a prized female child-killer.

I had no idea where I was going – the only words I had heard were 'Eastwood Park' – and all I could do was wait as the van eased its way into a steady rhythm. As I sat in that metal box staring at walls that were locking me in for the first time, my mind fixed on one thing: I was a murderer, a child-killer, and I was going to jail for life.

CHAPTER TEN

I heard the click of the lock soon after the van finally slowed to a halt at about 7.30 p.m. We had arrived at Eastwood Park prison in Gloucestershire. All I could see out of the tiny window were huge gates as heavy footsteps indicated other prisoners were being unloaded before me.

'Out you come,' a voice said as I sat, unwilling to move – at least I was safe in there, locked inside that tiny steel coffin.

I could not bring myself to step out of that van and towards my new future – a future of locks, cells, rules, fear and separation from everything I knew and loved. I felt like a husk – empty, drained and consumed by a nightmare from which I would never wake up.

'What's your name, age and address?' a woman officer asked as we stood in a mostly deserted reception area after I was led into a 1960s-style building. 'Please remove all your jewellery.'

As I slowly peeled off the mementoes of my former life – my watch, my shamrock necklace, my wedding ring – each item was listed on a sheet of paper. I felt sick as I slipped the gold band off my finger, that tiny final physical link with Terry gone.

After I'd been checked in, I was taken for another interview with an officer before being given a welcome pack – a see-through plastic bag containing a small packet of tobacco, rolling papers, matches, a £2 phone card, a pen, two stamps and a small notepad. I looked at it dully, my new worldly possessions.

With each box ticked and computer entry made, I was sucked into a new and alien world. It hardly seemed possible that I had woken up that morning at my mum's, hugged Claire on my way into court, said goodbye to Bill and Jacqui. Now I was here and it seemed utterly unreal. I started to sob once again as I was guided into a small cubicle like those you find at the swimming pool and told to wait.

Where are they going to put me? What is going to happen to me? How did this happen to me? I thought to myself. How are Terry and Jade? Is anyone with them?

Fear filled me about what was going to happen to me now I was in prison. Until that moment, it had been something I read about in newspapers or saw on the television, but now I was in it – and I would be here for life.

Soon I was taken to a nearby shower room where two female officers told me to remove the top half of my clothes. I walked behind a curtain, where I quickly took off the jacket of the suit I'd worn that day to court, my shirt and bra.

'Lift up your arms, open your mouth, lift up your tongue and turn around,' they said after pulling back the curtain, as one peered at me while the other checked behind my ears. I felt like a specimen in a laboratory. I was shocked when they told me to remove the rest of my clothes.

This time there was no curtain to shield me as I took off my skirt, underwear, tights and shoes while the prison officers silently watched. Hands hovering uselessly in a vain attempt to cover my humiliating nakedness, I could only submit to another inspection as the officers looked me up and down before turning me round to stare once again.

'Jackie, can you come down here and sort Angela out, take her for a shower and a hair wash?' I heard a voice shout after I was given a bathrobe and taken back to the cubicle where I had previously waited.

As I heard the harsh swish of the plastic curtain, an older woman wearing a grey sweatshirt and leggings came into the cubicle. She had a ponytail of long greyish hair and, judging by the dark circles under her eyes and lines on her face, had had a hard life. Looking at her clothes, I realised she wasn't an officer and shrank back for a moment. I had never met a prisoner before.

'Come on,' she said in a kind voice. 'You've got to come with me. You need to get into the shower. When anybody arrives here they have to have a shower and get cleaned. I'm Jackie. I work here in reception.'

I looked at her blankly. I didn't want to have a shower, to be told what to do any more – all I wanted was to be left alone, to wrap myself into a ball and let blackness overcome me.

But I silently followed Jackie and, after the shower curtain was closed and water began to fall over me, began to sob once again. I felt broken, heartbroken, empty. I was never going to be free, see Terry and Jade, live a normal life. I had no idea how I was going to survive.

Later, after we had become friends, Jackie would tell me she had never seen anyone so distraught during her time working in the reception area.

'I'll never forget the night you arrived,' she told me. 'You looked so lost.'

But back then she simply handed me a thin blue towel and took me back to the cubicle where she gave me a huge tracksuit top, black leggings, underwear and flip-flops before bringing me a cup of tea and some toast.

'You just need to eat something,' she said. 'I'm sure it's been a long day. Don't worry, you'll be fine.'

Certain tiny details stick in your mind when you look back and I will never forget Jackie's kindness during those first few awful hours in prison. I felt as if I was becoming part of a huge machine and she gave me a brief, comforting glimpse of the humanity that might be hidden somewhere inside it.

But for now all I could do was stumble after officers as they guided me here and there – an appointment with the doctor, silent walks down corridors with only the sound of the locking and unlocking of doors to accompany us, and finally into a cell on the healthcare unit.

It was empty, bare and cold. On my left was a long concrete slab with two hollow squares beneath it and a plastic mattress and pillow on top. There was also a small wooden table with a TV on it and, to my right, an alcove containing a stainless-steel sink and toilet. It stank of stale urine and I noticed that in addition to a hatch in the door there was another peephole to the back of the toilet – there was no escaping the eyes of my captors.

How did Terry and Jade hear the news? I wondered as I sat down heavily on the bed. What has he told her? Are they okay?

I made up the bed before sitting back down and staring around me. Desperate for some distraction, I turned on the television. It was the news and I was all over it.

'A mother was today given two life sentences for the murder of her two babies,' it intoned. 'Angela Cannings collapsed in the dock as she was jailed for life for smothering sons Jason and Matthew.'

As a reporter's voice gave further details about my trial, pictures of the prison van I had left court in were shown. As it sped away, photographers gave chase. It was me in there, I thought as I started to cry again.

It was like a dream. I couldn't believe it was happening. I quickly switched the television off and sat in silence, my mind numbly turning over the questions that crowded it.

'We are going to be keeping an eye on you all night – it's standard procedure,' a male nurse told me as he walked into the cell. 'I'll also get you something to help you sleep.'

Obediently I took the pill before lying down on the hard bed and waiting for sleep to wash over me. But it was no good. I couldn't still my mind. Over and over I heard the word 'guilty' as that awful moment in the dock replayed again and again in my mind.

I don't know if I can do this, I thought as I curled up and started to cry again. Am I really going to be able to get through this?

Hour after hour I lay there, sometimes slipping into a fitful sleep before being woken by the scrape of the door hatch and seeing a light burning white through my closed eyelids as the overhead strip was switched on and a nurse looked at me. I knew I was on suicide watch and it made sense. After all that had happened, I finally felt I was going to go under as I lay in that prison cell cut off from everything I knew and loved.

The next day I was led into the association room, where inmates spent time out of their cells, and was introduced to my 'lifer officer', who explained she was there to discuss my 'life sentence plan'. I looked at her blankly.

'Everyone sentenced to life gets one and it maps out a schedule for your time in prison,' she told me. 'Life doesn't mean life but I think you'll probably serve a maximum of fifteen years.'

Fifteen years? I silently screamed. Jade will be twenty-one, Terry will be sixty-three, I'll be fifty-three. I can't do it. I can't do it.

'You will know for sure how long your sentence will be when the Home Secretary sets your tariff recommending how many years you will serve. But in the meantime we must plan your sentence because it will involve different stages in different prisons,' the officer went on, apparently oblivious to the fear rising up in me. 'You will stay here at Eastwood Park for five to six months before being transferred to a prison with a unit for lifers. There are two with a unit for women – Durham prison and Bullwood Hall in Essex, and I will strongly recommend you go to Bullwood because it is nearer to your husband and daughter.'

'Please don't let them send me to Durham,' I told her. 'It is so far away. Terry and Jade will never get to see me.'

'I'm sure that won't happen,' she said, before telling me that I would be classed as a Schedule 1 offender because my crimes involved children.

'Angela, your convictions are sensitive with other inmates and we have some concerns,' she told me. 'Provision will be made to ensure you are safe.'

Fear contracted my stomach. I was going to have to be protected, kept safe. I was a target for other prisoners within those walls. As a child-killer, my conviction made me the lowest of the low among inmates and many would relish the chance to attack me, to express their hatred of my supposed crime in punches and blows.

Panic gripped me as I sat silently and looked at the officer. I wanted to grab her, plead with her to get me out, scream at her to save me. But I sat silently as she told me I would be kept apart from prisoners and eventually, hopefully, put onto a different wing.

'When can I see Terry and Jade?' I asked the officer as she led me back to my cell.

'I'll see what I can sort out,' she told me. The door slammed shut again and I looked around the empty room.

Nervously I searched the outlines of people visible through an opaque screen dividing the room where I sat from an adjoining corridor. Three days after coming to Eastwood Park, I was sitting at a round table surrounded by four easy chairs in a large prison visiting hall, looking for Terry and Jade. Minutes before, I had been led into the hall and given an orange bib to wear before being sat at one of about a dozen tables and told the visiting rules.

'You mustn't cuddle each other for too long, you must stay in your seat at all times, if anyone wants a drink they can go to the vending machines but you can't. You have an hour.'

I looked at an officer sitting on a raised platform and at others behind a counter at the front of the hall and wondered how I would cope with seeing my husband and daughter enter my brutal new world. Relief that I was finally going to see them wrestled with anxiety.

'Mummy,' I heard Jade shout as she ran across the hall and into my lap. I started to cry immediately as I put my arms around her – unable to be anywhere near as strong I had promised myself I would be – and through the tears saw Terry and Stephen walk up to us.

'Oh, Ange,' Terry said, as he looked at me wearing the same sweatshirt, leggings and flip-flops I had been given on the night of my arrival. 'You should have had some of your own clothes with you rather than those hand-me-downs. Why didn't we think of that?'

Terry's shock at my appearance was written on his face. He had last seen me five days before when I had said goodbye to him at the end of the weekend. Now pale, drawn and unkempt, I was a stranger from the woman I was then – scared but in control. Now I felt like a zombie and, however hard I tried, knew I couldn't be the Angela he loved. For the first time in the two long years since Matthew's death the strength that had sustained me had been sapped from me. I felt completely overwhelmed, unable to fight, hopeless – and I knew he could see it in me.

'I don't understand this,' was all I could sob as we sat there looking at each other. 'I've been stripped, they took my ring away and my watch. I was put into this. Why are they doing this to me? How could this have happened? Please get me out of here, Terry. Stephen?'

As I pleaded with them through the tears, they started to cry. We had never let our guards down before in front of Jade but that day we were incapable of hiding our grief.

'We will get you out of here,' Terry told me. 'We really will. But you're going to have to grin and bear it for a while. I need to talk to Bill about the timescale but it took twenty-two months to get you to trial so God knows how long it will take to get you out of here. I'm sorry, Ange, I don't want to make things harder for you but if I start to lie to you now about this then everything is going to become a lie and you don't want that. I will be in this fight as long as it takes but it might take a while.'

'But everyone thinks I'm a murderer,' I whispered. 'They think I killed Jason and Matthew.'

'At the end of the day, the people who care, and the people who know you, know you've done nothing wrong, Angela. One day all this will come right for us.'

But I couldn't find it in myself to believe him. After all those months of believing the system would not fail us, while Terry had said it would, he was now the one telling me it would work for us and I couldn't believe it. I didn't feel panicked or even angry at the thought that his reassurances were hollow, instead I felt numb. The only thing that mattered to me at that moment was my family and I longed to get up, go into a separate room and be on my own with them – no clock to keep an eye on, no social workers lurking, no prison officers watching over us.

'So how are Kellie and the kids? How was the journey?' I asked dully, as I tried to stop my tears.

'They're all fine, aren't they, Stevey?' Terry replied. 'It's lucky he came with us because he had a good idea where we were going. Getting in was a bit more difficult. They searched us, frisked us, even looked into our mouths. But Jade took it in her stride.

'So how about you, Ange? What is your cell like? How are you getting on without your watch? How do you know what time it is?'

'I don't until *EastEnders* comes on,' I replied, before telling them about my cell and the trees I could see over the back of a fence.

As we talked, Jade got off my lap and looked around before going over to stand by Stephen, looping her arm through his. I so wanted to pull her back to me but couldn't – I was allowed to stand up but not move anywhere – and all I could do as we sat and chatted was hope she would come back to me. She didn't.

'Go on, darling, give Mummy a cuddle,' Terry told her as an officer shouted, 'Five minutes.'

Familiar panic rose in me once again as I thought of Terry, Jade and Stephen going out of the door and leaving me in that hall. As Jade came over to cuddle me, I felt loneliness creep cold into the pit of my stomach.

'I love you, I love you, I love you,' I whispered over and over as I clung onto her, desperate to drive the words so deep within my daughter she could never forget. 'Be a good girl for Daddy,' I said, my voice thick with tears, before finally letting her go.

'Keep your chin up,' Terry whispered into my ear as he hugged me. 'I love you.'

Strangely it was Stephen I found the most difficult to let go of at the end of that visit because I knew he was going to have to look after Terry and Jade.

'Keep them safe for me,' I told him.

'Don't worry, Angela,' Stephen replied. 'I'll always be there for them. You know I will.'

How I forced myself to sit back down in my chair and watch

them go, I will never know. Each one – father, son and daughter – turned as they reached the door to blow me a kiss and I strained to drink in those last glimpses of them. Grief cut through me like a knife as I waited for my name to be called for the journey back to my cell.

One thing prison quickly taught me is that however alien something is to you, however grotesque, however sad, it is amazing how quickly you can slot into a routine. Within a couple of days of my arrival on the prison healthcare unit, I knew breakfast would be served through the hatch in my door each morning, I would stand placidly in front of the hatch later in the day to take delivery of my antidepressants and sleeping tablets, while at night I would patiently tick off the boxes on a menu card for the next day's meals. I even got used to waking up dripping with sweat after sleeping on a plastic mattress, eating the slop – anything from a greasy spaghetti bolognaise to stew with grey bits of meat floating in it – that was served up at mealtimes and forcing myself to make the occasional trip to the association room, where classes, mostly arts and crafts, were held.

'You're doing so well,' a woman said to me, as she inspected the frankly awful drawing I'd done of a bowl of fruit.

Jade could have done better, I thought darkly to myself as I returned her smile.

I'd like to say that tiny bit of structure comforted me but, to be honest, during those first few days in healthcare nothing pierced my grief. I felt like a pencil drawing half rubbed out, the lines all blurry, as I struggled to find my feet in the strange new world that was opening up before me. The sights, the smells, the atmosphere – prison's rules and regulations were so far removed from anything I had ever known.

I spent most of the time in my cell, avoiding even the odd occasion when we were allowed into the association room, preferring to keep myself to myself because I was scared. But as the days passed, I also became increasingly aware that I was different to most of the women on the unit. However awful I felt, I was still

165

aware of who and where I was. But looking around me, I became more and convinced I was not in a prison but a madhouse.

On the odd occasion I was in the association room I would always see a young girl rifling through the dirty ashtrays for other people's dog ends until she was led away by a nurse, while an older woman, who looked like a tramp, walked up and down muttering constantly to herself and wringing her hands. Most of the other women looked out of it – with dark circles under their eyes and vacant expressions.

The unit was like a cattle market during the day, echoing at times with the screams and shouts of inmates who weren't allowed out of their cells. I quickly realised there were women housed in cells hidden behind a huge steel door near the entrance who were suffering serious mental-health problems. The ones who were out and about, I thought, must be less serious.

But that all changed when I was moved into a double cell with a girl in her twenties. I think I was allowed to share a room on healthcare because most of the women did not know what day of the week it was, let alone that I had been convicted of child murder. But within days she had smashed up her side of the room. Nothing on mine was touched but I could only watch in horror as everything of hers was ripped, thrown and smashed. Face contorted in fury, she screamed as she attacked her possessions, and I stood rooted to the spot when the nurses rushed in. I had never seen anything like it. Later they reassured me she would never have touched me. But my first glimpse of the violence simmering under the seemingly orderly surface of prison life stayed with me.

She was replaced by a new cellmate, a Welsh woman called Paula, who told me she was in for a few months for drugs offences. It was a dark world I knew nothing about and which scared me, but as Paula explained she'd done what she'd done for money and was devastated at being separated from her two teenage sons, I could see that she, like me, was being cut from the inside out at the loss of her children.

All too soon, the moment arrived that I had been dreading ever since coming into prison.

'What are you in for?' Paula asked.

166

My stomach tensed and I took a deep breath before uttering the words I had never thought I would have to say.

'I've been convicted of murder. I am supposed to have murdered my two babies.'

'Oh my God,' Paula gasped, as I started to cry.

'I didn't do it and I'm not just saying that,' I sobbed. 'I did not do what they said I did to my babies.'

Paula was silent for a few seconds before she turned and asked me to tell her what had happened.

I found it hard at first but over the next couple of days I told her everything about Terry and Jade, our separation and losing Gemma, Jason and Matthew. My story poured out of me until eventually I finished telling it.

'You've just got to keep your head up and try to get through it as best you can,' she told me.

I looked at her in utter relief. I knew I would be a target for hate for years to come but at least Paula believed in me. I didn't know if anyone would ever do so again but just to know there was one person who had treated me with kindness was something I could hold onto.

For my two weeks on healthcare Paula and I gave each other a reason to keep going. Amid the grief and sadness, we'd find ourselves laughing at the same thing as we watched a soap, or giggling as we took apart our dog ends and made roll-ups with them – desperately trying to eke out every last drop from the welcome packs we'd been given. We even started getting friendly with some of the nurses, who'd slip us the odd fag through the hatch when we were really desperate. Sometimes at night I'd feel guilty because we had had a laugh that day. It felt wrong. But Paula was my saviour and I was devastated when I was told that I was being moved onto the main prison.

My trainers squeaked against the shiny lino floor as I was taken down a long corridor lined with cell doors. Each had a metal box beside it with a card sticking out of the top like a clocking-in card. Another journey into the unknown – hospital corridors, mortuary

167

corridors, police-station corridors, court corridors – but I knew this would end in a cell where I would be locked up for more than twenty-three hours a day. I had been told I was a Rule 45 prisoner – considered so vulnerable in the company of other inmates that I was only allowed out when everyone else was locked in – and my new segregated cell was one of three separated by a barred door from the main A-wing of Eastwood Park. As I walked into it, the card containing my details was slipped into a holder next to the cell door. It read 'A Cannings DT9868 Life'. I was now officially a numbered part of that system.

The room contained a wooden-framed bed with a thin mattress and a duvet on it, a cupboard and a table with a television. I forced myself to unpack the small amount of baggage I had with me to try and make myself feel at 'home'. As well as prison bits and pieces, my family had been allowed to send certain items in – things like clothes, stationery and stamps – and it was a relief to have some of my own things.

My most prized possessions were photos of Terry and Jade and the first thing I did was stick them to a huge pinboard on the wall using toothpaste. We weren't allowed drawing pins and it was a trick I'd learned soon after receiving my first package from home. Those photos were like the Crown Jewels for me. Tiny splashes of colour in an otherwise grey life that kept me going, snapshots of another existence which at night, as I lay on the verge of sleep, I could almost will myself into. Like some kind of religious artefact, those photos reminded me of why I had to have faith.

But that day they were more important than ever as I faced life in the main prison alone. I felt terribly vulnerable and a prison governor had even visited to reassure me I would be protected in segregation. But it took only hours to realise I didn't have to come face to face with other inmates to feel their rage.

Eastwood Park's A-wing housed mostly young offenders, girls aged from eighteen to twenty-one, who began to shout to each other from their cells as things started to quieten down late in the evening.

'Can you lend me some tobacco in the morning?'

'Did you go to the English lesson today? I've been stuck in my cell all day.'

'Can you keep it down? I'm trying to get some sleep here.'

'Oh shut it. Just stick your pillow over your head.'

'Has anyone been down to the laundry today?'

I lay on my bed listening to the voices. It was so different from the healthcare unit and my cell with Paula and I missed her. But as I listened to the shouts, I realised with a rush of fear that news of my arrival had already reached the other inmates' ears.

'What about those three at the end then?'

'What, down in segregation?'

'Yeah, they're all sick in the head down there.'

'There's one who killed her babies in there. What kind of fucking bitch does that?'

'Nonce,' another voice screamed.

It was the first time I had heard the word and it would haunt me for ever. I never got used to it. It made me feel dirty. I was being labelled a child abuser and it filled me with disgust.

I held my breath as the shouts got louder and louder and the girls demanded I speak to them. In the nights that followed the officers would occasionally walk down the corridor telling the women to stop. But they didn't do so often. Usually the women would carry on screaming until they fell asleep – sometimes not until one or two in the morning.

'Answer back, you sick bitch, say something.'

'If I ever get near you I'll fucking kill you. I've got a kid and I hate women who'd do that to their kids.'

'Yeah, watch your back, you twisted cow. You'll never know who's behind you.'

I was completely still, unable to move as the voices became louder and louder and the dark filled with screams.

'Sick bitch, sick bitch,' the girls heckled in unison and I lay there alone.

'Happy birthday, Angela,' Mum said, as the wheels of the tape softly spooled around. It was 22 May, my thirty-ninth birthday and five long weeks since my arrival on A-wing.

Terry had arranged for my friends and family to record the

messages they couldn't give me in person and I wept as my cell was filled with familiar voices – Claire, Mum, Dad, Brian, Bill, Tina, Jacqui, Kellie, Gill and Terry. In the background I could hear the low hum of chatter in the pub where they had met to make the tape. As I closed my eyes I imagined myself hearing those voices for real but all too soon I heard the stuttered whirr as the tape came to an end and I opened my eyes to see my grey cell again. This tiny room was now, quite literally, my prison, and I didn't leave it unless I had to. After that first night on the wing, the hysteria that my presence had created had not lessened in any way.

The inmates bayed for blood every chance they got. One of the other segregated cells housed a well-spoken arsonist who would sometimes answer them back but I never uttered a word. Initially on most days the abuse would be directed at us all and some were worse than others – if the girls hadn't had cigarettes, for instance, they got really bad. But eventually the abuse would always make its way back to me and I could sense how desperate those young women were to vent their hatred on me.

I had tried going into the exercise yard a couple of times but it was surrounded by cell windows and within minutes the chorus had started. 'Sick bitch, sick bitch' roared in my ears as I walked round the yard and felt eyes burning into me. I only lasted a couple of sessions before I refused to go out again and did the only thing I knew how to – hide.

Meals were brought to me in my cell and I only left to go to a church group once a week or to shower. Even that was an ordeal because while I only ever went when the other girls were locked down in their cells, the bathroom was like a trough – faeces and blood smeared on the floor. I would rush in and out as fast as possible. At first I couldn't understand how the inmates could live like that, but I soon realised many of the women in Eastwood Park were coming off drugs and simply didn't know what they were doing. I would hear them talking at night and it was obvious, even to me, what they were speaking about. It was clear that drugs were part of prison life, however hidden, and the odd glimpses I caught of my fellow prisoners convinced me of that.

Other than those quick trips out, I sat in my cell reading books, writing letters, watching television and listening to life on the wing. I could hear so much from my cell – doors clanking, music blaring, voices chatting, girls being sick, shouting for a light for their 'burn', crying, arguments and the constant murmur of televisions.

Thoughts crowded my mind during those long, solitary hours – I tormented myself with images of Terry and Jade without me or let irrational shame wash over me as I wondered what Gemma, Jason and Matthew would make of it all – their mother, a murderer. It felt like such an insult to them. But, once again, I forced myself to switch off those thoughts. Grieving for my lost life was almost as much as I could bear – grieving for my lost children as well would have been too much.

I was sitting in my cell one afternoon when faces appeared at the hatch in my door.

'Fucking bitch,' one screamed as fists started banging on the cell door.

'Look at her sitting on the bed as if she's done nothing wrong,' another shouted. 'You're the one who killed your babies, aren't you?'

I didn't say a word. Head lowered, I wouldn't even look at the eyes staring at me through the hatch. All I could do was pray an officer would arrive as I tried to calm the panic rising in me that somehow those girls would get through the door and rip me apart. I could hear them jostling for space outside, desperate for a peek through the hatch at the monster's lair, anxious to make the most of an officer's fleeting mistake, which had left the door to the segregated cells unlocked.

'Nonce,' a voice shrieked as I shrank back further towards the wall, trying to find a tiny corner in which to hide from their stares.

'Answer us. You're the one who killed your babies, aren't you?'

'I didn't,' I whispered.

'You fucking liar. That's why you're in here, isn't it? You got convicted so you did it. Liar.'

'Nonce.'

I could see faces straining at the grill, eyes searching every corner of the room.

'She's even got pictures of her babies up, sick bitch,' one shouted as she spotted a photo of Jade.

'That's a picture of my daughter,' I said as I raised my eyes to the door hatch for the first time.

I don't know what made me answer back – I just had to try to make them stop screeching the words that landed like hammer blows upon me. But it meant nothing. Screaming, those women were desperate to reach me – unable to give up this moment of victory as their quarry came almost within touching distance.

'Freak,' a voice screamed. 'Baby-killer.'

'Fucking nonce.'

'Back to your cells,' an officer suddenly shouted as the women continued screaming through the door.

'Come on. Show's over. Move,' another voice cried as the inmates reluctantly started to move away from the door. I heard their footsteps echoing down the corridor as the girls dragged their feet back to their cells.

I sat on the bed shaking. Then I turned my head to the cell wall and started to weep.

CHAPTER ELEVEN

'Why's Mummy gone? When's Mummy coming back?' Jade intoned as she stared in the mirror while Terry combed her hair.

She had caught nits soon after I went into prison and ridding her hair of the tiny creatures had become a nightly battle with her father.

'I don't want you to do it, Daddy,' she began to scream, as Terry held onto her shoulders and tried to carry on combing. 'Leave me alone, Daddy. Leave me alone. I don't want you to. Where's Mummy?'

Lunging her tiny frame at her father, Jade pinched and punched Terry, lashing out at his face and shoulders as she tried to vent the pain she couldn't find the words to express. But as he started to cry, she suddenly stopped and burst into tears.

'I'm sorry, Daddy. I didn't mean to do it. I don't know why I did it,' she told him as he cuddled her back to calmness.

All Jade knew was that I had disappeared on the day her brother died to become just a visitor to her home and now had gone for good. She was furious I had left.

It was summer 2002 and after just three months in prison I knew Jade was becoming ever more of a stranger to me. The care orders covering her had been lifted six weeks after I was convicted and social services had finally given Terry his life back. In fact, they had disappeared as quickly as they'd arrived, and offered him no support after his wife was convicted of murdering his children. John Pook was the only one who told Terry he was just a phone call away.

Now my husband and daughter were adjusting to a life stretching years ahead without me, and while I greedily drank in every detail about them during their twice-monthly visits to Eastwood Park – Jade's hair, Terry's expression, the clothes they wore, the colour of their cheeks, the look in their eyes – Terry looked uncomfortable and Jade confused.

He never told me the cards I sent each week often went unopened. He hid Jade's loss of interest from me and I in turn refused to acknowledge what was happening – clinging to the morning of 12 November 1999 when I was a proper mother. But there was nothing he could do to hide the sting when Jade refused to speak to me during my nightly phone calls home.

'Hello, darling, how are you?' I would say smilingly down the phone.

'Okay,' she'd reply.

'And what have you been doing today?'

'Just playing with my Barbie stuff. Here's Daddy,' she'd say breathlessly as I felt her attention drift and heard the phone drop.

'I can't make her talk to you, Ange,' Terry told me. 'She doesn't understand what's happening. You've got to let things be the way they've got to be.'

I felt devastated by the rejection, knowing that she clung to Terry for almost dear life and couldn't bear to be separated from her father to the point that she even slept with him, resting her tiny foot against his leg throughout the night as if to make sure he didn't leave too. But there was nothing I could do as my daughter drifted away from me. I was trapped. At times I could barely contain my anger when people reassured me things would come good.

'We'll sort this out,' my dad would say at the end of every phone call as I bit down the frustration rising in my throat.

No you won't, I wanted to scream. I'm the one having to live with this and it's not going to happen. They've done this to me. I'm not coming out. It's not all going to be all right. You can't make it all better by patronising me.

174

But while Jade let go of me in many ways, she also made it obvious she craved a mother figure in her life.

'I'm going to see Tiki, she's my new friend,' she would tell Terry. But soon Tiki's name would be replaced by Ursula, her mum.

'I'm going to see Ursula,' Jade shouted as she left the house. Without her own mother around, she clung onto other people's.

Meanwhile I was trying to get used to life at Eastwood Park. After eight weeks on A-wing, I had finally gone onto F-wing at the end of June. There are three regimes in prison: basic, standard and enhanced, each bringing with it a different level of privileges, and my good behaviour had convinced those in charge that I should go onto the enhanced wing.

It was a world away from my segregated cell. I now lived among the other women on the wing in a cell that boasted pine furniture and a porcelain sink, kettle and double glazing. There were even wing gardens to walk in, and I had a job – first envelope stuffing and then data-inputting in the computer room, which earned me £25 a week. The money went into my bank account and I was allowed £15 a week on my canteen sheet to spend on extras like toiletries, sweets, coffee, biscuits and cigarettes. Suddenly I could afford to buy rolling tobacco and a packet of ten straight cigarettes as a treat.

But the biggest change about life on F-wing was my fellow inmates. Tucked away from the main prison, the wing housed forty women ranging from a couple of teenagers to half a dozen inmates in their late fifties. They were all on enhanced status because of good behaviour. Whereas A-wing had pulsed with the pent-up aggression of young girl offenders, F-wing felt less threatening. As the weeks passed, I started to let my guard down, thriving in having some company at last and a little proud for pulling myself up a bit.

Much as life improved in some ways, there was a constant weight in my chest – a leaden lump that stifled my breath at times as I wrestled to push it down. Every day I struggled to understand what had happened to me, how it had happened to me, and each night I kissed a picture of Terry and Jade before tucking it under

175

my pillow and feeling tears fall wet on my cheeks in the dark. Outwardly I may have learned to adapt but deep down I still felt as stunned as I did on the day of my conviction. My response was simply to shut the feelings down, just as I had done after Matthew died. I knew I had to survive or go under, and to survive I couldn't allow myself to feel the true extent of what had happened to me.

What did I do to deserve this? I would ask myself over and over again as I lay in bed at night. Why did He let this happen to me? Will I ever get out? Will Terry and Jade know me if I do?

Somehow sleep still came easily to me but I paid a price for tumbling into such forgetfulness. Each morning I woke feeling almost normal before reality hit. Every day felt like a whole new readjustment to my new life. In addition to the big things, there were a million details about life in prison that I knew I'd never get used to – never being able to move anywhere without the sound of keys slipping into locks, never being able to lie in or pick at something you fancied out of the fridge, using plastic cutlery and mugs, eating at set times, lino on every floor, cheap plastic razors. But as the summer passed I tried to make the best of life on F-wing and focus on the chink of light that an appeal promised. I knew Bill and Jacqui were working on it and I forced myself to hope that I might one day be reunited with Terry and Jade.

It could not come soon enough because, as well as Jade's distance, being apart had put strains on my marriage for which neither Terry nor I had prepared. Tensions that had long lain dormant opened up in the wake of my conviction and for the first time we started to argue and snipe at each other. For instance, while a core group of friends and relatives kept him going, Terry was increasingly resentful that my family seemed interested in my fight but not his. He felt that he and Jade had been abandoned as soon as the drama of the trial was over and Jade in particular was being let down.

'Ange, they're just not taking any interest,' he would tell me on the phone. 'They say they'll come to visit and they don't. They say they'll have Jade for the afternoon and they cancel.'

I simply couldn't believe what he was saying and refused to listen. My family had supported me all the way – they wouldn't give up on Terry and Jade knowing how important it was to me that they were looked after. But however entwined Terry and I were on a day-to-day level, he forced himself to let go of the final strings of attachment to me in preparation for up to fifteen years alone. Initially his drinking worsened as he tried to cope with the fact that he was forty-eight and alone for the first time in his life. He still saw Stephen and Kellie, his parents, Steve Crouch, Steve Grant and Terry and Gill Chambers frequently, but they couldn't make up for the family he had lost. All the feelings Terry had had before the trial had been magnified by the verdict and he looked for comfort in the bottom of a brandy bottle. He'd been power-less to stop me being taken away and he fell even further apart with that final insult to his masculinity.

But by August 2002 he realised that, whether I was with him or not, life had to go on. The energy that had been poured into his work before Matthew died was refocused on the new council home he and Jade had moved to and he literally cleaned up his act. He scrubbed the house, put down a new wooden floor and came off the antidepressants. Finally Terry stopped waiting for me to come home.

'You're moving out this weekend so you'll need to start packing up,' an officer told me one Friday afternoon in the middle of August. 'You're off to Durham.'

I gasped as my head started to race and I looked blankly at the officer. Durham? It was so far away from my friends and family. I'd never see them. I wasn't supposed to be going there. That's not what they'd told me.

'What do you mean?' I asked dazedly.

'I mean you're going to be transferred to the lifers' unit in Durham.'

'But I've been told I'm going to Bullwood Hall. It's in Essex, much closer to my family. Durham is too far, that's where all the lifers from up north go.'

'It's nothing to do with me, I'm just the messenger,' came the reply. 'It's the Home Office who decides. There's nothing we can do.'

'But why are you doing this to me?' I started to sob. 'Why are you sending me so far away?'

'Like I said, nothing to do with us. You'd better start packing.'

I stumbled back to the cell, crying all the way. Durham? It was hundreds of miles away. How would anyone get to see me? It was just so far.

Voice thick with tears and panic, I phoned Bill and Terry to tell them the news.

'I'll get straight on to the Home Office,' Bill reassured me, before I rang home and the answer machine picked up.

'I can't go there, Terry,' I sobbed into the silence. 'I just can't go there.'

Even today Terry says it was one of the worst phone calls he ever got from me in prison – awful both because I was so distraught and because there was nothing he could do to help me. Yet again, all he could do was sit back as my fate was decided by others.

Three days later I was led into a cell at New Hall prison in Yorkshire where I was to spend one night before going on to Durham. Some things were familiar – like the metal holder with my name card in it at the side of the door, which read, as always, 'A Cannings DT9868 Life' – others frighteningly different. To reach the cell, I'd walked across a courtyard surrounded by accommodation blocks which echoed with the shouts and screams of women. It seemed like a zoo compared to the relative quiet of F-wing.

'If I have to stay in this fucking place much longer I'll go fuck-ing mental,' a voice screeched in a piercing northern accent.

I suddenly felt far from home. Nothing was familiar – even the voices – and I felt desperately lonely. Fighting back tears, I walked into a stinking cell to see a filthy mattress, dirty toilet and a burn-marked table with a wobbly chair. I sat down and thought of the girls back on F-wing. I'd found it such a wrench to leave them – particularly after they'd all trooped into my cell on my last night to sign my top.

I wonder what they're up to? I asked myself, as I glanced at my watch and realised they'd probably all be getting ready to go for tea.

Memories of those first awful weeks in segregation on A-wing washed over me as I thought back to the courtyard and the barely contained aggression in those voices. I felt sick, desperate for the minutes and hours to pass and to be back on the van again. I clutched a picture of Terry and Jade.

'You've got to come down for supper,' an officer told me after she unlocked the cell door.

'Please don't make me come out until I move on,' I pleaded. 'I can't go down. I just can't. I'm so scared.'

'All right, I'll get a tray of food brought up to you,' the woman replied as the door swung shut.

A while later an older lady came into the cell to deliver my food.

'Don't take any notice of what they say,' she said. 'Most of them are high on drugs. They don't know what they're doing.'

But I could hardly eat. All I could think of were those long nights on A-wing as darkness closed in.

'What you doing in there, new girl?' I heard a voice call from a cell window opposite. The inmates must have seen the light on in my normally unoccupied room.

'Answer back, bitch,' another voice shouted as I sat frozen on the bed. Suddenly there were bangs on the walls as girls in the cells either side of mine started to join in the taunts.

'You've got life, haven't you, so you must have done something serious,' a woman shouted, her voice muffled by the walls. She must have seen the name card outside my cell.

'Fucking speak out, bitch. You're a lifer. Answer me. What you in for?'

'Yeah, come to the window, bitch. Must have been really bad if you won't even come to the window.'

Voice after voice joined in – accents thick with northern and Scottish lilts – until, just as it did everywhere, news of my crimes filtered through. Someone must have seen the name card by my door.

'We'll get you, baby-killer.'

'Fucking nonce.'

'Don't show your face out of that cell because we're waiting for you.'

179

'Sick bitch. Sick bitch.'

Water started slapping against the cell windows as my tormentors became increasingly desperate to lure me out from hiding. But I remained stock still on my bed – hardly daring to breathe as the women's rage poured out of them and the noise got louder and louder.

That night seemed to last for ever – the only time in prison when I did not sleep a wink – and, as soon as dawn started to blur the edges of the black sky, the taunts started again. All I could do as I lay there and listened to the screams was wonder what I was going to find at Durham. New Hall and Eastwood Park might have housed teenagers with too much anger and energy to burn, but I knew I was going to a prison where Britain's most violent and dangerous women were held. I could only wonder what they would do to me.

Eyes down, I stood in a queue of inmates waiting to be frisked and run over with a metal detector on our way back to the prison workshop after lunch.

'Isn't that the one who murdered her babies?' I heard a voice behind me stage-whisper. 'She'd better watch her back. We don't like her sort.'

Two weeks into my time at Durham, it was the same everywhere I went – down to meals, to the showers, to work – I was always alone and always aware of being watched.

I kept my eyes down as I waited to go through security and, after walking across the yard to the workshop, collected a pair of scissors from the glass-walled security office. I sat down at a wide table to start cutting out a furry shape, which I would then sew up and stuff to make a cuddly toy, as the women around me chatted. I didn't speak to anyone except the odd word to the inmate sitting next to me, a girl called Louisa who I knew was considered a high security risk because she was accompanied everywhere she went. Across the other side of the room, more inmates sat at long, narrow tables making party hats – I'd had to smile when I thought of the looks on the faces of all those party-goers if they knew where their hats had come from – and I could hear the hum of their voices as I bent my head to work.

Suddenly a scream cut through the air.

'You fucking bitch,' a girl shouted as she stood up and scraped back her chair. 'Do you think you can get away with saying that to me?'

'Go on, get her,' women screeched in encouragement as they sensed blood. The girl lifted her chair and threw it at a woman sitting opposite.

Instantly blood ran red across her face from a gash on her forehead.

'Just ignore it,' Louisa said, as I looked on in horror. 'If you look up you might get involved. Keep your head down.'

Obediently I lowered my eyes as I heard the thud of officers' feet running across the room.

'She fucking deserved that,' inmates shouted as the woman was dragged away by two officers.

'Any more trouble and you'll all be on lockdown,' an officer shouted as the woman was frogmarched out of the workshop.

My hands shook as I tried to work and asked myself: How long will it be before they come for me?

The thought had been with me every waking minute since my arrival at Durham. I'd soon realised that F-wing at Eastwood Park had lulled me into a false sense of security. Gone were the friendly atmosphere, kindly officers and homely cell. Durham was brutal, basic and only the strongest survived its tough regime.

The prison lived up to its fearsome reputation in every way. From the outside it looked like a grey fortress, with barbed wire running along walls and an exercise yard surrounded by a high fence. Inside, it felt cold and dank. Even the cells looked as if they had been carved out of the wall, like tiny caves, and the only daylight in mine came from a small barred window, high up like a castle window with the wall sloping up to it. At night I could hear dogs barking in the kennels below and men shouting to each other in Durham's male wings – sounds which only increased my fear.

The prison atmosphere was also hard, brittle with pent-up

aggression, and a strict security regime was in place to stifle it – dogs, cells, strip and body searches, split association times to stop inmates socialising and continual lockdowns were among the measures intended to keep us under control. Officers patrolled everywhere, barking orders into walkie-talkies and herding us like animals back into our cells when trouble erupted – as it did nearly every day. To me, the place felt like a powder keg waiting to go off. Retribution was swift if inmates attacked each other, which they often did, or anything went missing that could be used as a weapon, like a pair of scissors from the workshop.

'Get back to your cells,' the officers would shout as they bundled women into their rooms. It sounded like a riot.

It wasn't just me who suffered. Everyone who came to visit me in Durham had to be security-checked to get in, an exhausting process. Mum, Brian and my auntie Roberta; Dad; Gill Chambers and her parents; Stephen and Kellie; Claire, Kevin and Andrew – all were frisked, had their thumbprints taken and were photographed for an ID card. They even had their footwear checked. One of Dad's friends, who wore a built-up shoe, had trouble getting in until he managed to convince the guards he wasn't hiding something in it. He was furious.

But it wasn't the brutal regime that threatened to break me. It was fear. Where the aggression towards my crime had once been openly directed at me, it was now like a hidden enemy. I was never spat at or pushed, punched, hit or stabbed. Instead, my fellow inmates expressed their hatred of my crime with stares and whispers. It's hard to explain – almost the stuff of the playground – but it was infinitely more terrifying than anything I had experienced before. Like the fear when you catch a glimpse of the darkness as you close the curtains at night and a shiver runs down your spine as you wonder if there's someone outside watching you, or being terrified by an old black and white film as your imagination fills in the gap when a shadow passes across a wall. I tried to talk to Terry and my family about it and they could hear in my voice how terrified I was but there was nothing they could do. It was very upsetting for them. All we could do was wait for news from Bill about when I might be transferred. I kept asking prison officers when it might happen, but although they told me they would be requesting a transfer for me down south, it seemed it might take months to arrange.

As each day passed, I felt more and more terrified. I wondered when and where I would be on the receiving end of the violence that simmered just below the surface of life in Durham. Arsonists, killers and robbers were housed on the four floors of the women's wing – those whose violence had earned them a place in one of Britain's most notorious prisons – and I was terrified to find myself among women who looked so hard, so unforgiving, so brutal. Hair scraped back, eyes dark and piercing, aggression etched on their features, they looked at me with hatred.

'You've just got to get through each day and keep your head down,' an inmate called Alison told me one day.

She lived in a cell opposite and was one of the few girls who were friendly towards me, not seeming to care what the others thought.

'The women in here have murdered someone, beat the shit out of someone, set fire to something, robbed someone at gunpoint, killed their partner. They're that kind. You need to look after yourself.'

Her words were in stark contrast to the homely cell Alison had created for herself during several years in Durham – complete with a budgie, and certificates decorating her pinboard for all the education courses she'd completed in prison.

'I hate the place,' she told me. 'It's a cold environment, no mistake, and you've got to keep on your guard.'

Durham was a harder place to hide than most. For instance, there was no dining hall. Three times a day I had to climb down four flights of stairs from my cell to the servery to get my food before going back up to my cell. I felt watched every step of the way as women gave me cold looks and turned their backs as I passed.

'Watch out, sick bitch,' the whispers seemed to follow me everywhere.

I clung onto any tiny gesture of friendship from women on my floor – walking with Alison down to meals whenever I could or

183

scurrying after her as she went to shower, anxious never to be alone. Climbing down the stairs I passed through the prison floors – knowing that each contained a different 'grade' of prisoner. Arsonists and the most dangerous inmates on the ground floor where a close eye could be kept on them, younger girls and women doing shorter sentences on the ones, anything from drugs to murder on the second and thirds, while my floor housed lifers and women who had committed violent crimes like armed robbery.

I struggled to understand how I had ended up in such a place. I tried to fill up my day as much as possible with work, chapel visits and making story tapes to send home to Jade. But I couldn't be busy every moment of the day and as soon as things slowed down my mind was flooded with thoughts of Terry and Jade. I was tormented by the life that should have been mine and was desperate to be closer to them.

But I had been told that it would be at least six months before I could be transferred to Bullwood Hall. Until then I was stuck in Durham and, naïve as it sounds, I struggled with shock to be living among the kind of people I had only read about before in the pages of a newspaper – like Marie Therese Kouao, the woman who had murdered her niece Victoria Climbie. But by far the most notorious prisoner was Rose West.

Her cell was on the threes, in a corner out of the way under the stairwell, and I would occasionally catch a glimpse of her plodding along to collect her hot water from the urn before evening lock-in, or in the exercise yard walking in a continuous circle alone, never stopping, never speaking to anyone. I had thought she would get constant abuse but the other girls explained that while she'd got a lot of it at first, things had quietened down over the years because she never answered back.

One Wednesday afternoon about a month after arriving at Durham, I was sitting staring blankly at a computer screen, trying to work out what to do. I'd transferred from making cuddly toys to doing database work – a move which had pleased me because my wages had gone up from £6.50 a week to £10 – but it was early days and I was stuck.

'Are you all right?' a voice asked.

I looked up, surprised that someone was actually talking to me, and found Rose West standing beside me.

'Yeah, it's not too bad. Hopefully I'll get the hang of it one day,' I gulped.

'You will. You'll work it out,' she told me and was gone.

I continued staring at the screen, my heart beating.

How on earth did I end up here with her? was all I could think as she padded away. How did this happen to me?

I held my breath as the phone rang, willing Terry to pick it up. He'd been out for the past two days and I was desperate to speak to him.

'Hello?' he said, as my heart beat with relief.

'It's me.'

'Hello, my darling.'

'Where have you been? I've been trying to get you and you've been out. I've spent two days trying to get through and nothing.'

'Just out and about, Ange. I'm sorry we missed you but we can't spend our lives waiting by the phone.'

'But, Terry, I have to speak to you. You don't know what it's like in here. I'm so scared. I know it's hard to be in to wait for the phone all the time but I've got to talk to you.'

My voice trailed to a whisper as I heard the familiar sounds of home – the murmur of the television, Jade's chatter, Cindy barking – in the background. All I wanted to do was climb through the phone and touch Terry.

'Ange?' he asked.

'Yeah, sorry,' I replied, as I breathed deeply to push my tears down. 'I just feel so afraid. I can't tell you what it's like in here and it isn't getting any better. Is there any news on when you can visit?'

''Fraid not,' said Terry. 'I don't know how I'll get all the way up there. It took Stephen and Kellie nearly seven hours to get up there and they looked like they'd run a marathon when they got back. It's bringing me down trying to arrange it all. I'm afraid it will be too much for Jade and we don't even know when she'll be allowed to see you.'

185

I'd been heartbroken to discover after arriving at Durham that as a Schedule 1 inmate – someone who had committed an offence against a minor – I must be security-checked to see Jade. The police and probation service also had a hand in deciding whether I would be allowed to see her and it seemed to be taking for ever.

'But can't you come without her?' I asked, anger pinching my voice. 'I really need to see you.'

'No, Ange,' he replied. 'We've kept the family unit going this far and we can't break it up now. Jade's always come with me to see you and I don't think it's a good idea to change things. Anyway, I couldn't come without her. She can't be more than about two inches away from me at the moment. If I go for a shower she asks me where I'm off to and she's even playing up when people come over to see us. It's like she doesn't want anyone else near me. I just can't leave her. But we'll visit soon enough. Bill says it won't take long to get the security clearance through.'

I silently bit down a spurt of liquid anger that filled my veins as jealousy rushed through me. Can't you forget Jade and come to me, I wanted to scream, before pushing the thought down.

'Well, hopefully it won't be too long,' I spat. 'I can't wait to see you both. How is she?'

As Terry chatted, frustration rose again inside me. I was dependent on prison officers, probation officers, governors, Home Office officials, everyone but myself, and now it felt even my husband was letting me down.

'I've got some photos to send you,' I heard Terry say as his voice penetrated my thoughts.

'Oh lovely,' I replied. 'What of?'

'Well, Ange, we've had a bit of a breakthrough this week,' he said before pausing. 'Jade's learned to ride a bike.'

My heart sank – another milestone I'd missed, another moment that could never be recaptured, another memory I would never have.

'That's great,' I replied, as I felt my voice falter. 'That's really good news. I didn't realise you were going to try it with her so soon.'

I thought back to that thrilling moment as a child when your shuddering progress becomes smooth and you realise for the first time that you don't need your parents any more to get past the end of the road, that you've taken your first step towards independence. Jade had done it without me by her side.

'I can't believe I'm here,' I whispered as the units on my phone card ticked down. 'People are looking at me all the time. It's violent. I'm seeing things I've never seen before. Please get me out of here. Please, Terry.'

'You've got to prepare yourself to be there at Christmas,' he replied. 'Bill's telling me you might still be there then. But there will be a tomorrow. You'll get out of there. Don't give up. I love you, Ange.'

It's hell on earth, I wanted to scream but instead stayed silent. 'Bye, love,' I whispered, as I heard the click on the other end of the line.

I turned round and started the solitary walk back to my cell.

A month after arriving at Durham I was given the news I had been dreading – the BBC were planning to screen *Angela's Trial*, the documentary we had cooperated with, at the beginning of October. Panic rushed over me as my mum told me on the phone. During all those weeks in Durham I had tried to keep my head down, be as inconspicuous as possible, but I knew it would be impossible if the programme was shown. I would be even more of a target. The threat of violence that had hung over my head every second of every day must surely be realised. I was convinced I would be killed.

Desperate to get it stopped, I rang Terry and pleaded with him to ring the programme producers.

'You've got to make them see, you've got to make them stop it,' I cried down the phone. 'They get so jealous of other people getting their case highlighted in here and if you don't get it pulled I fear for my life, I really do. I'll be beaten to a pulp. You don't know what it would mean for me up here. Please, Terry.'

'I'll see what I can do,' he told me. 'I'll make them listen to us.

I'll tell them that if they go ahead with it they'll have to live with it for the rest of their lives. I'm sure they'll stop it.'

But his reassurances meant nothing and I went to talk to a prison governor about my concerns. I also asked to be put on the healthcare unit but was refused. It felt as if there was a gun at my head and I was pleading with someone not to pull the trigger.

Days later some of the TV listings magazines mentioned the programme and featured my picture. I felt the news go through the prison once again – a shiver of excitement and hatred that rippled through the wings. I could not stop thinking about what was going to happen to me – as I lay in bed at night, as I walked downstairs to the canteen, going across to the workshop – I waited for it.

Exhausted by uncertainty and anxiety, I was told one thing by my family and another by a governor. One said the programme was going to be postponed; the other said it wasn't. I didn't know what to think.

One day, as I stood waiting to collect my hot water, a woman approached me. I knew who she was. Her name was Donna Anthony and she too had been convicted of murder after Professor Meadow gave evidence against her following the deaths of her two babies. She had dark hair, was in her twenties and had been in prison for four years.

'Don't worry about it,' she told me. 'Keep your head up high and go about your business. You'll get through this.'

Then she was gone.

The day before the programme was due to be shown, a governor told me the BBC had agreed to postpone it. I felt almost sick with relief at the news but it wasn't enough to rid me of the anxiety that had now blurred my mind.

'She's got something to hide,' girls hissed when they discovered the documentary wasn't going to be shown. 'Baby-killing bitch.'

CHAPTER TWELVE

It wasn't to be in Durham that my fears were finally realised. Violence was unleashed against me when I dared hope I might be safe.

I left Durham a week after it was agreed the documentary wouldn't be shown and days after Bill applied for a judicial review at the High Court about the decision to send me there. He and Jacqui suspected the authorities weren't keen on sending me to Bullwood Hall because Sally Clark was also imprisoned there and they feared that together we might become a cause célèbre. But the threat of legal action certainly changed someone's mind and I left Durham soon after an inmate who was due to be released had hanged herself within those austere, grey walls.

But my relief about going to Bullwood Hall was tinged with worry about what I would find there. The Essex prison was closer to home but I was apprehensive about another set of rules, another regime, because I had quickly learned that no two prisons were the same.

Within hours of arriving, though, it was obvious how different Bullwood was. The mechanics of prison life were similar – a strip search and property check were the first things that occurred – but the atmosphere was a world away from Durham. The lifers' unit looked like a wooden chalet, rather than a medieval fortress, and the prison officer who greeted me in reception wore a T-shirt and tracksuit bottoms – infinitely more relaxed than the shirts and ties I was used to. There was even the reassuring presence of laundry hanging on a clothes horse in the association room.

It must be all right here if people are hanging their washing out and not worrying it will be stolen, I thought to myself as I was led up to my cell on the first floor.

It was bare but there was a wooden bed, corner pine unit with a television on it, small cupboard and a bathroom complete with a shower, toilet and porcelain sink. I couldn't believe it as I walked in – it might have been a bit shabby but it was clean.

'I'll get you a sheet for the window,' the male officer who'd taken me up told me. 'We'll have to sort you out a curtain but it will do for now.'

It was a world away from what I had known and I was tempted to let a small part of me relax after all those long, fearful weeks in Durham. But I knew that however much regimes differed, prisoners did not when it came to inmates like me. Outside Durham, Bullwood Hall contained the only unit for women lifers and I feared they would be as brutally unforgiving as the other prisoners I had encountered.

My heart sank when I walked into the dining hall later that day and realised we had to eat with the other wings. Bullwood housed many young offenders and I tried to steel myself against the stares and whispers as I collected a tray of food. Exposed and alone, I realised that for the first time I was actually among the young women who had taunted me at both Eastwood Park and New Hall. Before I had been hidden from their view in a cell but now I was face to face with them. I felt sick as I pushed my tray away before heading back to the lifers' unit.

I didn't really mix that evening. I needed time to assess what the atmosphere was like, who I needed to be on the lookout for, what the girls' reaction to me would be before I could start to let my guard down.

The only people to introduce themselves were an older woman called Alicia, who occupied the cell opposite me, and a woman called Rose, who I knew had made a special effort to say hello because her cell was nowhere near mine.

190

She seems nice, I thought to myself as I fell asleep. Maybe it won't be all bad here.

'Angela, I think you're wanted downstairs,' a voice called from outside my room.

It was my second night at Bullwood Hall and lock-in was in five minutes.

Perhaps one of the officers wants to see me, I thought as I walked to the end of the landing where a girl was hovering by the 'kitchen' area, which housed a sink, toaster, cleaning cupboard and hot-water urn. I recognised her from a couple of hours earlier when I'd queued up to leave the unit for the dining hall. Standing with another inmate, who wore a black-and-white-checked bandana on her head, the pair had stared at me intently.

They're young to be on the lifer unit, I'd thought as the bandana girl walked up to where I had sat down on the stairs. Silently, she had stood in front of me and motioned a kick.

I forgot the incident later as I sat at supper with Alicia and some of the other lifer girls. None of them spoke to me but at least they weren't being openly hostile and I went back to my room feeling almost hopeful. Being ignored was far better than what I'd encountered before.

But as I walked to the top of the stairs, I noticed the girl was still staring at me. Looking straight ahead, I tried to ignore her. I turned to go down the stairs, and saw her bandana friend standing motionless in the middle. I tensed, knowing what was coming – the screams, the threats, the abuse from these young women so full of hate.

Suddenly the bandana girl's arm arched in front of her as a single scream filled the air.

'Bitch,' she cried, as a burning sensation covered my throat and chest. Seeping through my thin vest top, boiling liquid sent hot poker needles of pain stabbing through my skin. Gasping in shock, I looked up to see the girls running off.

'Oh my God, what's happened?' someone cried as I stumbled into the association room.

All I could smell was coffee and I realised what had hit me.

'Please help me, please help me,' I sobbed as officers ran towards me.

One on each side, they lifted me up under my arms and pulled me out of the room as the other girls were locked down.

'We've got to get this cooled down,' the officers told me as they peeled off my clothes and guided me into the shower cubicle.

I gasped as freezing cold water hit me, stunned the threats had finally been made real. I couldn't believe that after all the months of whispers it had actually happened. Again and again the cold hit me as officers threw jugs of water over my scalded skin, anxious to rid it of the heat.

'Just stay still,' the officers told me. 'It's quite a bad burn. Stay calm, Angela, we've got to get it cooled down.'

I stood in my underwear sobbing as I bent my head to look at my burned body. My chest, breasts, throat and chin were lobster red.

'Can you remember who did this to you?' an officer asked me as another put her radio to her mouth and requested help.

'I don't know.'

'Can you remember what she was wearing?'

'A black-and-white-checked thing.'

'What, a bandana?'

'Yes. There was another girl – young with a ponytail.'

I stood under the shower obedient as a child, shivering and passive, frozen with disbelief that this had happened – the bright red scars of my shame scorched livid across my pale white chest. I was shocked by the randomness of the violence. After all that waiting, I'd expected to know. But I hadn't. So how could I prepare myself for the next time?

I seemed to stand in that shower for ever, time suspended, my mind racing, as the officers tried to cool the burns. Eventually they stopped dousing me and two gel cushions were pressed to my chest before I was given a towel and a loose pair of trousers and top.

'We've got to get you over to healthcare,' someone said as I was led out of my cell.

Shocked, I could feel the pain intensifying as the water's soothing cold seeped out of the burns.

'Nobody deserves to be treated like this,' a nurse said in disgust as she inspected my injuries. 'Whoever did this needs to be out of this prison.'

But her words offered no comfort. Instead I sat in silence and sobbed as she massaged thick white cream onto my chest, breasts, throat and chin.

Later, as I lay in a bed on the healthcare unit, there was a kick on the door. I looked up to see a pair of eyes staring at me through the hatch.

'If I'd done it, I'd have made fucking sure I did you in, baby-killer,' a voice hissed.

'I can't go back,' I told the officer as she sat on my bed in healthcare. I'd been on the unit for ten days and didn't want to return to the lifers' wing.

'But you can't be here for ever, Angela,' she replied. 'You've got to get back into a routine.'

'I don't want to go. I feel safe here. I'm away from everyone. I don't want to go. Please don't make me.'

'What happened to you should not have done,' the officer reassured me. 'But, as the governor told you, the girls involved in the attack have left the prison. You can't stay here for ever. You've got to get back to the wing and try to start settling in.'

I stared at the bouquets of flowers sent by family and friends. Bill and Jo Briggs had been to see me a few days earlier and I'd seen shock written across their faces.

'This should never have happened,' Bill said quietly as he took a statement, as the local police had also done. Terry too was horrified when I had rung to tell him.

'I wish I could be there for you,' he told me, and I knew he felt crippled by his inability to help.

The burns to my chest and throat had started to heal and over the coming months they would shrink and become pale. But to this day there is still a patch of puckered white skin on my right breast.

'Angela, you must come back,' the officer said gently.

I looked at her.

'All right,' I replied with a sigh, knowing I couldn't hide for ever because wherever I was I'd be found and attacked again.

'You'll be fine,' the officers said as they walked me back to the unit. 'You're doing the right thing.'

Every step I took carried me closer to what I dreaded but, like the night I was attacked, the officers helped me put one step in front of the other when all I wanted to do was stay still.

As we walked onto the wing a girl I didn't know looked up.

'All right?' she said as we passed.

Head down, I hardly caught a glimpse of her.

'How are you doing?' I heard another voice say as we walked by.

'I'm okay,' I replied.

I barely registered what they were saying. Fear rushed over me as I walked back up the stairs where I had been attacked on the way back to my cell. It felt strange being back. I hadn't had a chance to get used to the unit and now I was convinced I would never be comfortable there. All I could do was watch and wait for someone else to come at me.

But I was surprised later that night when two girls from my corridor came into my room to see me.

'Keep your head up and you'll be fine,' they told me before leaving.

Their reassurances were echoed the next day when several women popped their heads round my door as they left for work.

'This doesn't happen on this wing. We're not like that.'

'We just want to get on with things and we can't believe it's happened.'

'It's disgusting. Don't think we're all like that.'

I was shocked but it seemed as if my worst fears might not come true after all. The women appeared genuinely unhappy about what had happened.

Gradually I learned the rumour had gone round before I'd arrived that a baby-killer was coming onto the wing. Hysteria had pricked sharp through the veins of the women and, as the two girls who attacked me started threatening to do it, they were egged on by an angry chorus.

Several inmates had been punished after the attack on me and their privileges had been withdrawn. Retribution was also swift for the two girls who actually did it – and not just from the prison bosses. Apparently an inmate nicknamed Mad Maggie was still down on segregation after knocking out the teeth of the girl who'd acted as a lookout. In Maggie's eyes, you didn't turn on girls in your own wing. You didn't shit on your own doorstep.

A few days later I was in my room again when she appeared at the door. Small, with hair pulled back and a stocky, slim body, she spoke in a thick Glaswegian accent.

'All right?' she asked.

'Yeah, fine now,' I replied before adding, 'Thank you for what you did. For sticking up for me.'

'S'all right. It doesn't matter what anyone's in here for, you just don't behave like that. It's out of order and she needed to learn.'

With that Maggie turned and left my room as quickly as she'd arrived. She didn't seem mad at all. It might not be my way, but there was a kind of logic in what she said. Other inmates hadn't meted out such bloody punishments but I knew many agreed with her – they might not like my crime but we had to live together.

Soon after arriving at Bullwood Hall, I began to see Sally Clark on the lifers' wing. Catching glimpses of her from afar, I could see she was pale, thin and looked as I felt – haunted. But, however linked our names have since become, we did not get to know each other back then. All I knew was that Professor Meadow had also given evidence against Sally and that a second appeal against her conviction was due to be heard because a first had failed. But I'd been told we weren't allowed to discuss our cases and, anxious not to put a foot wrong, I didn't disobey. We simply glanced at each other in passing and nodded hello whenever we saw each other. I remember seeing her on one occasion with her husband and son and being filled with hope that she would be able to go home. But I didn't dare think about it too much.

195

As I had at Durham, I set about making myself as busy as possible and started my first job as a wing cleaner earning £8 a week. I was worried about working in the main prison and so was allowed to stay where I felt safe. The only time I had to venture out was for meals and I can safely say that during my time in Bullwood I gulped down every one in record-breaking time.

Each morning, after being unlocked at 8 a.m. and eating a breakfast pack in their cells, the girls would line up to go off to work. After shouting their room number and being ticked off a roll-call list, they headed all over the prison for the laundry, gardens, kitchens, gym, education unit or library – a couple even worked in the prison's hairdressing salon.

But I stayed on the wing and worked quietly with an Indian lady. It gave me a lot of time to think and Terry and Jade were never far from my thoughts. As the end of 2002 approached, I struggled as much as ever at being separated from my family.

It was a strange kind of grief. I had longed to be with Gemma, Jason and Matthew but had also known I never could be because they were gone. But the loss of Terry and Jade tormented me for exactly the opposite reason. They were alive, on the outside where I couldn't be, living their lives without me, and at times my sadness was physically painful.

What are they doing now? I would wonder as I kissed their picture and settled down to sleep. Why am I here? I should be with them.

Anger was another emotion I grappled with. In many ways I was still in denial I had been branded a child-killer but, as the months passed, I thought more and more about it. Rage and frustration grew steadily inside me and it sickened me to think that to the outside world I was no different, worse even, than some of the women I saw in prison. How had the justice system let me down so badly?

But I knew I could never express my feelings. My fellow inmates had been convicted of anything from arson to murder and there was an unwritten, but strict code which decreed you had to keep yourself together, whatever the circumstances – everyone was wading through their own personal difficulties and they didn't need to see yours written over your face in sobs and sadness.

As much as I wanted to, I knew if I expressed my anger or cried my way through my time inside I would never be thought much of and so, once again, I hardened myself. Where I had frozen myself in the years before my trial, I was now aware of shutting down even further. Every ounce of softness and vulnerability was squeezed out of me as I fought to fit in. Before prison I had at least had the company of family and friends; now I was completely alone and had to look after myself.

Fitting in was crucial, keeping my emotions buttoned down key, and gradually everything became more and more locked down inside me. Even my body responded and it shut down to the most basic functions. I felt hungry, I felt tired, but that was it. I was aware of the odd lesbian relationship inside but it struck me that many of those girls were simply grabbing onto affection more than anything else. It certainly never occurred to me. My love life with Terry had disintegrated long before my trial but in prison I became utterly sexless. In odd moments I would long for the warmth of a hug from one of my family but mostly I forgot what it had ever been like to feel the physical reassurance of someone you love. As time passed I began to look the most masculine I had ever looked – at 5 feet 2 inches it was hard – but I made little effort with my appearance and my very features seemed to sharpen slightly. My body became a shell, no more, and while I still washed it and fed it, I felt completely cut off from it.

But it was the emotional shut-down mirroring the physical that was possibly the most harmful. I gave up all hope. Most weeks I had a visit from someone – Claire, Mum and Brian, Terry and Gill, Gill's parents, Stephen, Kellie and their children, Dad, Tina and Andrew, Brian's daughter Miar, Ally, Steve Grant and Steve Crouch – and everyone urged me not to give up, that the appeal would soon be heard, that I would be free.

I'd get letters too from complete strangers telling me the same thing. They'd started when I was at Eastwood Park and I ended up writing to half a dozen people quite regularly. By the time I'd sent letters to them and my close relatives and extended family –

all my aunties, uncles and cousins – I spent a lot of time writing and the other girls were amazed by the amount of post I got. It was a highlight of the day and I received at least three or four letters to enjoy. Some days there were eight or nine and it always cheered me up. The letters from strangers came from all over the country – a man in Durham, women in Sheffield, Liverpool, Wales, Portsmouth, Essex, Wiltshire and London. People from my past also wrote, such as the mother of one of Jade's old school teachers, and I even got a letter from Virgin boss Richard Branson telling me he'd read about my story and offering to help my case in any way he could. Terry even ended up speaking to him on the phone. Those letters uplifted me and left me feeling humble because people I didn't know had bothered to take the time to write to me. They believed in me.

But while they all told me not to give up, I didn't allow myself to consider the possibility of getting out. My conviction had rid me of any faith in the legal system and I simply didn't believe I would ever be freed. Bill and Jacqui continued with the job of preparing my appeal and, when I saw them on monthly legal visits, they too reassured me they were doing all they could. But I would always end each visit with the same words – 'Don't forget me. Promise me you'll get me out' – because part of me felt that eventually people would forget.

What I didn't know then was that Bill and Jacqui were also struggling with doubts because it wasn't just me who felt crushed by the system. They had seen the founding principle of British justice – innocent until proven guilty – turned on its head and had no idea how to right the wrong because they faced the same problem they always had – no one could explain how my children had died. They knew they would never be able to come up with a magical reason why Gemma, Jason and Matthew, like other cot-death babies, had simply stopped breathing. Every possible theory about my children's deaths had been put forward at my trial to contradict the idea that the loss of three babies must equal murder, and it hadn't worked. My legal team couldn't put forward more theories and hope to win me my freedom. They had to have something new. But there was nothing.

Deep down Bill and Jacqui were still convinced the key to my case lay in genetics. But, as Dr Patton told them, without more significant information it was difficult to do any more than had already been done. All they had was a hunch, a family history and another medical theory. It might have been used to convict me but there was little chance it was going to get my conviction over-turned. They were as trapped as they ever had been.

Of course they confided nothing of their fears to me during our meetings. Instead Bill continued to be the calm, steady presence he always had been as I listened blankly to his reassurances. But deep down I had given up. I was in prison for something I hadn't done and it was unimaginable, a living nightmare. I knew there was no point wasting any more hope.

Of course I longed to cry in the anonymity of my dark cell, to shout from the rooftops – 'I didn't do it' – but such talk was frowned upon in prison. The faith those girls had in the system amazed me but they believed that if you had been convicted, you must have done the crime. I was shocked by just how judgemental they could be of their fellow criminals. It was like a hierarchy of crime. I lost count of the times I heard young girls laughing about mugging an old lady for drugs, before adding, 'Those lifers, they're sick in the head.'

Not all the women on the inside were bad, though. Many had ended up there simply because of bad choices, often to do with men, which had made them spiral out of control. Women who'd helped a boyfriend cover up a crime, aided a man who dealt drugs, been abused as children and become involved in prostitu-tion and drugs – they were all at Bullwood, and while some were to be avoided, many were not.

I can honestly say that having been in prison, I feel many women need help not punishment. Full of self-hatred, some will use anything – a phone card, a CD – to cut themselves repeatedly. I knew one girl who almost slashed her arm in two and refused to allow the wound to be sewn up. My eyes were also opened to the amount of domestic violence there is. I met women who were glad they'd rid themselves of an abusive partner and accepted they had to serve their time, women who'd been used as punchbags by drunken men and snapped after years of abuse, women who'd fought back in a moment of terror.

As the weeks went on and I was left alone, I started to inch ever so slightly out of my shell and become part of the wing. And it was then that I met Rose, the woman who had said hello to me on my first night there and who would be holding my hand, my dearest friend, on my last.

Rose was serving life for murder. She'd been jailed for life two months before me after being convicted of killing her partner. He'd been violent towards Rose during their relationship and one night she'd grabbed a knife to defend herself and stabbed him. He died from a single wound.

She was forty-two, with shoulder-length mousy, slightly curly hair, and had one brown eye, one blue. In prison for nearly two years by the time we met, Rose had learned the ropes and was willing to teach me.

We got to know each other during association as girls went into each other's rooms to have a cup of tea and a chat. Soon I discovered Rose was yet another example of looking beyond the label. She had a great sense of humour, was very knowledgeable – especially about prisoners' rights and health matters – had a lovely singing voice and could play the guitar. But it was her sense of humour that made us really click and we spent more and more time together.

I don't know what it was but from the start I instinctively knew I could trust her. She'd suffered over the years from depression and breakdowns, was a mother herself, and yet, while many women around me had similar stories to tell, there was a seam of utter compassion in Rose that was unique to her. As time went on I showed her pictures of Terry, Jade, my family and friends, and she recognised that I was lost because I'd had such a normal life – a husband, a daughter and a loving family.

'You're going to get good days and bad days – I get them all the time,' she'd tell me as we sat in my room – me drinking tea, Rose always coffee – after the day's work. 'I was in Holloway and it was the pits. At least here you've got your own room and a bit of privacy. The way I see it is that we've got life sentences and either you can accept that fact or not. If you do, you've got to make good use of your time; if you don't, all you'll do is sit in your room and wallow and that's the worst thing. You've got two people out there who need you more than anything and you've got to stay focused for them.'

But much as I tried to listen to Rose, I felt increasingly worried about the approach of Christmas. I wondered how I would ever be able to get through it, and I knew Terry felt the same.

'It feels like it's getting rammed down my throat everywhere I go,' he told me on the phone at the beginning of December. 'I just want it to be January. Christmas means sweet nothing to me. I just want it over with.'

'I know,' I replied. 'But you'll have a nice time with Jade.'

I knew my assurances would not work for him – Terry and I still spoke to each other every night on the phone but we had drifted apart and become argumentative with each other in a way we had never been before. It upset me but I pushed the truth away. Terry and Jade were my reason to keep going and I refused to acknowledge what was happening.

What I didn't know then was that as he faced Christmas on the outside, Terry was struggling with uncertainty about whether our marriage could survive. I was allowed a visit once a week for two hours and saw him and Jade together once a month. But as he sat in traffic on the M25 at the end of a ten-hour day on a dark winter's night, with Jade sitting tired and scratchy beside him after visiting me, he wondered how we would cope. He'd never been a great driver, preferring always to stay close to home, and he found the 300-mile round trip a hurdle which he doubted he could keep jumping over in his depressed state. Terry might have accepted life without me but he was still deeply unhappy and crippled by loneliness.

He poured his thoughts into letters to me, long rambling letters which went on for pages about how black he felt. But I didn't reply. I couldn't bring myself to write down what I felt. It seemed so artificial – I wanted to hear his voice, to talk to him – and, however much he asked, I didn't put pen to paper. Page after page, he told me how hard life was and I couldn't write back telling him that I was finding it difficult too – he had enough on his plate. But the fact that I wrote to friends and family became another wedge driven between us.

'Can you send me in some stamps and envelopes please? I've run out,' I'd ask.

'Well, I can, but are you going to use any of it to write to me?' he would snap, anger making his voice hard.

'I'm sorry, Terry, I can't – I just can't.'

'But these calls aren't enough for me, Ange. I'm writing to you two or three times a day sometimes and you find the time to write to everyone else so why can't you write to me? We get on the phone, you talk and talk about your day and then you're gone. It's just not enough.'

'But I need to speak to you on the phone. It's such a relief for me. I look forward to it all day.'

'Well, just bear in mind that when we do it's entirely on your terms, Ange. I sit here and wait to hear from you and then when you do I can't get a word in edgeways. If you write to me then I'll know you're really thinking of me instead of these quick calls.'

'But I think of you all the time, Terry. I never stop thinking of you and Jade. I love you but I don't want to write, I want to hear your voice. It's hard enough to send a card to Jade each week – I just can't do it with you.'

It was an argument neither of us would ever win. Each lost in our own pain, we refused to consider the other's.

A week before Christmas 2002 I spent my first whole day with Jade. As well as the weekly visits from friends and family, children were also allowed into the prison for one day a month to see their mothers. I could hardly wait to see her as I waited in the visiting hall. It had been decked out with a huge mural of snow-capped hills in front of which Father Christmas would later sit to give out presents. The chairs and tables had been put at the sides of the hall and there was a huge space in the middle where we could play games. There was also a table covered in crisps and treats for the children.

'Mummy,' Jade shouted as she spotted me.

'Hello, darling,' I said, as I scooped her into a hug. 'How was your journey?'

'Oh, you know, long,' Terry replied. 'We didn't sleep too well at the bed and breakfast last night but at least we're here on time, which we wouldn't have been if we'd driven up today.'

Jade tugged at my sleeve.

'What are we going to do today, Mummy?' she asked.

'We're going to play lots of games and Father Christmas might even come to see you if you're a good girl,' I told her, before turning to Terry. 'Thanks for bringing her up. I'll see you later.'

My heart squeezed in pain as he turned to leave. Terry should be with us but instead he was going to spend the day on his own because adult relatives were not allowed in on the children's visit.

Jade looked as pretty as ever in a sparkly top and jeans. Everyone had made a big effort to make the children feel as comfortable as possible – even the officers were wearing ordinary clothes, with just a name badge to distinguish them. As ever, Jade seemed to take everything in her stride.

'It's my birthday soon, Mum,' she told me solemnly.

'I know sweetheart,' I replied. 'You're going to be seven. You're getting so big.'

It was a lovely day. We played games, had lunch, stuffed ourselves with cakes and treats, danced to a disco, smiled at each other in the flashing coloured lights and laughed when the bubble machine sprang into action. And, of course, there was the all-important visit from Father Christmas.

After eight long months apart from Jade, it was such a joy to be with her again for more than just one stilted hour in the visiting hall. You never know what you've got until it's gone and just to be able to move around freely with her, to touch her, to have a few hours in which to watch her properly, filled me with happiness. I drank in every second with her, desperate to absorb and hang onto that happiness in some tiny corner of me.

But it was almost more than I could bear. Part of me might have been happy but another wanted to weep every time Jade smiled.

Why am I here doing this with her? Why aren't I at home with her? My mind whirred as I tried to push the thoughts to the back of my head.

Just try to enjoy yourself, one voice shouted in my head, as another screamed back: But how can you? How can you have fun with Jade in a prison?

How did you get here, Angela? How did it come to this? You'll never be a proper mother to Jade here. Face it.

I don't know how I must have seemed to Jade or if she picked up on the battle going on inside me. But if she did then she didn't show it, and seemed as excited as any six-year-old would be with too much sugar rushing through their veins and presents to open.

'Now when you're back at home with Daddy, you mustn't forget to clean your teeth after all those sweets,' I said, as we sat playing with the doll Father Christmas had given her.

I smiled weakly at 'our' joke – Jade could never understand why I was so bothered about her teeth.

'I really miss you, Mummy,' she said as her blue eyes fixed on me.

'I miss you too, darling,' I said and bent my head to kiss the top of hers, hearing the doors of the visiting hall open in preparation for the children to be picked up.

Face hidden, I tried to hold back the tears. I wanted to be happy mummy, the mummy that Jade had known since Matthew's death, the mummy who didn't cry in front of her.

'I'm sorry I can't be closer to you. I know it took a long time to get here.'

'I wish you could come home, Mummy. Why do these people in the big building think you've done something when you haven't?'

'I don't know why they said it, darling. But they've put me here now and I've got to stay. Remember Bill? Well, he's our friend and he's trying to help me to come home one day. And I will come home one day, Jadey.'

Forcing my voice to be artificially bright, I smiled at her: 'Now I need a big hug and kiss because Daddy's going to arrive in a minute. I really hope you enjoyed today. Did you?'

'Yes.'

She climbed onto my lap and I pulled her to me, squeezing her tightly as I tried to gulp back my tears. But I couldn't stop them as Jade started to cry. However distant she had become, I knew she wanted to be with me. For a brief moment that day a tiny door had been reopened and I wanted to scream with grief that it was about to be closed again.

'Daddy's here,' I said as I saw Terry arrive and we silently walked towards him. Jade was wracked with sobs as he took her hand.

'Bye bye, darling,' I whispered as I bent down to kiss her.

'Bye, Mummy,' she cried, as she clung onto me for a final time.

Terry took her hand and they turned to walk away. I think my heart broke a hundred times as I watched them go.

Christmas came and, with Rose's help, went. I tried to enjoy it as much as I could – entering the wing table tennis, darts and pool competitions – but trying to have fun made me feel almost guilty. I also knew I was going to have to try and say goodbye to Matthew for a second time because two weeks into the New Year Terry had arranged for a memorial service to be held for him.

As time had passed, Terry had become more and more pre-occupied with putting Matthew's name alongside Gemma, and Jason's on their headstone in the churchyard at Winterbourne Gunner. He said he couldn't bear to think of something happening to him and his three children not being 'together' and I agreed with him. I too wanted to hold my own memorial for Matthew away from police stares.

'It will be a way of saying goodbye properly, Ange,' he told me one day on the phone. 'His funeral was a mockery compared to what Gemma and Jason had. He deserves a proper goodbye.'

On 15 January 2003 – more than three years after Matthew's death – some twenty friends and relatives gathered in Winterbourne Gunner church as I stood in the chapel at Bullwood Hall. I'd started going to Mass soon after meeting the prison Catholic priest on my arrival at Bullwood and the chapel seemed the one place where no one judged me. John Walton had written to the prison requesting my release to attend the memorial but he'd been refused, and so I stood with Rose in the chapel as the chaplain ran through the same service that John was overseeing at that very minute in Winterbourne Gunner.

I looked down at a white rose I was clutching in my hand – just like the ones I had laid once for Gemma and Jason, and the people I loved were laying at that moment for Matthew.

'Angela, would you like to light the candles now?' the chaplain asked.

Blindly I walked to the front of the chapel with Rose and we each placed a flower on the altar. Desperately, I tried to visualise Terry and Jade, my family and friends, John Walton, the church-yard where the headstone stood, as I lit a candle. But as I tried to tap into the sadness I knew was hidden somewhere I felt completely hollow. Even as I kept telling myself I had to say goodbye to Matthew, I couldn't – because to say it would be to accept both that he had gone and I was here, in prison, convicted of his murder. I might be facing life in jail but however long I was locked up I knew it was something I would never be able to do.

CHAPTER THIRTEEN

I was woken by the sound of a door clanking open, footsteps clicking down the corridor and the rustle of plastic. My heart skipped a beat in the early morning still of 29 January 2003 as Sally Clark left prison for the second day of her appeal. Like all prisoners, she was carrying a standard issue bag containing her possessions in case she was freed, and it crackled as she walked past my door.

Please let it be me soon, please let her go home, I whispered to myself as I lay in bed listening to the footsteps disappear.

The atmosphere on the wing was thick with anticipation. The girls had kept the television on all the previous day as Sally's lawyers revealed that vital medical evidence had been 'kept secret' when she was convicted of smothering eleven-week-old Christopher and shaking eight-week-old Harry to death. Home Office pathologist Alan Williams, they told the Court of Appeal, had failed to disclose vital blood test results that proved Harry had been suffering from a potentially fatal bug when he died. Like Sally's first son Christopher, whose death had first been put down to a lung infection until his mother was accused of killing him, Harry had died of natural causes. Keeping the information secret had seen Sally wrongly jailed. And all because, as in my case, no one thought it was possible a loving parent could lose more than one child to cot death. In fact, Sally's lawyers told the court, instead of 73 million to one the likelihood of losing two babies was closer to between one in 100 and one in 400.

While the girls waited impatiently for news, I tried to put the hearing out of my mind. All I could do was pray Sally would be allowed home, but I refused to let myself invest too much hope in her appeal. I had always known Professor Meadow had given evidence at her trial but while our cases shared similarities, they were also very different. The loss of Sally's babies could be explained, and I knew I would never be in the same position.

I was out in the corridor when a shout went up on the wing.

'She's going home,' girls cried. 'Thank God.'

Sally was free. Her conviction quashed by the Court of Appeal.

My heart caught in my throat as I watched the television. As well as criticising Dr Williams, the judge had also described Professor Meadow's one-in-73-million statistic as 'grossly misleading'.

'It should never have been put forward at all,' Lord Justice Kay told the court. 'Its potential effect when it was manifestly wrong was, I think, huge.'

Interestingly, Mrs Justice Hallett, who had overseen my case, was one of three judges overseeing the appeal.

As Sally walked onto the steps of the court with her husband Steve, she looked drawn and gaunt as she spoke to the cameras.

'Today is not a victory,' she said. 'We are not victorious. There are no winners here. We have all lost out. We simply feel relief that our nightmare is finally at an end.'

Relief flooded over me as I watched her speak, a free woman wiped clean of the shame of murdering her children. Someone had listened at last. Maybe the tide was turning.

But as I stood there I realised my happiness was tinged with envy. Hot and stabbing, it rose up in me and twisted in my chest as I pictured myself standing on those steps with Terry. I turned and left the girls to their celebrations.

'Ange? Can you hear me?'

Rose's muffled voice filtered into my bathroom.

'Yes,' I replied as a giggle rose up inside me.

'Ange?'

Crouched on the toilet, I was trying to 'talk' to Rose via our sink pipes. With Sally's release had come cell changes and Rose and I had been delighted when we were given adjoining rooms. But I thought she'd gone mad earlier that day when she suggested we chat via our bathroom sinks.

'What are you on about?' I asked as we sat at lunch.

'We can talk via the pipes,' Rose told me. 'The other girls do it all the time. Let's give it a try.'

Standing up, I bent my head into the sink. Rose might be tall enough to sit on the loo and get close enough to the plughole to talk but I wasn't.

'Yes. I'm here,' I replied. 'I can't believe we're doing this.'

'I can hear you now,' came Rose's hollow voice as it echoed up. 'At least we can talk now when we're locked up. Don't knock it, girl. How are you doing?'

'Oh you know,' I replied. 'It's been a pretty bad day. The doctor's given me some new tablets to help try and calm me down. But I don't know if they'll work.'

'They will, Ange, they will,' Rose's voice told me as I smiled once again at the plughole.

Turning I walked back into my cell and lay down on the bed. I'd been in prison for nearly ten months and was at my lowest ebb. I'd been on antidepressants since being convicted but had now been prescribed another drug to control anxiety – what I didn't know until later is that it was an anti-psychotic drug which could have had serious side effects, far too strong for my needs. But being given drugs wasn't unusual. Every woman was on something. I'd felt increasingly paranoid in the months since I was attacked, as if I was being watched all the time, and there were moments when my heart beat so fast I thought it would burst out of my chest. My feelings seemed determined to make themselves felt – however hard I tried to deaden them.

I turned over and pulled a photo of Terry and Jade out from underneath my pillow.

'Goodnight,' I whispered before kissing it and tucking it back in its hiding place. Every day continued to be a struggle as I fought not to be drowned by the anger that filled me at my

209

wrongful conviction and the longing for my husband and daughter. Staring up at the blackness, I waited for sleep to wash over me.

However much I wanted to give up, though, Rose simply wouldn't let me. As February stretched into March she forced me up and out of my cell. I'd moved jobs and started work in the laundry, which I enjoyed. It was hard but I got on with the girls there and soon my wages rose from £9.50 a week to £12 as I moved to stage 3 responsibilities, which included logging the laundry, checking machinery and reporting maintenance problems. But Rose still wouldn't let me sit around when I wasn't working.

'You've got to keep yourself busy,' she'd tell me as she dragged me off to the gym where I pounded out my anger and frustration on the rowing machine. With her help I joined the prison choir and had my hair done. I also went to church once a week and started reading the Bible – desperate to find a way through all that had happened to me, I used the lessons learned in childhood. In some ways I drew comfort from it, but however hard I tried I couldn't find it in myself to put my faith back entirely in God. I was still too angry with Him. The prison officers also encouraged me to keep myself busy. Dwelling on things wasn't acceptable at Bullwood – inmates either had to work or do education courses, which included literacy, maths, hairdressing, art and computer studies. I didn't do those but my boss Mr Roe helped me work my way up the laundry certificate levels to gain more responsibility. He was a fantastic man – I always said that if he had been on the out I'd have worked for him anywhere. He wouldn't have any messing about but earned our respect with his fairness and sense of humour. Other officers were also kind and, unlike some I had met in other prisons, treated us like human beings. This respectful attitude extended throughout the prison regime, and even the food at Bullwood was the best thought-out and most nutritious I encountered in the prison system.

Outside work and activities, Rose also continued to teach me to fit in. I soon realised that I'd been too naïve at the beginning, too trusting, and steeled myself to be more wary. But while I got on with the girls and joined in, I was always aware of where I was and some small part of me remained on guard.

With Rose, though, it was different. In her I found the human contact I craved and our friendship slowly deepened to the point where she was the one person inside prison with whom I had the same relationship I would have had on the outside. It wasn't tainted in any way by being inside those walls. People move on in jail, you don't allow yourself to get too close, but Rose and I overcame that to have a real relationship and it was precious.

Soon we started looking out for each other. Where I had people to send me in money or things I needed, Rose had no one, and I would buy her the odd packet of cigarettes or jar of coffee. On Mother's Day I sent her flowers and we also spent hours poring over the Avon catalogue together. What Rose did for me was to listen. She sat for as long as it took me to unravel my fears, talk about my worries and let out some of what had remained buried for so long. Night after night she sat as I poured everything out – how we had been forced to live after Matthew's death, the uncertainty in the run-up to my trial, my anger with social services, my rage at what had happened to me.

I talked in a way I never had before. On the outside I had always been aware of how other people were affected – Terry was grieving, Jade was confused, my parents and siblings upset by what was happening to me – and those considerations had kept some part of me in check. I wasn't the only one suffering and I had kept things back just as others had done.

But in a prison cell with Rose I was finally able to explore my feelings without the fear of hurting anyone. Selfish as it sounds, it was simply about me, and she gave me the love I so craved, the softness I needed to trust myself to finally talk about my lost children. Perhaps the most important conversations we had were about Matthew. I'd been allowed to go through the natural processes of grief with Gemma and Jason, but with him I'd been too busy clinging onto the remnants of our life, dealing with the nightmare that had engulfed us. I'd frozen inside.

With Rose's help I took the first steps towards grieving for my son. I couldn't do it completely. I still haven't. But finally I allowed myself to let go of a little of the control I'd exercised over my feelings for so long and thaw inside bit by tiny bit.

'He was such a lovely baby,' I said as I started to cry one night. 'So smiley, so happy and Jade adored him. It's what hurts most in a way because it was one of the best things about having them. She just loved Matthew so much. I'd take them to Tesco and she'd go around in the trolley telling everyone he was her brother. I was so proud. It seemed as if finally we'd be happy. Jade doted on him. She was only little but you could see just how much he meant to her. And then we lost him and now she has no one.'

'I can't imagine what it must have been like,' Rose replied softly. 'And I can't understand how anyone thinks the way you were treated was right.'

'No,' I sobbed. 'And now I'm here and the longer it goes on the more I know I'm losing Terry and Jade. I can feel them slipping further from me.' My voice faltered as the tears hushed me to a whisper. 'I don't know what to do, Rose. How to get them back. There's nothing I can do in here and it's breaking my heart.'

'Ange,' she said as she looked at me. 'I don't know how and I don't know when but one day you will be with them again and you've got to hang onto that thought. You can't let yourself go under. Terry and Jade are out there and you've got to keep going for them. You have to keep strong, you have to keep well and you have to believe that somebody somewhere will let justice be done.'

At first I didn't listen to Rose's pleas. But as I gradually poured out the emotions that had remained buried for so long, I began to let myself dare feel them. Rose gave me sympathy, love and companionship. But there was one gift more precious than any other – she brought me back to life. Finally I allowed a flicker of hope to alight within me.

Elsewhere Terry too had formed a friendship that would become his lifeline. Some months after I'd been sent to prison he was contacted by a woman called Penny Mellor. A housewife and mother of eight, she talked nineteen to the dozen down the phone at him.

'I know she's innocent, Terry,' she told him in a rush. 'She didn't do it and you've got to help get her out.'

Terry was taken aback by this stranger. He didn't know who she was, what she wanted. But he quickly learned, because Penny never does anything slowly, that she campaigned for families whose children had been taken into care on the basis of medical theories like those that had convicted me. Completely 'unqualified', her medical knowledge was encyclopaedic and that, combined with her terrier-like pursuit of the facts, meant lawyers acting for families had begun to take real notice of what she had to say. Penny had even been imprisoned for eight months in March 2002 after being convicted of conspiracy to abduct. Phone calls she'd made to a family accused of making up illnesses in their children had been traced after the grandmother took the child abroad to stop her being taken into care. To some Penny was an abuse denier, a woman unhinged by zealotry, but to others she was a glimmer of hope in the darkest of times and for many families their best hope of proving their innocence.

As she dragged on cigarette after cigarette during daily phone conversations, Penny opened up a whole new world to Terry. She told him about her work, about the system that had wronged us and, for the first time, he realised we were not alone.

'There are other parents just like you out there, Terry, and in some ways you're lucky,' she told him. 'Parents accused of abuse in the family court don't go to prison – they lose their children for ever when they're taken into care. There's a core group of doctors who give evidence in these cases, so-called expert witnesses, and some see abuse everywhere. They work on the premise that parents are guilty until proven innocent, and because cases in the family courts are held in secret, behind closed doors, bad evidence has been allowed to flourish because no one has questioned their word. It was only a matter of time before the criminal trials started.'

Terry could hardly believe what he was hearing. Until then we had thought that, apart from the Clarks, we were completely alone. But not only did he learn this wasn't the case, it also seemed that in some ways we were fortunate.

'If you'd been accused in the family court, you'd have lost Jade for ever,' Penny said simply. 'There a judge only has to decide that on the balance of probabilities you abused your child – it doesn't have to be proved like it does in a criminal case. Jade would have been taken into care and that would have been it.

'I know of families who've lost three children to adoption on a doctor's say-so, mothers accused when their baby died who had a subsequent child taken from them by police twenty minutes after they gave birth, a father who had no doctor to speak up in his defence when he was accused because the word of the others is seen as so powerful, parents whose children have been genuinely ill and it wasn't picked up.

'And because the family courts are closed to anyone except the judge, the lawyers and the parents – supposedly to protect the child – no one can hear the evidence or criticise it. At least Angela has the chance of a criminal appeal in public. It's almost impossible in the family court. If you appeal there you're basically saying a judge made the wrong decision and it's very rare for a judge to overturn their colleague's decision.

'So you've got to remember it could have been worse, Terry. I don't know one parent who wouldn't swap places with Angela in order to get their child back.'

Just as Rose had done with me, Penny wouldn't let Terry off the hook as she told him day after day that he must fight and do all he could to help win me an appeal.

'You don't realise how important you are,' she would say. 'You're the human face of this case. Angela's inside and Bill is doing the legal work. But you're the person ordinary people will relate to. You've got to start working with the media, you've got to turn public opinion around. The ball has started rolling with Sally Clark and now you've got to help convince the general public that Angela's innocent too. Most of my families don't have that luxury, Terry. If you'd been accused in the family courts you couldn't be identified, show anyone documents about your case, because of the secrecy. You'd be committing a criminal offence.

214

'But you've got the chance to get out there and start fighting. Use the media, use whatever voice you've got, to scream about what's happened.'

Like me, Terry was initially reluctant to listen to Penny, but gradually he began to realise that he could be my voice and turned to the handful of journalists who seemed genuinely interested in my case. Soon after Sally was released, two articles appeared in the national newspapers.

'Sally's free . . . now end MY wife's nightmare' said the *Sun*, while on the same day the *Daily Mail* asked: 'Angela too was jailed for killing her babies. Is she also innocent?' Two weeks later a documentary appeared on BBC2 called *Cot Death Mothers: The Witch-Hunt*. In it reporter John Sweeney raised questions about Professor Meadow's work in my, as well as Sally's, case.

I felt torn about the coverage. As the year rolled on, Terry did more and more media work – appearing on television, speaking on the radio, in newspapers and magazines. Part of me celebrated him being so proactive, and after all the 'baby-killler mum' headlines it was a relief to see supportive articles. But I also knew the reaction I'd get within the prison walls. Every time my name was mentioned in the press, the jeers would start again when I appeared in the canteen and the girls would be restless for about a week afterwards. Just because I was finally prepared to hope, it didn't mean I wanted to take on the rest of the world.

As 2003 rolled by, I continued to see Terry every four weeks and Jade on monthly children's visits. There had been a scare they might be cancelled after it was discovered drugs had been smuggled into the prison in a baby's nappy. But there were no more problems after a warning letter was sent to every inmate telling us the visits would be stopped if it happened again.

Jade had changed so much from the little girl I'd left at pre-school on the morning of Matthew's death. She was seven now and remembered little about the time when I'd been at home. Life for her was all about Terry, while I was someone with whom she shared the threads of an emotional bond but little else. In some ways she responded to me just as she always had done – flinging herself into my arms when she arrived as I covered her in kisses. But when the initial excitement was over, it was almost as if she knew that although something was expected of her she didn't quite know what. Our relationship on an everyday level had completely disappeared. Even after Matthew's death I'd had enough contact with her to see some of the tiny ways in which her growing up had changed her – such as the foods she liked, or the TV programmes she watched. But now I knew none of that and every month I missed pushed us further apart. At times Jade would ignore me for the whole of a visit, too busy making peppermint creams or painting to talk to me.

But it wasn't just her who withdrew. In some ways I did too, because while I desperately wanted to be part of her life, another part of me shrank back because of the environment I was in. I couldn't be a real mummy when I saw my child in the association room of a prison. Awareness of where we were, of how my feelings had to be hidden in that place, clashed with the knowledge that I might be separated from Jade for years to come and I felt almost afraid to let go with her. Ultimately, though, I knew that without those visits our relationship would have been lost for ever and I was grateful for them.

In March, Terry and Jade, and Stephen, Kellie and their six-year-old son Lindon, to whom I was particularly close, came onto the wing for one of the two annual family days each inmate got. A different lifer had one every Wednesday and to me it felt like Christmas Day. I had spent weeks saving up my canteen money to buy the kids chocolate and treats and could hardly believe I was going to spend a whole six hours with them. It was the only visit we were allowed on the actual wing and it was a chance for me to show them a bit of the unit.

What I hadn't bargained for, though, was that such a long time together meant it was far harder for us to keep up the pretence than usual.

'Well, it's better than a normal visit,' Terry said with a sigh. 'About 80 per cent of the other relatives on those look like people you'd see on TV. They're scary.'

216

'Stop it, Dad, don't wind Ange up,' Stephen replied. 'It's not all that bad.'

'No. No, it isn't. It's good to be together today, isn't it?'

We fell silent as we watched Jade and Lindon play.

'Jadey,' I called to her. 'I've got a video here. Would you like to come and see it?'

'No thanks, Mummy,' she said, head down, intent on her game.

'Well, how about a game of table football?'

'I don't want to,' Jade replied.

'Or why don't we play with the dolls' house?'

'I'm fine here, Mummy.'

I looked up, embarrassed. I was desperately trying to make the day work but another part of me didn't want to have to. I felt somehow ashamed the people I loved were seeing my real life in prison, that what should have remained hidden was now out in the open. It felt wrong and I'd never felt like such a stranger to them as I did that day, showing them my cell and the laundry where I worked.

All too soon the familiar dread descended on me as the day drew to a close and I prepared to say goodbye.

'I wish you weren't here, Mummy,' Jade said to me as Terry gently pushed her towards me. 'I wish you weren't in the big building and could come home.'

'So do I, darling,' I said, throat tight with tears as I bent to kiss her. 'So do I.'

'Bye, Ange,' Kellie whispered as she hugged me. 'Look after yourself. You'll be out of here soon enough.'

'I hope so,' I replied. 'I hope so.'

I cried my eyes out when I got back to my cell. If the system hadn't defeated me, then that day I thought my emotions might. I'd tried so hard to be something I wasn't – the same old Angela – but I knew it was just an act. I felt sad, lonely and yet again disbelief surged through me that I was being made to live this life when I had done nothing wrong.

It was the end of a long June day in the laundry and I was looking forward to getting back to my room and sitting down. I opened the door to the lifers' unit and started walking upstairs when one of the girls ran up to me.

'Have you seen the news?' she shouted, eyes bright, breathless with excitement. 'She's been acquitted, Angela. Trupti Patel is free.'

I gulped as a rush of disbelief gripped my chest.

'What?' I whispered.

'She's out, Angela. Not guilty.'

Without a word I walked towards the association room where girls rushed towards me shouting.

'Have you seen?'

'She's just like you and they said not guilty.'

'You're walking, Ange. You're walking. You're out of here.'

Just as they had been on the day of Sally's release, the girls were on a high and I could almost touch the excitement in the air. It was pandemonium.

As women rushed up to me smiling their congratulations, others ran over to officers and shouted: 'What's the matter with you? She shouldn't be here.'

I stood in the middle of it all, unable to take it in, hardly daring to.

Like me, Trupti Patel had lost two boys and a girl to cot death, like me she had one surviving daughter, and like me she had been accused of murder. Her trial had been going on for about a month and I had followed every step. Dread had gripped me when I realised Dunkels was the prosecuting counsel and Professor Meadow was a witness. He told the court 'the most probable diagnosis is asphyxia caused by an adult, either by smothering or by restriction of chest movement' and said it was unusual for a third child to die without reason being found.

'In general, sudden and unexpected death does not run in families,' he intoned.

But a week later my heart lifted when Trupti's grandmother, Surajben Patel, told the court that she had lost five of her twelve children in infancy.

The eighty-year-old, who had flown in from a village in India, spoke through an interpreter as she was asked if she knew what had killed her children.

'No,' she said simply. 'This is something God takes care of. We leave it to God.'

It had taken the jury just ninety minutes to deliver a unanimous not guilty verdict.

Rose looked at me.

'It's just a matter of time, Ange, just a matter of time,' she said.

I stared at her, desperate to let the girls' optimism sweep me up but too scared to join in. Hope's tiny flame was still alight inside me, shored up a couple of months earlier by reading the Court of Appeal's judgement in Sally's case. Bill had sent it to me and I had sat up until midnight reading all thirty-eight pages in one sitting. Seeing those words in black and white had made me feel for the first time that I might stand a chance against all those eminent, educated doctors and it pricked new interest in my appeal. Justice had come so close to me – Sally had lived just a few doors away – but I took my lead from Bill.

'The Clark judgement will do us no harm,' he told me as we sat together on legal visits. But he was cool in his optimism and so I too was cautious. All my hopes were pinned on Bill, I quite literally idolised him, and so I didn't go off the deep end because he didn't. Always calm, always balanced, he never once gave me false hope.

The attitude of the girls on the wing had also changed after Sally's conviction was quashed. I'd never protested my innocence but suddenly they started treating me differently. They could see I was just an ordinary woman and, because they seemed friendlier, I relaxed and started to mingle more, which I think convinced them further. The BBC documentary *Angela's Trial* was also finally shown while I was at Bullwood. Now the girls seemed to be completely behind me. But as much as I wanted to join in their euphoria, something held me back. I was still in prison. It wasn't me walking free.

I looked at Rose.

'Sally's been released, she lost two babies. Now Trupti Patel's been acquitted. She lost three. But what does it mean for me? I can't go there, Rose. I've spent fourteen months in prison being treated as the lowest of the low, adjusting to life in here, and I'm not sure if I can let myself show I'm hopeful.

'It's there deep down inside. But I can't show it. To do that would make it real and what will I do if I don't get an appeal? Life in here carries on and I mustn't let myself get too swept away.'

'Okay, Ange,' Rose replied. 'Let's go and have a cuppa.'

A few weeks later I rang home one afternoon.

'Hello?' said Terry as he picked up the phone and I could tell immediately something was wrong.

'What's happened?' I asked. 'Are you all right?'

'It's Cindy,' Terry replied, his voice thick with sobs.

'What's the matter?' I asked urgently.

'She's dead, Angela. She collapsed yesterday in the garden and was bad again this morning. I knew something was really wrong but didn't have any money for the vet so I had to ring him and get an idea of how much it would cost before he came across. It was awful. I've just buried her in the back garden.'

Cindy was my dog and had been at my side throughout everything. She had been with me during all those walks with Gemma, Jason, Jade and Matthew in the pram, and again when they died.

'Well, she was seventeen – a good age,' I said, my voice flat. 'Have you heard from Mum about when she's going to visit?'

'Ange,' Terry said, disbelief and frustration straining his voice. 'What's wrong with you? Don't you care? Cindy's dead. Your Cindy. And you can hardly bring yourself to waste any time on it, let alone cry about it. What's happening to you? How can you be so cold? The Angela I know would have cried her eyes out.'

'Look, Terry, if I was at home with you I would be, but I'm not, am I?' I hissed. 'I didn't see her. I didn't see her die and I can't start breaking my heart. I've told you, I just can't in here.'

'I can't believe you're being so heartless,' Terry replied. 'I'm here. I've had to worry about her, worry about money, worry about burying her and you're not saying a thing.'

For just a moment I almost weakened but stopped myself. Prison had hardened me so much that even with Terry I couldn't let myself go.

As my first year inside had rolled into the second, and the

summer of 2003 turned towards autumn, I knew we were drifting further and further apart as man and wife. We were still friends, we still chatted as we always had, but the closeness, the tiny intimacies, such as saying 'I love you' at the end of each phone conversation, had been stripped away. Our worlds were now completely separate. Mine was in prison, his at home in Salisbury with Jade and we each struggled to find a way into the other's.

'Thank God we were friends before we became lovers and whatever else has gone we'll always be friends,' Terry would say as we sat together on a visit.

But whatever he said, I refused to admit to myself how bad things had got. Of course I was aware of the distance, as I was with Jade, but they were the anchor I clung onto and to admit how far we had drifted would have been too much. To the outside world Terry was my devoted husband, fighting for my life. But he was fighting for Angela, the woman he knew was innocent, not Angela, his wife. It was as if, after nearly twenty years together, chasms had suddenly opened up between us that we had no idea how to cross. Jealousy was one.

As my friendship with Rose and Terry's with Penny deepened, we had each become increasingly resentful of the 'intruder'.

'Rose really made me feel better today,' I'd tell Terry.

'I envy you that, Ange – that you've got someone to talk to, someone to get a bit of TLC from,' he would reply. 'I just feel so lonely out here. I wish I had more adult company.'

'I don't want to be here, Terry,' I'd snap. 'But I've found someone who's genuinely concerned for us as a family. Can't you be happy for me? And anyway, you have got people. You speak to Gill Chambers every day, Stephen, your mum. You're not completely alone.'

'I don't mean it like that, Ange. I'm glad you've got someone, I really am. It's just I'd like some adult company sometimes rather than Jade all the time.'

'I've got to go – there's a queue for the phone,' I'd say suddenly, frustration rising up in me. I knew he was still crippled by sadness and rage and was drinking to try and numb it. But I was stuck inside a prison and there was nothing I could do. It was all so different to how it had been for so many years before Matthew's death. Before that, we'd talked about everything, shared it all, but now I just couldn't find the words.

'Bye then,' Terry said, as I put down the phone and felt guilt wash over me. I hated leaving it on a negative note but I'd got to a stage where I didn't know what else to do.

At other times he'd chat on about Penny and my guts would twist with jealousy. I could hear her words in his and, although I knew she was happily married, I could have screamed. I was beside myself when Terry and Jade went to stay with Penny and Andrew, her husband, for a weekend. Who was this woman? Why was she spending time with my child when I couldn't? It was probably one of the few times in all those years when Terry and I almost had a stand-up shouting match.

'But why have you got to go?' I asked angrily.

'Because it will be good for Jade,' he replied. 'Come on, Ange, Penny's got eight kids, a husband. You'd really like her. She calls a spade a spade.'

Frustration rose once again inside me – that I was still inside when Sally Clark and Trupti Patel were free, that I couldn't be a proper wife and mother, that I had been convicted at all. Pushing it down, I calmed my voice and carried on talking to Terry.

As the summer turned to autumn and then towards winter, I became increasingly frustrated by the fact that nothing seemed to be happening. Trupti Patel's case was almost identical to mine, it seemed, and yet I was still inside. Where once I had been able to push down my anger, there were now times when I felt it would overwhelm me. I knew Bill and Jacqui were doing all they could, working with experts on my case and looking at new research about multiple cot deaths. I'd also seen Mr Mansfield on a couple of legal visits, who'd reassured me that everything was continuing as it should, but I felt so cut off from it all.

Other people too were trying to win me my freedom. I'd first met BBC reporter John Sweeney before my trial and knew he'd been following my case ever since. As well as mine, he'd reported on Sally's case and those of other falsely accused parents, and he had raised many questions about Professor Sir Roy Meadow's work since first reporting on it for BBC Radio Five Live in 2001. In the months following the Trupti Patel verdict, the press had taken up the mantle and the almost unimaginable had started to happen – the reputation of this world-renowned expert had come under fire. Momentum was also building among the press and public alike that something had gone seriously wrong in cases like mine. But my separation from the real world meant I knew little of this and the small amount I did pick up hardly registered.

But while the weeks and months seemed to roll by with no significant changes to my case, two things happened in October that forced me to sit up and take notice. Firstly – and finally – my appeal date was set. Bill and Jacqui were hoping up-to-date research about multiple cot deaths and new reports from expert witnesses would convince the court to free me. Bill was his usual measured self when he broke the news and told me it was going to be held at the end of November. But almost as soon as relief washed over me, I felt panicked – this was my chance to clear my name and if it failed I didn't know what I would do.

The other thing was that John Sweeney went to Ireland to research my family history – with quite extraordinary results. Until my appeal was granted, Bill, Jacqui and all the experts working on my case, including Professor Patton, were working for nothing because the majority of legal aid funding isn't granted until a case is won. They still believed my Irish family tree was the key to my case but were unable to go to the costly lengths of flying over there to research what was essentially a hunch. But John, backed by BBC documentary funding, was able to do so and he and his producer had gone to Dublin in the hunt for clues. There, after trawling through ninety-three record books in the General Register Office, they had discovered something that Bill believed could only strengthen our case – as well as the five cot deaths we already knew about, there had been three other infant deaths on the Irish side of my family. My great-grandmother Sarah had lost a baby, my grandmother Harriett had buried two children. The information was sketchy but the cause of death for two of the babies was given as 'debility' – a term that, according to an Irish genealogist, covered cot death. Shrouded in secrecy, no one in the family knew about the deaths because they had never been spoken of, but as some families have a history of heart disease or cancer, this new information seemed to prove my Irish bloodline was predisposed to SIDS. There had been eight cot deaths in four generations of my family. A BBC1 Real Story documentary called *Angela's Hope* was broadcast on 3 November and all I could do was watch and, indeed, hope that the judges would be convinced.

It was almost more than I could bear when my appeal date was changed from November to December. Buoyed up by the press, Terry kept telling me I was going to be freed, but I refused to allow myself to be carried away and the delay played on my paranoia. The days dragged by but all I could do was force myself to wait and carry on with life as normal. Deep down I might be hopeful but I also knew I couldn't count on anything. It had gone wrong once and could do so again. Those were the longest weeks of my life. Night after night I lay in my cell wondering if the judges would listen – and how I would ever cope if they didn't. It was far worse than waiting for my trial because then I'd had no idea about what was waiting for me. Now I knew and felt desperately scared. It was my last chance. The only thing of which I was certain was that if I was not freed I doubted I would make it through another Christmas without Terry and Jade. When the possibility of bail was raised I had said no – I didn't want to taste freedom only to be put back inside if it all went wrong.

A week before my appeal, nervousness tightened my stomach as I sat in the visiting hall waiting for Bill and Jacqui to arrive for my final legal visit. We had an hour to tie up all the loose ends. But as they walked through the door I could tell immediately that something was wrong. They had such serious looks on their faces as they walked towards me – Bill smartly dressed in a suit with his white hair swept back and Jacqui, as ever, looking a million dollars.

'Hello,' I said with a weak smile as they sat down.

'Angela, I won't beat about the bush, there is something I need to tell you,' Bill replied.

My heart sank as I looked at them and Jacqui leaned forwards to take my hand in hers.

'What's happened?' I whispered.

'We've got something to tell you,' Jacqui said softly as she turned her gaze to Bill.

'Angela, you have a half-sister,' he said in serious tones.

I looked at him blankly.

'It seems your father had a liaison some years ago and she has contacted us in the light of the John Sweeney documentary.'

For a moment I hardly knew what to say, then I burst out laughing. I couldn't believe it. My dad? A secret daughter?

'You know what?' I said, choking. 'It doesn't surprise me at all.'

'We need to explain to you how significant this is in terms of your appeal,' Bill continued. 'Her story is very interesting in terms of the genetic side of your case because one of her children had breathing problems from birth. She is your half-sister, Angela, a close genetic relative, and her children suffered similar problems to yours. It is very important.'

'Surely it has to mean something,' I replied, struggling to take it all in. A half-sister I never knew I had? What must Mum be thinking? Tina, Claire, Andrew?

'We think it is and we will use the information at the hearing. But this lady doesn't want to be identified. She grew up with her mother and stepfather and doesn't want any media attention that will rake up the past and cause trouble, so we must respect her privacy.'

'Of course,' I said. 'Whatever she needs I'm happy to go along with. The most important thing is that she's come forward.'

'Yes it is, Angela, yes it is,' said Bill. 'This is a very significant step forward.'

As I looked at Bill, I saw real hope in his eyes for the first time. Until that day he had always been guarded, never wanting to give me false confidence, but in that moment I realised he was finally truly hopeful. He'd always said we needed a 'silver bullet' to help win my release. Now it seemed that at last we might have found it.

CHAPTER FOURTEEN

It was 5.45 a.m. and I looked up at the bare walls of my cell. The prison was silent and the sky outside black as I sipped a cup of tea. It was lonely being up at that time – even the hot water hadn't come on yet and I'd shivered under a lukewarm shower. My appeal started in less than five hours and my stomach swooped every time I thought about it.

Two weeks ago I'd done a property check and everything that wasn't vital – like the good-luck cards lining every surface of my room, and needlework things – had been sent out to Terry. My remaining belongings were in two see-through prison-issue plastic bags, which sat in the middle of my room alongside an overnight bag containing things like a nightdress and toiletries I'd need during the five days of my appeal.

Keep calm, I told myself as I lit a cigarette with shaking hands.

I looked up at the black jacket hanging near me. It belonged to Rose and she'd given it to me the night before.

'When you're done with it you can send it back to me,' she said as I handed my duvet cover to her just in case I didn't return. 'It will be a lucky jacket then because you'll have been wearing it when you get out.'

Nervously, I fiddled with the silver crucifix around my neck. Mum had sent it in to me and I wore black trousers and shoes and a striped navy top with it. Twenty months after being convicted, I was suited and booted once again to face court.

I thought back to my last visit with Terry two weeks ago. He'd looked like a tramp as he walked unshaven into the visiting hall wearing tracksuit bottoms and a baggy jacket, his hair a mess.

'Sorry, Ange,' he'd said as he sat down. 'I took a sleeping pill after I had a couple of brandies last night and dropped off again when I'd taken Jade to school this morning. I woke up late and had to jump straight in the car.'

Tears started sliding down Terry's face as he spoke and soon he was sobbing uncontrollably. He simply could not stop himself and I tried to comfort him as best I could as officers looked across at us. I touched his arms and hugged him briefly but of course I couldn't hold onto him for too long because of the visiting rules.

'What's happened?' I asked.

'It's our last chance,' he replied softly, as he looked up at me. 'All this time I've been so convinced but I'm scared now. If this appeal goes wrong, what will we do?'

'Please, Terry,' I said gently. 'You've got to try and hold on. You must. We've got to get through this together.'

But even as I said it I could feel my sympathy was tainted by frustration and I fell silent. I wanted him to be there for me, I was so afraid. The rest of that awful hour was spent trying to soothe Terry as he sobbed his heart out but I couldn't seem to get through to him.

I was devastated when I got back to my room and told Rose. It was so hard to see him so upset, so filled with doubts.

'You've gone through Matthew's death,' she said. 'You've gone through being charged, you've gone through being arrested, you've gone to prison, you've gone through shit here and this is just another stage you've got to get through, Angela. Don't give up now.'

After that Terry had bounced back to the optimism that the media coverage had instilled in him. But as I sat on my bed on the morning of my appeal the glimpse of his desperation played on my mind. However hard I tried to push the thoughts away, I was wracked with doubts. Would Terry still want me if I got out? Would Jade want her mum back? Would our family survive? Or had things gone too far? They simply couldn't have, I told myself. I hadn't gone through all this to lose them now.

At 6.30 a.m. I heard the click of the lock as the door to my cell opened. As I walked out an officer leaned towards the holder by my door and removed the card containing my details so others would know I was not there. I hesitated outside Rose's door and gave it a quick tap.

'See you later,' I said in a low voice before I was taken downstairs and across the courtyard to the reception area, where my property was unpacked and checked. I was then body-searched, handcuffed and taken out to join other prisoners in the waiting van – or sweat box as I'd learned to call it inside.

I felt sick as the lock slid shut on the door to the all-too-familiar steel box. I'd been told the journey to London would take about two hours, but I didn't know either Essex or the capital very well and so didn't really know what to expect.

Thoughts rushed around my head.

What will the court look like? How's Mr Mansfield feeling? Will I come back here tonight? Will they let me out?

Although the appeal was listed for five days and I was due to return to Bullwood Hall each night, I knew the judges could make a decision at any time and so I would never be quite sure if I would return or not.

Under the bottom of the door I was handed a packet of sandwiches. Egg and two types of cheese – everything I hated.

As the van got under way the officers started talking to the driver.

'Parky today, isn't it?' one voice said to all of us locked up into cubicles as another piped up, 'Are you all right back there, girls? Do you want a light for your fag?'

'Yes please,' I shouted. An officer passed a lighter under the gap at the bottom of the door, which I used before handing it straight back.

My mind continued racing as the van thundered down the motorway. I could hear Radio 2 playing and Terry Wogan's chirpy voice – it felt so strange that for so many people it was another ordinary morning.

Some time later I saw the London Eye through the van

window, and after a few minutes an officer said, 'We'll try and get round the back so they can't see her.'

As the van slowed up, it seemed as if a million camera flashes had started to go off outside the blackened windows. The press were out in force.

Oh God, I thought to myself. This is it now. Keep yourself together, girl.

An officer opened the door and cuffed me again before leading me down the steps at the side of the van. I could hear rustling and voices but kept my eyes fixed on her back as I followed her through a door, down a step and along a corridor into another where there was a table covered in files. I gave my name and was led down to the cells.

'We'll have to be quick,' someone said as I looked at my watch. It was 10 a.m. – there was just half an hour to go before my appeal finally began.

'All rise,' a voice said as I heard the swish of the judges' robes and walked into the dock.

My breath caught in my throat. I was in the most impressive room I'd ever seen. This was the High Court in London – Britain's most important court – and the surroundings were suitably grand. A high ceiling towered over me and dark wood panelling covered the walls. There were also rows and rows of books and a thick carpet on the floor which hushed all noise to a whisper. The dock was barred but felt more like a pulpit, looking down as it did across the room and the glossy dark wood seating where the public and legal teams sat. Above me to my right the three judges who were hearing my case sat next to each other at a long bench looking down over everyone. If the atmosphere at my trial had been serious, then it was a thousand times more so here. The judges sat like birds on a wire, an air of calm but absolute authority hanging around them like a second skin. Each wore scarlet robes and a white wig and the two closest to me were men. I would later learn that the one nearest me was called Mr Justice Pitchers and the man in the middle, who was in charge, was Lord

Justice Judge. I looked along the line to see a woman sitting farthest away, Mrs Justice Rafferty.

As I looked down and saw Dunkels sitting there once again, I felt intimidated, like a bird in a cage.

My eyes darted to Mr Mansfield and Jo Briggs, who sat on benches along from Dunkels, and I could see Dad with his friend Roland Revell directly behind them. On the opposite side, behind the prosecution team, were Claire and Kevin, Tina, Andrew and my mum and Brian. But try as I might I couldn't see Terry. Eventually I found him right at the back, sitting alongside Terry and Gill, Stephen and Kellie, and Gill's mum and dad.

Why are they all the way back there? I thought to myself. I want them closer.

At least I could see the people I loved this time, but it was a bittersweet moment as I gazed at their faces. I just wanted to reach through the bars and touch them, pull Terry to me. As the court settled down I prayed this was the final journey I would have to make without him.

Mr Mansfield stood as he opened my case and told the judges the whole prosecution against me had depended on the evidence of Professor Meadow. My conviction, he said, was now unsafe, in part because the paediatrician's standing had been undermined by the outcome of the Clark case.

'Without Meadow, this case would not have got off the ground,' Mr Mansfield told the court. 'The Crown's case was fundamentally to depend on Meadow. At the trial, we say the jury must have been impressed by this particular witness.'

My heart swelled as I watched him speak. I looked at Jo, Bill and Jacqui sitting with him – they'd worked tirelessly for this.

In commanding tones Mr Mansfield reminded the judges of Professor Meadow's assertion at my trial that it was 'very, very rare' for two babies to die of SIDS in the same family and accused him of getting the Sally Clark statistic in 'by the back door'.

'His dependence on rarity is misleading,' the QC said. 'It is as misleading as the statistic he used in the other case. What he was doing was getting it in by the back door because that's what he was meaning – one in 73 million. He didn't say it, but he didn't have to.

'Some of the important points that were being raised by this important witness have to be at least doubted. Were the trial to take place now, it's unlikely the Crown would call Professor Sir Roy Meadow, or if they did it would be done with a health warning.'

The minutes ticked by as Mr Mansfield addressed the court and accused the jury in my trial of acting unreasonably by accepting Professor Meadow's evidence and that of Dr Ward Platt when thirteen other experts said the causes of my babies' deaths were natural or indeterminable. But the three-in-one theory had 'pervaded' the jury and 'bedevilled' the case.

'The jury was provided with ample material which we said, and does, render this conviction unsafe,' Mr Mansfield said. 'The jury could not have excluded the possibility that there was a natural cause of death, albeit unknown.'

There was no forensic evidence Jason and Matthew had been smothered, he told the court, but yet I'd been asked to explain the natural, but unknown, cause of their deaths.

'It was impossible to overcome the prejudice which exists,' he told the court.

And finally, thankfully, Mr Mansfield dismissed the illogical premise upon which the whole case against me had been based – that, free of psychiatric illness, I had given birth to my children simply in order to kill them. It was one of the aspects of the case I had found hardest to bear.

'It beggars belief,' Mr Mansfield said and added, 'This conviction doesn't make sense. There was no disorder, nothing in the background, nothing in the family history to suggest this was a woman who was bent on killing.'

I slowly let my breath out as he sat down. I knew I was in the best possible hands, but would the judges listen?

The phone rang a couple of times until there was a click, a pause and I heard Terry's voice.

232

'Hello?' he said.

'It's me,' I replied.

I'd got back to Bullwood at about 7 p.m. after the hearing drew to a close and felt exhausted.

'So how did you think it went?' Terry asked.

'Oh you know,' I replied uncertainly.

'I feel confident,' he said. 'From the questions he was asking, the one in charge seems to be on your side. I feel odds on you'll walk because of him.'

'I don't know, Ter. I can't go there. Let's just see what happens.'

There was a pause.

'I got really annoyed at lunch,' I said, anxious to change the subject and determined not to get my hopes up too high.

'Why's that?' Terry asked.

'Well, first I couldn't eat the food they brought me and then they gave me coffee instead of tea. It really got on my wick. I felt like saying to them, I know it's not the Ritz and I know I'm in prison but talk about human rights. Can't I get a ruddy cup of tea? I don't ask for much. I haven't eaten a thing.'

'Poor Ange.' Terry laughed down the phone as I smiled at my annoyance. Even in such a serious situation, I couldn't bear to go without my food.

'So how's your hotel?' I asked.

Terry, Stephen and Kellie, Terry and Gill and Gill's parents were all staying in a hotel close to the High Court. It was being paid for by the *Daily Mail* newspaper because Terry had made an agreement with them that I would speak to them exclusively if my conviction was quashed. I'd felt uncomfortable about being paid – was it right to take money? What would people think of us?

'I don't like it, Terry,' I'd said as we discussed it. 'Our children died and we're going to take money. It feels wrong.'

'I know, Ange, but we've got nothing,' Terry replied. 'I worked hard for thirty years and we've had everything ripped away – jobs, house, insurances, pension money. We've got nothing left and we need this to start rebuilding our lives. We can use it to buy a house. I don't want us living on the social for the rest of our lives. We need to be practical, Ange.

233

'Also, don't you want to tell our story? Don't you want people to know what happened to us? If you do the interview then millions of people will know.'

And so I had agreed.

When we finished talking I went back to my room, looking forward to seeing Rose. We'd been given special permission to visit each other when the girls were locked in.

'Oh, Ange, you look knackered,' she said as she hugged me. 'Tell me all about it.'

I was too scared to cry that night as I told her about the day.

'I don't know if this is going to work,' I said. 'I'm just not sure. Will they listen to me?'

'It's only day one,' she replied. 'You've got to have your say and then the prosecution has theirs, that's the way it works. But they haven't got the evidence and the judges will realise that. Remember we've just got to get through each day.'

We chain-smoked our way through the next hour as I recounted what had happened at court.

'Don't forget to knock on my hatch,' Rose said as she was leaving. 'Open it and I'll wave to you. You will get out of here, Ange. It's got to work and it will work. You're innocent. They'll have to let you go.'

After she left, I sat back down on my bed and pulled a picture of Terry and Jade out of my overnight bag. 'I've got to get home to you,' I whispered.

As much as I understood that in any case there has to be a prosecution as well as a defence, I could hardly contain my anger the next day when Dunkels rose to once again label me a murderer.

I had been convicted, he told the court, because of 'compelling' evidence. I was alone with my children when they had breathing problems and alone again with them when they died.

'SIDS could have occurred at any time of the day or night, anywhere or when anyone was about,' he said. 'Yet these incidents only ever occurred in the morning when the applicant was alone with her babies.'

Yet again, my 'unnatural' behaviour was twisted against me – phoning Terry on the morning of Matthew's death instead of an ambulance and running to ask Gloria Peacock for help on the morning of Jason's breathing difficulties instead of calling 999.

'It is the Crown's suggestion that for her to behave in this curious and detached way was not the instinctive way one would have expected a mother to behave,' Dunkels boomed.

Rage rose up inside me as I sat in the barred dock looking down at the man who would return to his comfortable home that night as I sat in a prison cell.

This is my life, I wanted to scream. Of course I was alone with them – I'm their mum and their dad was out at work, it's what happens in millions of families. Who are you to tell me how I should have reacted when I found my children dead? How can anyone tell me what I should have done? Have you ever, for even a second, tried to imagine how it felt to lose three children? Don't you think I've replayed those days again and again in my mind wondering where I went wrong?

But Dunkels heard nothing of what was screaming through my head as he continued telling the judges why I should remain locked up.

'The jurors had ample opportunity to do what juries are best designed to do – to assess her and decide on her credibility,' he said. 'Seeing her and listening to her, the jury had to decide: "Can we be sure this mother was capable of smothering her own babies?" and they decided that she was and that she had done so.'

Again my mind raced. They didn't know what was going on, I thought. Even the doctors couldn't agree. All they heard was smothering and, like most people, they thought the odds of my babies dying naturally were longer than them winning the lottery.

Finally Dunkels dismissed Mr Mansfield's earlier statement that it was illogical that I'd had my children in order to kill them.

'She may have thought she could overcome those feelings that she had in the past,' he said.

Didn't he think someone might have noticed me grappling with murderous impulses over so many years? My doctor, my health visitor, my priest, the successive medics we'd met in hospital, my family, my friends, my husband? Once again I could only sit and stare as logic flew out the window.

The girls at Tesco had more common sense, I thought to myself as the van crawled slowly through the heavy Friday night traffic on the journey back to Bullwood.

That weekend was the longest of my life as I waited to go back to court for day three of the appeal on the Monday. I felt as if I was teetering on a ledge with freedom and life on one side, death and imprisonment on the other, and I had no idea which way I was going to fall. The other girls were keen to find out how it was going but I retreated into my cell. I couldn't allow myself to get too caught up in their enthusiasm because this time next week I might still be here. I even refused to go down to the dining hall and was given permission to have meals sent to my cell. I knew my case had been all over the TV and papers and didn't want all the looks and abuse that I still got from girls on other wings at mealtimes again. Instead I spent most of the time quietly with Rose, only venturing out to Mass on Saturday morning where prayers were offered for those in appeals.

Please God, I pleaded with Him. Please let the judges see the truth.

But by the time we returned to court on Monday, I was filled with dread – that tiny flicker of hope inside me battered by a weekend of doubts and questions.

What happens if we go through the whole five days and the judges still don't make up their minds? I kept asking myself. They let Sally Clark out after two days. This is day three and they've said nothing.

As Monday slid into Tuesday I kept looking at the judges, trying to tell what they were thinking from the questions they asked and the way they looked. But they were completely impassive. Other than that I could only sit in the dock and listen as the prosecution and defence laid out their cases once again. It was as hard as it had ever been to listen to but I forced myself to focus on my family and friends sitting so tantalisingly close. As I sat in the dock, I looked down at them in turn. Terry, who nodded reassuringly at me each time we locked eyes; my dad mouthing as ever, 'You'll be all right, love', still convinced the justice system would look after me; Andrew scrabbling for his phone when it went off by accident, and Stephen snoring during some of the drier medical evidence. Life carried on as normal.

Just as it had been at my trial, much of the medical evidence was dense and complicated. But I was pleased to see Professor Patton again as he presented the new evidence about genetics.

He told the court that a genetic disorder could have been responsible for Jason and Matthew's deaths and revealed the new evidence that John Sweeney's programme had uncovered. The judges listened closely as he told them about Sarah, Harriett and my half-sister.

'It strongly supports a genetic case for the infant deaths,' he told the court.

But nausea washed over me when Dr Ward Platt went onto the witness stand on Tuesday. I could not understand how after all this time when everyone said my case was so strong, he was still prepared to give evidence against me.

His conviction scared me as much as it ever had and, as the day drew to a close and I got on the van to start the journey back to Bullwood, I was convinced I wasn't going home. The judges were taking so long – surely if they thought I was innocent they'd have stopped the whole thing rather than letting it go on, just as they had with Sally? While everyone else still seemed to be buoyed up by optimism, I felt bleaker than ever.

That night the girls gathered outside my room just before lock-in. They knew the next day was the final one of the appeal and wanted to say the goodbyes they felt sure were due. I didn't quite know how to respond as each one in turn filed into my cell to hug me goodbye.

Martika from the gym; Alicia from next door; Claire and Nathalie, who I worked with in the laundry; Tracy, Martika's best friend; Jo, who had the most infectious laugh I'd ever heard; Angela, a lovely older lady; Chrissie, a lively Liverpudlian girl who slipped cards underneath my door when I was ill; Anne from the kitchens where Rose had got the girls to bake me a cake to celebrate my fortieth birthday back in May – each came in to say goodbye.

'You go for it, girl. Get in there. You're going to walk tomorrow. You're going to go. You really deserve to.'

And finally there was Rose.

My throat tightened as I looked at her standing in front of me. Whatever happened by tomorrow night I would either be sitting in a prison cell again or with Terry – each prospect frightened me for different reasons.

'I'm really going to miss you, Ange,' Rose said tearfully. 'I don't know what I'll do without you.'

'If it's positive tomorrow then I may not be here,' I replied. 'But you will never know how much you've done for me and I will never forget that. I'll always be your friend, Rose. I will always be there for you. Thank you so much – you've kept me going.'

Strange as it sounds, I dreaded the possibility of leaving her. She had become my second family inside those walls and I hated the thought of not seeing her again, not sitting down for a good gossip after work, not hearing her giggle with me as we took the mickey out of a television programme.

'I'm just going to miss you so much, Ange,' she said as we hugged each other.

'I'll miss you too,' I replied, my voice thick with emotion and confusion making my head ring. Was this really goodbye?

Just after 6.30 a.m. the next morning I flipped open the hatch in Rose's door as I left my cell.

'I'm off now,' I said.

She was crying as she lay in bed.

'You're going to go. You're definitely going to go,' she replied in a faltering voice.

My heart squeezed as I looked at her sitting there. I couldn't bear to think of her so sad.

'I don't know, Rose,' I replied. 'I just don't know.'

Utter disbelief as I am taken into Winchester Crown Court on 19 February 2002 to stand trial for the murder of my babies.

The photograph of Terry and Jade that I kept under my pillow every night while I was in prison. When I felt like giving up I would look at them and will myself to carry on.

Handcuffed, I am led into the Appeal Court (where?) on 4 December 2003 for the start of my appeal against the life sentence.

The court sketch drawn during the hearing of my appeal. I was trying to make sense of what was going on around me and just praying hard that I would be allowed to go home.

My prayers are answered and on 10 December 2003 I walk out of court
a free woman, surrounded by Terry, my family and friends. I am
bewildered but filled with overwhelming relief that my innocence has
finally been proven.

TOPFOTO

Terry and Penny Mellor, who gave Terry tremendous support while I was in prison, join protesters outside the General Medical Council HQ in 2003.

TOPHAM/PA

Committed to supporting families who have lost their children to the Family Courts, I join campaigners outside the High Court in March 2004.

With my stepson Stephen on his wedding day.

Back home in 2004 and spending family time together.
Terry and Jade show off their singing skills to Meatloaf.

I never dreamed I would be holding Jade again while she was so young. This photograph will always have happy memories for me, but it is tinged with sadness for the lost four years of her childhood.

Me, Terry and Jade with our trusted and loyal friend Shadow.

Terry and me. It has been a long, difficult journey, and one that is continuing, but we are still taking it together.

I steeled myself not to cry as I walked into reception to pick up my bags. An officer behind the counter started to smile.

'Well, it's judgement day today,' she laughed. 'Now let's get you off. We don't want to see you back here tonight. We want some good news today.'

'I'll see what I can do,' I said with a weak smile as the handcuffs were put on and I was led to the van.

As the journey got under way, I sat frozen with fear about what was going to happen.

Please, judges, listen, my mind raced. Please give me my life back. If I have to come back here tonight I'll die. I can't do it.

'Do you want a fag?' an officer asked above the roar of the van.

I nodded.

'Here's one, keep yours for yourself. I've been watching your case and I think it looks good.'

She slid the cigarette under the door.

'I just want to go home,' I sobbed as I lit it.

The only thing I knew for certain was that I did not think I would cope if I returned to Bullwood Hall that night. I couldn't think about getting out – it was staying in that frightened me.

Later as we arrived at court, I heard another prisoner on the van shout, 'I hope you get out, girl,' as she was taken off, before the officer who cuffed me said, 'Good luck. Fingers crossed.' It seemed everyone believed I was going to walk out a free woman that day. But I knew the court had made the wrong decision once. It could so easily happen again.

Later that morning Dr Ward Platt finished his evidence and my final expert, Professor Robert Carpenter, was called to give his. He was a medical statistics expert from the London School of Hygiene and Tropical Medicine who had reviewed the latest information on cot deaths and prepared a report for my legal team. He believed the chances of my smothering my children and leaving no telltale signs were just 5 per cent. He was also going to talk about as yet unpublished research that children like mine who suffered breathing attacks were ten times more likely to suffer cot death.

I knew he was an important witness but I was taken aback when a frail-looking old man with white hair and a walking stick approached the stand.

Is he going to be all right? I thought to myself as he settled down.

Suddenly a high-pitched squeal filled the court.

'Would the person responsible for that mobile phone please switch it off?' Justice Judge said sternly to the court.

'Would you mind resetting your hearing aid, Professor Carpenter?' Mr Mansfield cut in as the doctor started to fiddle behind his ear.

It seemed to take for ever as he sorted himself out and my nerves were in pieces by the time he'd finished. I wasn't sure how the judges were going to take to this.

But from the moment Professor Carpenter started speaking, my worries melted away. It was as if a young, vital man had leapt out of his ageing shell and into the courtroom. Professor Carpenter was so thorough, so quick and he had an answer for everything Mr Mansfield or Dunkels put to him. The Court of Appeal is a highly intellectual place – full of books, case law and precedents, with fine minds having what is often essentially an academic argument about law – but Professor Carpenter was more than up to the task.

He told the court Jason and Matthew were at high risk of dying from cot death and said it was likely they were hypersensitive due to an allergy, genetic defect or a response to risk factors. He also condemned Professor Meadow's interpretation of the statistics about the likelihood of three children in the same family dying of cot death as a 'travesty'.

'The occurrence of a third sudden unexplained death is rare but not unknown,' Professor Carpenter said. 'And more often than not all three deaths are due to natural causes.'

His passion for his subject was obvious – he'd have shamed many twenty-somethings with the depth of his feeling – and I could sense, from the questions they asked and the way they did it, that the judges respected him. I was in absolute awe.

240

Only five minutes until lunch, I thought as I looked at my watch and saw it was 12.55 p.m.

'The court will adjourn,' Lord Justice Judge said as he and his colleagues rose and left.

'This is a bit odd, isn't it?' I said to the security guard as we shuffled into the corridor and I lit a cigarette.

'Yes,' she replied. 'But we'll be going off for lunch soon.'

As I took another drag, the words 'All rise' boomed out from the court once again and I hurriedly stubbed out the cigarette before walking back into the dock. Sitting down, I looked across at the judges and it seemed to me that the woman almost smiled for a moment. A rush of nerves washed over me.

As Lord Justice Judge started to address the court, I realised the atmosphere in the court was tight with tension. I searched the faces of Bill and Mr Mansfield below me for clues but they were staring straight ahead. I couldn't understand what was happening. Why weren't we stopping for lunch?

Through the confusion I forced myself to listen and heard the judge tell the court that infant deaths were 'at the cutting edge' of medical knowledge with new discoveries being made all the time.

'The door never seems to be closed to new views on what may or may not cause cot death,' he said gravely. 'We are here on the edge of known science and research is absolutely continuous and producing new results and opinions on a daily basis.'

I sat holding my breath – terror rising up inside me. What did he mean? That until they knew for certain what had killed Jason and Matthew they weren't going to release me?

My heart pounded as Lord Justice Judge told the court my appeal had raised a number of issues in the public interest about cot deaths.

'We shall therefore take time to reflect on the terms of our judgement,' he added and fear welled up in me once again. Did that mean there would be another wait until they decided? 'But the appeal is more directly concerned with the convictions of Mrs Cannings,' he went on as my heart pounded.

For a tiny moment, as the judge took a breath, the world seemed to stop.

'We have reached a clear conclusion and we don't need to reflect on that,' he said, looking down at the court. 'These convictions are unsafe and accordingly they will be quashed and Mrs Cannings will be discharged.'

My hands flew to my mouth as I heard shouts of 'Yes' while someone screamed, 'She's free.' There was clapping and a rush of noise as the judges rose to leave the court and journalists scurried out hurriedly bowing their heads.

I staggered back on one foot as I watched the judges go and tried to mouth 'Thank you'. I don't know if I managed to or if they saw me. I hope they did. And then, in a rush of red robes, they were gone. I was free.

I was stunned, shocked and, as I looked across at Terry, one thought filled my mind: Let me go now.

But as I watched my family and friends hug each other I couldn't feel their instant excitement and joy. It felt as if a huge balloon I had carried stretched to breaking point inside me since the day Matthew died had finally popped. Relief was the only feeling that flooded over me as I turned to leave the dock. It rushed through my veins for the first time in more than four years. I was going home to Terry and Jade.

'We've got to take you back to your cell until we get all the paperwork sorted out,' the security guard said.

'Can't I see my husband?' I asked.

'No,' came the reply as I was led back downstairs. 'We need to get formal permission from the prison that we can release you.'

My mind still reeling, relief immediately gave way to panic as I realised they weren't letting me go. I didn't understand it. My conviction was unsafe and yet I was still a prisoner.

As I was locked back in the cell, there was only one thought in my mind: I hope they let me go again. I stared around. Ridiculous as it sounds, I couldn't quite believe I was free. After all the waiting, it was as if my brain was refusing to let the judge's words sink in.

As a security guard brought my lunch in, he smiled at me. 'Well done. Congratulations. It's good to see justice being done.'

'Thanks,' I replied. 'But can't I come out of the cell?'

'No,' he said, as my heart sank again. 'We have to think of your safety. There are prisoners here going back and forth to court.'

I looked at him in amazement. An hour ago I was one of those, a convicted murderer, and now I wasn't being allowed out for my own protection? It was surreal.

A few minutes later I was taken into a small room where Bill, Jacqui and Jo Briggs were waiting for me. I could hardly speak as I looked at them.

'We've got there,' Bill said as he hugged me. 'It was hard work but we said we'd get you home. That was my promise.'

'I can't believe it,' I told him. 'Thank you so much.'

I felt overwhelmed as I sat and looked at Bill, Jacqui and Jo. They had stuck by me and words could not do justice to how much I owed them.

'Shall we go and have a drink to celebrate?' Jo said, smiling, as we sat dazedly and discussed events.

I felt almost embarrassed as I told them I couldn't go, that we had to leave to do the newspaper interview. They seemed to accept it but then, as now, I felt awkward that I appeared ungrateful. It was a hard couple of hours for me as I told the people who had fought for me, who cared for me, that I couldn't be with them.

'Where's the big man then?' I asked.

Mr Mansfield walked in.

'So how are you?' he said.

'I don't know really,' I replied. 'Shocked.'

'Well, we seem to have a result here today, Mrs Cannings,' he said with a smile. 'You know the media are going to want to hear from you so it might be wise to write something down.'

'Will do,' I told him and a few minutes later I was returned to the cell.

A security guard gave me a pen and paper and I tried to think about what I wanted to say. But my mind just couldn't seem to take it all in. The relief I felt was unlike anything I had experienced before. Otherwise I felt completely dazed by what had happened and was just desperate to see Terry.

It seemed like I sat there for an eternity until I was finally taken out of the cell and told it was time to fill out the final bits of paperwork.

I was led into a huge office where a Christmas tree and decorations signalled that the world was getting ready to celebrate. On the wall was a huge whiteboard listing all the court names and numbers. As I looked up, I suddenly saw my name at the top. 'DT9868 Cannings' it read, with one word next to it: 'Acquitted'.

That's me, I thought. It's actually happened.

And for the first time, seeing those words in black and white, I finally realised I was free – the world knew I was innocent, that I hadn't killed my sons.

'Well done, you. How do you feel?' said a smiling security guard as he rifled through some papers. 'Can you sign for your property please? And I need to give you your £59 discharge grant.'

I looked at him blankly. I hadn't seen money for so long and it looked so odd.

'It's what everyone gets when they leave prison,' he told me. 'It's supposed to get you started.'

I thought back to all those poor girls in Eastwood Park – drugged up, without friends or family, and a criminal record. How far would they get on £59?

'Oh,' said the man as he scanned another sheet. 'You've got more to come than that. It's money from your prison savings account.'

He handed me £110 and I thanked everyone before lifting up my property bags and walking out into a corridor where Terry was waiting with two journalists from the *Daily Mail*.

Shaking and crying we moved towards each other and hung on as if for dear life.

'It's all over, Terry,' I sobbed. 'It's finished. I'm back.'

He looked at me, hardly able to speak through the tears.

'You're free,' he whispered.

I couldn't believe he was standing in front of me again. He was finally here and we could hug each other for as long as we liked without a prison officer telling us to move apart.

We were ushered into a small side room and there, once again, we held onto each other for what seemed like for ever. But I've got to admit it – even in that emotional moment, the practicalities of life forced their way into my head. He's put on weight, I thought to myself as I hugged my husband properly for the first time in twenty months and realised he felt more plump than the Terry I knew.

Soon my dad walked into the room and we broke apart.

'Well, Angela,' he said in his soft Irish brogue. 'I told you we'd get there in the end.'

'You did, Dad, you did,' I told him as we hugged, and my mum and Brian, Tina, Andrew, Claire and Kevin, Roland Revell, Gill and Terry and Gill's parents arrived – followed by Stephen in floods of tears with Kellie.

'Get this down you, girl,' she said as she handed me a small water bottle. 'It's brandy. I thought you might need it.'

I can't remember much of those first few minutes with all the people I loved – finally able to hug them and touch them, talk to them with real smiles on our faces. There were tears, there was a lot of talking and I stood among them all, hardly daring to believe it was real.

One of the *Daily Mail* reporters arrived a few minutes later and explained we were going to walk out onto the steps on the Strand at the front of the High Court where I would say a few words. He also introduced us to a minder who was going to look after us. I was gobsmacked. Was everyone really so interested in me?

Our footsteps clicked on a beautiful tiled floor as we walked through the cavernous entrance hall to the High Court towards a huge set of dark wooden doors. As we passed a security check, I looked out to see a stone porch and beyond that what looked like hundreds of reporters and photographers.

'Oh my God,' I said as I ground to a halt.

There were cameras, microphones, men on stepladders, photographers jostling for space and reporters with their tape recorders and notebooks poised. Banked up seemingly four foot

245

deep and about thirty foot wide on the street outside the court, they were all waiting for me.

Terry squeezed my hand reassuringly as the *Daily Mail* reporter told me, 'Just say what you've got to say and then we'll go. Don't worry. We'll look after you.'

Shaking, I walked out of the porch beside Terry into the cold grey light of a winter's day, with my relatives and legal team behind me. Suddenly there was an amazing burst of light as hundreds of flashes started going off and photographers shouted, 'Angela, Angela, over here' as they struggled to get a picture of me looking into their lens. All I could hear was the rush of traffic on the road a few feet away. I hadn't been outside in the real world for so long and it seemed so noisy.

My legs shook as I unfolded my piece of paper and started to read in a quaking voice. The media pack moved closer to me, straining to hear my words as people crouching at my feet with microphones in their hands jostled to get nearer.

'On 12 November 1999 we lost our precious son Matthew after having previously lost our precious Gemma and Jason,' I said. 'We thought we had been through enough heartbreak. Then there was the police investigation, a trial then conviction. These last four years have been a living hell. Finally, today, justice has been done and my innocence has been proved.

'There are two special people in my life, my husband, Terry, who has stood by me and always believed in my innocence. He is my soulmate. And our very precious daughter who over these last four years has been our inspiration.'

I looked up.

'So how do you feel, Angela?' a voice shouted.

'Did you ever give up hope?' another screeched.

'What are you looking forward to now you're free?' someone else roared.

'Just going home to be mummy,' I said.

As the questions rained down, we turned and walked back into the court where we said goodbye to our friends and family. Again I felt so sad that I couldn't go to celebrate with them all.

Soon we were taken out of a side door and into a waiting car.

It was a condition of the deal with the *Daily Mail* that we had to spend a couple of days with them during which I'd tell my story. When it was all done, we'd finally be able to go home. Angela Levin, the journalist who was going to write my story and who had written to me in prison, was in the car with Terry and me.

'Hello,' she said, and smiled.

I could hardly take it all in as the car moved off. I simply sat there and stared at the cars, the people, the shops – real life so close once again.

Someone passed me a mobile phone and I took it – there was one person I hadn't spoken to yet and I was desperate to. Frustration overwhelmed me as I phoned Terry's parents' house and no one picked up.

'Give it ten minutes and then she'll be back from school,' Terry told me. 'Mum and Dad will be picking her up now.'

The time seemed to drag on and on as we waited until Terry tried the number again.

'Hello, darling,' he said with a smile. 'Mummy's coming home. I've got someone here to speak to you.'

I took the phone with a shaking hand.

'Hi, darling,' I said. 'It's Mummy. I went to the big building today and the people said I could come home.'

Suddenly Jade started to scream on the end of the line. 'She's free, she's free, she's coming home to me,' she sang.

Her voice pierced my disbelief. It was finally true. I was going home to my daughter. I was free.

CHAPTER FIFTEEN

It was dark when we drew up outside a small cottage in the West Midlands countryside. This was where we would be staying for the next two days to do the *Daily Mail* interview and, as well as half a dozen cottages, there was a large house across the driveway, which I would later discover contained a dining room for guests.

Terry and I had a cottage to ourselves and we walked in to find a stone fireplace in a comfy sitting room with a spiral staircase winding upwards to two bedrooms. Up a step was a dining area with the kitchen running off it.

It felt wonderful but strange. In the five hours since the judges had quashed my conviction, my brain was still racing to catch up. On the way up to the cottage, we'd stopped at a service station for a sandwich and it had been one of the oddest experiences of my life. Being in the real world once again had made me realise just how quickly you slide into an institution's regime. As I stared at all the food laid out for people to choose, I'd been bewildered – what flavour drink to choose? What sandwich? The lights were so bright, the colours so vivid, the noise so loud, everything seemed exaggerated, and I couldn't believe how much things cost when I looked down at my sandwich and saw £3.50 marked on the packet. I'd got used to earning £12 a week.

'Look at the prices, Ter,' I'd said to him as we sat down.

I was acutely aware of all the people around us as we ate, all getting on with another day when I'd just been released from a life sentence for murder. Would I ever be one of them again? But looking down at my china cup and plate, I realised that the tiny details of normal, ordinary life were becoming mine once again.

Now I was in this wonderful cottage and almost had to pinch myself as I looked at the washing machine, the small Christmas tree in the window and felt carpet under my feet. Everything looked amazing to me – like I'd stepped into a film set full of colour and light. I felt like an alien but each step I took into the real world – eating at the service station, walking into the cottage, sitting down later with Terry to eat and unfolding a napkin before taking my first sip of wine in twenty months – gradually reconnected me to real life.

It must be true, I thought as I watched Terry tuck into lamb stew. I must have been released. This can't all be a dream.

But I didn't feel excited or ecstatic. The only feeling still coursing through me was relief – that I was at last alone with Terry, that we would be seeing Jade tomorrow and that in a couple of days we would finally be going home together. Jade wasn't with us that night because we hadn't known if I would be released or not, but she was due the next morning. I also felt a little uncomfortable at being among strangers and leaving my family behind. But the *Daily Mail* team were respectful and gave us some time together and I reminded myself that I'd agreed to do the interview for practical reasons.

'I had no idea I was going to be released when the judge started talking – I didn't know what was happening,' I told Terry. 'I still can't really believe it.'

'I had no doubts,' he replied. 'There was such a feeling you were going to walk from people in the know that I was ten to one on sure you would.'

'But I keep thinking someone will walk in and tell me it's all been a mistake and I've got to go back to Bullwood Hall.'

'They won't,' Terry said. 'This is it now. You'll never go back there again. We're really here, Ange, and I never thought we'd get this back so soon. I thought it would be years until I saw you again. No social workers, no prison wardens, no solicitors, no police officers, no one to tell us what to do. We've survived.'

I looked at Terry and felt a little more of the tension in my body ease away. He was right. We were here and we were going to survive. All those doubts I'd had in prison were wrong – we were strong enough to cope with this.

'Thank God for those judges,' I told him. 'I'm just so glad we're back together. It's what kept me going every minute of every day.'

Later we climbed the spiral staircase and rediscovered each other. It felt strange after such a long time but wonderful and I knew it was the same for Terry. I thought back to the last night we spent together before the verdict. Where there had been doubt and fear, there was now certainty and hope. I was free. They hadn't broken us.

I was filled with an almost physical ache to see Jade when we woke up the next morning. Terry and I had had a lovely night together but it was as if some vital part of us was missing and I kept jumping every time the phone rang because Steve Grant, who was driving her up from Salisbury, kept calling with progress reports.

My attention was temporarily diverted by the arrival of the newspapers. I couldn't believe how big the story was. Every paper carried it either on their front page or soon after and the headlines screamed at me.

'Mother accused of baby murders is freed' said the *Daily Telegraph*, while the *Daily Mirror* said, 'Hi darling . . . the people at the big building say I can go home'. There were also articles examining whether prosecutions like the one against me would be brought again, and questions about Professor Meadow now that three cases in one year that relied on his evidence had collapsed.

'I can't believe it, Terry,' I said to him as we looked at it all.

'I've been trying to tell you, Ange,' he replied. 'Everyone is behind you. The newspapers and the TV have only given us support. They've been fantastic and look where it's got us. I kept trying to tell you while you were inside but you were so cut off from it all you just couldn't see. This is massive. Your case is massive.'

I looked at him, unable to take it all in. It just seemed so odd that I, Angela Cannings, a mum from Salisbury, was at the centre of this storm. I'd been separated from it all in prison and it would be a long time before I finally realised just how high profile my case had become.

My heart pounded as I looked out the window and saw a car pulling up.

'It's Steve, Steve's here,' I said, my voice trailing off.

I could hardly breathe as I went to stand in front of the doorway to wait for Jade. But as I did so a shadow flitted across my mind.

Will there be a social worker here? I thought as I fought the urge to look over my shoulder.

After four long years I could hardly believe no one would be watching Jade and me together and realised with a shudder that it seemed almost stranger to see her without someone observing us than it did with. I simply couldn't believe social services would leave us alone that easily and, however irrationally, part of me feared they would keep on watching, that they'd never let us go.

Suddenly the porch door opened and, in a blur of blonde hair and smiles, Jade ran towards me.

'Mummy, Mummy,' she said as my arms closed around her.

Happiness rushed through my veins as I held onto her as tightly as I could and relief once again flooded over me. Finally it was real – I was out and I had my daughter in my arms again. The last piece of the jigsaw to make my happiness complete: without a social worker watching us or a prison officer making sure we didn't break the visiting rules. I'd waited for this moment every minute of every day since Matthew's death and now, at last, she was mine again.

'I've come home and I'm not going away again, Jade,' I said, before spinning her round.

My eyes drank in every detail of her as I put her down and she walked over to give Terry a kiss. Her hair, her blue eyes, the gap in her front teeth, the pretty pink T-shirt she was wearing – I could hardly believe she was here.

'Can I look around, Mummy?' she asked and I smiled at her – here was the Jade I knew, nosey as ever.

251

She walked over to the stairs and started to go up as I followed her – determined to climb the steep steps alone. But as we made our slow progress upwards, she put her hand back towards me a couple of times as she faltered on a step and called for me under her breath.

'It's all right, darling,' I told her. 'I'm right here behind you. I won't let you fall.'

Conscious that if we returned home we would be deluged with well-wishers, we decided to go to Penny and Andrew's for the weekend after doing the *Daily Mail* interview and leaving the cottage. Terry was anxious for me to meet them and I was happy to go. I wanted to avoid waiting press, the knocks on the door, the endless phone calls, the real world, because I was still trying to adjust to being free. But part of me was also worried. I still didn't know what to expect of this woman who had formed such a strong bond with both Terry and Jade.

But from the instant I saw Penny I knew we would be friends. Small and with a broad smile, she talked nineteen to the dozen, sizzled with energy, smoked like a chimney and had an infectious laugh that matched the glint in her eye.

'So you're finally here,' she said as we first locked eyes. 'You've done it. Well done.'

Any doubts I had disappeared as we sat down together and started to chat. Penny and Andrew were both so warm, so open, that I couldn't help but like them, and by the time we left their home to make our way back to ours I knew I had made friends for life.

I felt nervous as we drove along familiar streets on our way back to our house in Waters Road. We were going to have just a few hours there before leaving again because we'd booked to go on a week's holiday the following day. But I knew that when we did return I'd have to settle in properly. I'd never lived there – Terry and Jade had moved in after I was arrested. I'd only ever been a ghost mum for just a few hours at a time.

We put on the bare minimum of lights as we stumbled through

the door and the first thing I remember is staring in surprise at the sitting room – it was smaller than I remembered.

'Do you like the laminate I laid?' Terry asked, gesturing to the floor.

'Yes,' I said uncertainly as I looked up towards the kitchen door, waiting for Cindy to rush through and greet me. But suddenly it hit me that she wouldn't, and I walked up to the patio doors to see the cross marking the grave Terry had dug her at the end of the garden.

She's not coming back, Angela, I told myself as sadness washed over me. Prison had robbed me of so many things – even my ability to feel at times – and it was only as I stood at the window looking at her grave that I realised Cindy had gone. I thought I'd feel so happy when I got back home but now all I wanted to do was cry as I tried to imagine life without her. Her absence echoed around me as the realisation pricked that I was not returning to a carbon copy of the life I had once had.

Turning back to the kitchen, I walked in to see my washing machine, my ironing board, my kettle – at last some familiar things – and noticed with surprise how clean everything was. Terry had only ever cooked a few meals before Matthew's death and now here was his home, spick and span.

He's become a proper little housewife, I thought to myself. I never thought I'd see the day.

There are a million tiny readjustments to be made when you come out of an institution and, while you prepare yourself for the obvious, there are countless others for which you cannot prepare. The roaring noise a kettle makes, the softness of carpet under your feet, the dull cold of a steel fork in your mouth after months of plastic cutlery, and as I stood staring at our suitcases, I realised there was another one to be made – try as I might, I couldn't remember what clothes I had.

It had been so long since my belongings were in one place – there were some in Waters Road, some at Mum's and some at Claire's – because my life had been scattered to the winds as I

253

moved from home to home. But even so it felt strange when I realised that I did not even know what clothes I owned, and in the end the cropped trousers, T-shirts, underwear and toiletries I packed for myself in preparation for our holiday came out of my prison bags – just a swimsuit, sarong and a couple of tops were unearthed from my former life.

As I opened drawers to look for my things, I realised Jade's clothes were scattered amidst everything in our bedroom. I knew she only had a small wardrobe in her tiny room but I was still surprised to find so many of her things mixed in with our clothes. There were dresses half on and half off hangers, dollies' clothes scattered around and T-shirts of hers lying on top of my shoes. Jade's clothes – be they clean or dirty – were scattered everywhere. Terry had always told me that he struggled with her clothes and I knew she put her own away, but this was ridiculous.

We'll sort it out when we get back, I thought to myself. There's plenty of time now.

Part of me enjoyed packing, putting back on the familiar coat of wife and mother by doing something for Terry and Jade, but I was also aware that I felt almost stressed by it.

'There's so much to do,' I said to Terry as he appeared in the room. 'We're leaving at three in the morning and I must get all this sorted out.'

Terry looked at me.

'Look, Ange,' he said coldly. 'I've had four holidays with Jade since you were gone and so you don't need to tell me what to do. I'll leave you to it but I'm quite capable you know.'

Upset tightened my throat as he left the room. Why was he lashing out at me? I just wanted to do something normal, start being a mum and a wife again. He'd never touched a case before I went away and now I was back to do it – surely he was pleased?

I sat on the sun lounger and stopped myself from pinching my arm. If I'd done so every time the feeling had washed over me in the past few days, I'd have been black and blue. We were in Tenerife, the sky was blue, the weather warm and Terry and Jade were in the pool together. It should have been perfect but still I felt almost cut off from it all. Just over a week before, I'd been in prison, and I couldn't believe what had happened in such a short space of time. My mind kept racing back to Bullwood Hall as I wondered how Rose was. I'd sent a message to her via an officer at the Court of Appeal but I still hadn't spoken to her and I couldn't put her or prison out of my mind.

'Come in, Mummy,' Jade shouted as she jumped in and out of the water and clambered onto Terry's back.

I was still taking in all the changes in her. She was so different to the little girl I remembered. I think part of me had expected to get back the three-and-a-half-year-old I'd been separated from on the day of Matthew's death. But Jade was now nearly eight and so different to the child I'd left behind when I went into prison. A year in a child's life is worth a decade of an adult's and it was slowly beginning to sink in just how much I'd missed of my daughter.

'No, darling,' I called to her. 'Mummy's going to stay here. I'll just watch you and Daddy.'

'Okay,' she shouted before plunging into the turquoise water once again.

But while I smiled on the outside, deep down I felt uncomfortable, almost scared to join Terry and Jade. Something held me back from going to them. Where I had once worn a bikini and loved to get a tan, I now cowered in a swimming costume and sarong. I felt terribly self-conscious – white, pale and more bulky after working out in the prison gym – and inside I didn't feel any better. Everything was lovely – the beach, the hotel, the sun – but I felt anxious, as if I'd gone from being a pauper to a princess in the blink of an eye. If I was unprepared to be convicted, I was just as unprepared to be released, and found readjusting to life on the outside far harder than I'd ever expected. It's an odd feeling to spend nearly two years imagining yourself somewhere with every fibre of your being and then feeling like you don't quite fit in when you finally get there.

As the days of the holiday had passed, I had begun to feel almost lonely – the one feeling I never thought I'd experience when I got back to Terry and Jade. He and I chatted on as we always had done but he seemed so withdrawn and uneasy. I'd also been shocked to discover that he now drank every night. Soon after arriving, Jade had spotted a poster advertising a children's disco and I'd agreed to take her. But on the first night we went down Terry had said he wouldn't come.

'But why don't we all go together?' I asked him as Jade got herself ready.

'No, no, I'll stay up here,' he replied. 'You take her down and I'll watch some telly. I've looked after her for four years so I'll leave her to you for a night, Ange.'

We left him nursing the first of his evening's brandies, and every night after that was the same – Terry stayed in the room while I took Jade out. I felt hurt. I thought we'd come on holiday to be together and he didn't seem to want to be with us.

There were differences in Jade too. I was surprised, for instance, that she dressed immaculately and did her hair exactly so, amazed that a seven-year-old could get it looking so neat. She seemed so independent and it hurt me a little when I realised how much she didn't need me any more in a practical sense. But her maturity was also contradicted by childish behaviour – she crawled into our bed every night and used a dummy to get to sleep.

'Why is she using it?' I asked Terry one day.

'Well, she started on it when you were in prison,' he replied. 'She was playing with dollies and she saw some and wanted one for them. Then she started using it herself and it's the only thing now that will get her off to sleep. It's a comfort to her.'

I didn't say anything to Terry, aware that I couldn't expect to start laying down the law again after he'd been on his own for so long. Instead I told myself that things like the dummy and Terry's drinking would be sorted out when we got home.

Things will work themselves out once we get back to normal, I told myself as I lay in bed. Maybe Terry's just a bit out of sorts like I am. We all need to get used to each other again. Everything will work its way right. We're back together, that's all that counts.

*

256

We arrived home in the early hours the day before Christmas Eve and flicked on the lights in the house.

'Look at all the presents, Mummy,' Jade exclaimed, her eyes wide with excitement.

Sitting underneath a beautiful tree in the corner of the room was a pile of packages. Decorations and a welcome-home banner covered the ceiling and in the kitchen was all we would need for our first Christmas together – a turkey, ham, vegetables and chocolates. Unknown to us, my dad, Claire, Tina and Steve Grant had rallied round while we were away and got us ready to celebrate.

'Oh,' I said as I stood looking at it all in amazement and felt gratitude rising up inside me. 'I can't believe it. They've made sure we won't want for anything.'

Terry didn't look as pleased.

'Well, your family have managed to come round to the house now that you're out of prison,' he said under his breath as he walked into the kitchen.

I looked at him in confusion as guilt bubbled up inside me. I did not understand why he seemed angry and I'd felt very aware ever since leaving the Court of Appeal of only saying a rushed hello to everyone before leaving to do the newspaper interview. People of course knew we'd had an obligation to fulfil, couldn't afford to say no and wanted to tell our side of the story. But it had nevertheless felt strange.

It was lovely that we were ready for Christmas, but I had mixed feelings about the time of year. Two weeks on from being released, I still didn't feel ecstatic, full of the excitement I'd expected to feel. I still only felt relieved and was worried that after the difficulties with the holiday, Christmas would be another time when we'd be under pressure to be 'happy'. We were still like newborn chicks, feeling our way through being back together again, and I just wanted to get back to normal, boring, everyday life. But I couldn't do anything about the time of year and so I pushed the thoughts out of my mind.

I've never received so many flowers as I did that day and the vases overflowed as more arrived. Two hampers were also sent by well-wishers. One, stuffed with wine, cheese, chocolates, conserves and pickles, was from Richard Branson. Yet again, I was stunned by his kindness. The other was from Philip Schofield and Fern Britton, the presenters of ITV1's *This Morning*, who'd sent a bottle of champagne with chocolates. I felt grateful that people with such busy lives could be so thoughtful.

We'd also received a mountain of post – more than a hundred letters – and later that day Terry and I sat down to go through it. Once again I realised that people we didn't even know had taken the time to write. Envelopes simply addressed 'Angela Cannings, Salisbury' by people anxious to congratulate us had reached their destination. I felt overwhelmed. From the moment I was convicted I had always believed that everyone, everywhere would be against me, and my release hadn't rid me of the feeling. But as I opened more and more letters, I felt filled with relief that there were a lot of people out there who believed in my innocence. With each word from a stranger, confidence grew inside me that one day I might be free of the awful label that had been attached to me.

I picked up a brown envelope and started to open it.

'Don't,' said Terry. 'Don't open it, Ange.'

'Why?' I asked.

'Because it won't be nice,' he told me. 'Leave it. You don't need to read that.'

But I didn't listen as I tore open the envelope to see a single sheet of paper inside. Silently I pulled it out and looked down.

'We'll get you, baby-killer,' it read.

I sucked in my breath as my heart started to hammer. How could I have been so stupid as to believe the whole world would be convinced of my innocence? To some people I was still the same baby-killer bitch I always had been – no matter what the Court of Appeal said. Just as it had done in prison, fear trickled down my spine as I realised that I'd never know who they were or where they were.

Terry grabbed the letter and tore it up, trying to reassure me – as the police did later when he contacted them about it – that there was nothing to worry about. But that single sheet of paper sparked a paranoia it would take months to get over. In the weeks to come, I'd refuse to go into town alone, aware that there might be eyes watching me – never sure of who was a friend, and who was an enemy.

Terry, Jade and I spent Christmas Day alone together, still greedily protective of our time and desperate to savour the moment. But in truth, while there were moments of pure joy – Terry still remembers watching Jade rip open her presents with me beside her, no social worker watching or agreement hanging over our heads – it wasn't the happiest day. We were still too raw, trying to adjust to life together. There had been something to fight for so long – first an arrest, then a trial, then the appeal – and it felt almost strange to face each other once again without having to look over our shoulders. Real life lay before us like a blank canvas and we were slowly edging towards living it.

'I'm glad the day has finished, Ange,' Terry said as we sat together in the evening. 'Ever since Matthew's death Christmas has always reminded me of him and the only thing I see in my head is you walking through the door with Claire at seven thirty in the morning that first one.' He looked at me. 'We've got a long way to go,' he continued softly. 'A long way to get this family back to normality. Jade's so distraught with it all she can't be more than a few feet from us and so she's in between us all the time. And I know there's a distance between the two of you. The bond is still there but you don't know each other any more. But we'll get through this, even though it will be a long road. I love you.'

Anxiety rose up in me. Of course I knew things were different – that Terry was drinking, that Jade went to him instead of me when she got tired or fell over – but from what he was saying it seemed the mountain we had to climb was higher than I'd ever imagined.

'It's going to be hard,' I said to him. 'But we'll get there. Remember, survive or go under.'

My breath formed clouds in front of me as I walked up the path to St Mark's Junior School with Jade and Terry. Term had started a couple of weeks before and I was beginning to enjoy taking her in each morning. After looking forward to the beginning of school, I'd been overwhelmed by nerves on the first day of term. All I could think about was the poisoned letter and, as I'd looked around at the other parents, I'd wondered how many of them felt the same. After all the publicity, I feared everyone knew my face and my concerns seemed justified when I walked into the playground and realised people were looking at me.

'It's good to see you back,' a couple of mums, who I'd known since before the trial, had said.

But otherwise people seemed to hang back and paranoia twisted its knife again within me. As the days had passed, though, more and more parents had started to ask how things were going and I'd slowly realised they hadn't been looking at me with hatred, just uncertainty about how to react to someone just like them who'd been through such extraordinary events. Now I loved walking Jade into school, silently celebrating inside each day that there wasn't a social worker walking six paces behind us, that I was out in the open, free at last.

I'd also enjoyed organising the celebrations for Jade's eighth birthday a couple of weeks into January. We'd taken about ten children to Salisbury cinema to watch *Peter Pan* and I'd revelled in booking the tickets and organising the party bags. Finally, with no one telling me where, when or for how long I could see my child, it felt as though I was becoming a real mummy again and my heart could have burst as I watched Jade sitting with her friends, eating popcorn and enjoying the day.

'Beautiful, isn't she?' Terry smiled as he turned to me.

'Oh yes,' I replied as the lights went down.

'Why do we have to sort my clothes out, Mummy?' Jade asked as we sat on the bed one January night preparing to sort out the wardrobes and drawers in the bedroom I shared with Terry.

'Because this is what mummies do,' I replied as I leaned to open a wardrobe door. 'Every so often they have a clear-out and we need to have one. Look at all these things. You've never worn some of them and others are dirty. We've got to organise things a bit.'

Jade fell silent as we started sorting clothes into piles.

'I wish you'd leave my clothes alone, Mum, and stop messing around with them,' she suddenly snapped.

'Well, they're all over the place and we've got to organise them,' I replied firmly.

'No they're not. I've put them where I know they are.'

'But some of them are in Mummy and Daddy's drawers, Jade, and we've got to sort them out.'

'But I know that's where they are. That's where I put them.'

I fell silent as I carried on pulling clothes out from the wardrobes. There were so many odds and ends all over the place – under Jade's bed, in our room – and I'd decided to gather everything together and put it all in one of our wardrobes because she just didn't have enough space in her own room.

However angry Jade was about the changes, I was determined to get this one tiny thing sorted out. Life was settling back into a normal routine after the holiday and Christmas and I was anxious to start being a proper wife and mother again. To me, that meant looking after Jade and Terry in a practical way and, however much I might only be starting to dip my toe in the water of their emotional distress, I was determined to look after them once again.

'Here you are,' I said, gesturing towards the wardrobe. 'This is where all your things will go now, all together. Look, there are drawers underneath the wardrobe where you can put your socks and pants and things like that, and you can hang things up too. You decide where everything goes, but it's just better for us all if it goes in one place.'

'I don't want my stuff in there,' Jade shrieked angrily. 'I like it where it is.'

I fell silent as she shouted – pushing down my hurt that she could lash out at me with such aggression in her voice. Even though I was the adult, it was hard to be at times when I realised just how different Jade was from the sunny little three-year-old I remembered. Of course, I'd picked up on her anger in prison when she would refuse to talk to me over the phone. But, after just a couple of weeks at home, I was shocked by its strength.

Calm down, I told myself as I carried on sorting. You've only just got out and you're going into Jade's stuff to organise it. She's going to find it hard. You've both got a lot of readjusting to do.

Silently I carried on separating Jade's clothes from mine and Terry's – trying to create order in a world turned upside down by the authorities, the very people who were meant to protect it.

Panic rose in me as we walked towards the Court of Appeal. It was 19 January 2004 and Terry and I were back in London to hear the judgement in my case. When anyone has a conviction quashed, the judges explain their reasons and today I was going to find out why they had decided to free me.

Rushes of fear kept spiking up inside me as I irrationally wondered if the judges would say they had made a mistake and I must return to prison. But I forced myself to stay calm as we walked into the court past waiting photographers and cameramen and I felt Terry's reassuring bulk beside me.

There were lots of familiar faces milling around as we waited to go into court. John Sweeney and other journalists I knew, John Batt, Sally Clark's adviser, who had advised Bill and attended parts of my trial, and of course Bill and Jacqui. But I tried to block them all out as we filed into court and took our places on long wooden seats like those I had looked down at from the dock just weeks before.

Hush descended as the three judges who had overseen my appeal hearing walked into court, bowed their heads and took their places at the bench.

Maybe they'll say they were wrong, that you've got to go back to prison because it's all been a mistake, the voice once again screamed in my head.

But everything fell away as Terry and I were handed a copy of the judgement and I felt its thickness in my hands. Here in black and white were the reasons why I was free, why my convictions for murdering Jason and Matthew were unsafe – but would the judges exonerate me or see my freedom as a technicality? I knew that within the academic confines of legal judgements, those who made them often made their feelings clear about the person they were dealing with. I held my breath as Lord Justice Judge started to read.

He started by saying that my case was unusual because the central issue was whether my children had been killed, whether a crime had been committed at all.

Relief flooded over me as he said those words.

They've finally listened to us, I thought to myself as he moved on to talk about the two possible approaches to three infant deaths in one family – think dirty or keep an open mind.

The first approach, he said, amounted to believing that lightning did not strike three times in a single place and almost any other piece of evidence – such as a mother not behaving in a supposedly 'normal' way – could be used against someone. The second – keeping an open mind – was the correct one, he added, because, as many experts believed, the lack of a currently known natural cause did not equal murder.

Again, I could only feel relief as I listened to him talk. So much of what he was saying reflected what we had said all along – these different approaches were just as Terry had described, they'd thought dirty in my case and I'd been convicted from the moment we lost Matthew.

I couldn't take my eyes off Lord Justice Judge as he read in slow and even tones that 'there was no direct evidence and very little indirect evidence' to suggest my children were the victims of crime, before going on to mention the cases of Sally Clark and Trupti Patel.

My heart slowed as the learned judge described Professor Meadow as 'an expert witness of great distinction' whose 'flawed evidence' at Sally Clark's trial had undermined his high reputation and, 'also demonstrates not only that in this particular field, which we summarise as "cot deaths", even the most distinguished expert can be wrong, but also provides a salutary warning against the possible dangers of an over-dogmatic expert approach.'

Emotion swept over me once again as Lord Justice Judge referred to Professor Golding's evidence at my trial about the fashion among some paediatricians that more than one SIDS equalled deliberate killing.

'If that is the fashion, it must now cease,' he said bluntly.

As the minutes ticked by it seemed that every assumption that had haunted my case from the start and 'proved' me guilty in so many eyes was being dismantled before me as I sat clutching the judgement. The attitude everyone had had towards us, the police, CPS, doctors and lawyers, and their assumption of guilt, which had forced me to prove my innocence – all was stripped away as page after page was turned.

The judges made it clear that constant advances in the understanding of infant deaths lay at the heart of my case – that cot death was surrounded by 'mystery' and the cause of some deaths which were now unexplained might one day be found. There was a 'realistic possibility', they said, of a genetic cause for the deaths of Gemma, Jason and Matthew because: 'What may be unexplained today may be perfectly well understood tomorrow.'

I became more and more transfixed as every aspect of the case against me was systematically examined – the expert evidence, the disagreements at my trial, the lives and deaths of my children – until the judges concluded their overview with the words: 'Our study of the details so far has not demonstrated any single piece of evidence conclusive of guilt.'

Relief washed over me as I heard those words – finally the world knew there was no evidence against me other than disputed test results and conflicting medical theory. The Crown's case, as the judges said, had depended on the pattern of deaths and breathing problems in my children – a pattern, they went on to say, which did not exist as they highlighted its inconsistencies – Jade had survived, Gemma had not had breathing problems before she died, Jason's had coincided with the arrival of the health visitor and Matthew had not had an ALTE at all – I'd called for help because I'd panicked when he was simply being sick.

And after reviewing the new evidence about multiple cot deaths they simply added, 'What is abundantly clear is that in our present state of knowledge, it does not necessarily follow that three sudden unexplained infant deaths in the same family lead to the inexorable conclusion that they must have resulted from the deliberate infliction of harm.'

Lord Justice Judge added: 'While the speed of research is gratifying, one unintended consequence is that it sometimes creates doubt about what were once thought to be certainties. And what was confidently presented to the jury as virtually overwhelming expert evidence providing the necessary proof that Jason and Matthew's death resulted from the infliction of deliberate harm, should now be approached with a degree of healthy scepticism.'

The Crown's case – which hinged on the rarity of three baby deaths in one family – had been undermined by 'significant and persuasive fresh evidence' that was not before the jury.

As I sat in the courtroom and the minutes turned to hours, I felt increasingly moved. This was no dry legal document but one written in a language I could understand and mentioning each of my children, Gemma, Jason, Jade and Matthew, by name. They were no longer exhibits, objects to be prodded as the ultimate proof of my guilt. As page after page was read out, I felt as if some of the horror of my trial was washed away as my children became individuals again and, within the formal confines of their judgement, the judges seemed to reach out to Terry and me and acknowledge our family tragedy. I felt touched by their humanity.

'The appellant invited us to consider a number of other facts which, again in a common-sense way, were relevant,' Justice Judge said as the clock hands ticked towards their third hour and I almost wanted to cry out with relief that someone had at last mentioned common sense – those vital words. 'No one doubted that each of these babies was a wanted child, blessed with love, affection and care from both parents. There was no suggestion of ill temper, inappropriate behaviour, ill-treatment, let alone violence, at any time with any of the four children. Although three of them died very young, Jade did not. Of itself, when four infants are said to have been deliberately harmed, that is an unusual feature. It is distinct from the additional fact that if it was indeed right that the appellant had tried to kill each of her four children

265

there was an absence of the slightest evidence of physical inter-ference which might support the allegation that she had deliberately harmed them.'

Emotion once again rose up inside me as the judges spoke about the notion that I had known I might try and kill my chil-dren – flying in the face of evidence from both the 'distinguished' psychiatrist who had examined me and my family and outsiders 'about the love and care' I bestowed on my children.

I cannot describe how it felt to hear those words. It still fills me with gratitude that someone in authority acknowledged I was a good mother, who had loved her children. As Lord Justice Judge read those passages, I felt some of the dignity that had been stripped by every other figure in authority – police, social workers, doctors, lawyers and the prison system – returned to me. They did not make up for everything, nothing could, but the humanity and kindness those judges showed, and the intelligence they applied to the whole issue of multiple cot deaths, humbled me.

As we turned towards the last page of the judgement, I held my breath once again as Lord Justice Judge said he and his colleagues were satisfied the deaths of my children in the future may come to be regarded as natural, due to a possibly genetic cause.

'"Never say never" is a phrase which we have heard in many different contexts from expert witnesses,' he said gravely. 'That does not normally provide a basis for rejecting the expert evi-dence, or indeed conjuring up fanciful doubts about the possible impact of later research. With unexplained infant deaths, how-ever, as this judgement has demonstrated, in many important respects we are still at the frontiers of knowledge.'

I sat silently, little prepared for his next words – which would send waves through the legal and medical worlds that are still being felt today.

'In cases like the present, if the outcome of the trial depends exclusively or almost exclusively on a serious disagreement between distinguished and reputable experts, it will often be unwise, and therefore unsafe, to proceed,' Lord Justice Judge told the court. 'In expressing ourselves in this way we recognise that

266

justice may not be done in a small number of cases where in truth a mother has deliberately killed her baby without leaving any identifiable evidence of the crime. 'That is an undesirable result, which however avoids a worse one. If murder cannot be proved, the conviction cannot be safe. In a criminal case, it is simply not enough to establish even a high probability of guilt.

'Unless we are sure of guilt, the dreadful possibility always remains that a mother, already brutally scarred by the unexplained death, or deaths of her babies, may find herself in prison for life for killing them when she should not be there at all.

'In our community, and in any civilised community, that is abhorrent.'

I had little idea of the impact of those words as I walked out of court with Terry. The judgement in my case had made legal history – bringing to an end cases like mine that rested solely on evidence from medical experts who were unable to agree on a cause of death. Mothers like me, left facing a black hole of grief when their children died and no one could explain to them why, would no longer be asked to explain the impossible or face prosecution unless there was proper evidence against them.

The judgement echoed into the highest corridors of power. As Terry and I walked through the echoing Court of Appeal, officials in the office of the Attorney General Lord Goldsmith – the man in charge of the Crown Prosecution Service – were preparing to launch a review of 297 convictions of parents for killing a child under two during the previous decade. The hunt for possible miscarriages of justice was the biggest of its kind in legal history. The following day Harriet Harman, the then solicitor general, announced the review would extend to cases in the family courts in which parents had had children taken away on the basis of contentious theories – finally a ray of hope for all those families accused beneath a shroud of secrecy. Nearly 30,000 cases would eventually be looked at.

But I knew nothing of all this as I stood with Terry. All I could feel was relief that finally the system that had wrongly convicted me had exonerated me. I hadn't slipped through the net on a technicality – the judges had said in the strongest possible terms that the whole premise of the case against me had been bad from the start, that I was a good mother to my children.

'Justice has been done,' Terry said softly. 'For the first time someone in authority has recognised you did nothing wrong, that we lost three children, not just objects they could drag into court when they felt like it.'

'I know,' I said as I took Terry's hand.

Bill, Jacqui and Jo Briggs walked towards us.

'In legal terms, Angela, this is a very important day,' Jo told me. 'This is a landmark judgement and it will be used in courts up and down the country for a long time to come.'

With Bill and Jacqui beside us, we walked out to the waiting crowd of media.

CHAPTER SIXTEEN

'Is that the last one, Ange?' Terry shouted as he carried a box towards a van parked outside our house.

'Yep,' I called, as I looked around our empty living room. 'There's just a couple of small ones but we can take them with us in the car.'

It was a hot Sunday in late April and we were leaving Salisbury for a new life in Cornwall. Stephen, who was working as a removal man at the time, was helping us, and as I looked out the window I saw Terry wave him off. We would follow in the car with the newest addition to our family – an English setter puppy called Shadow.

This is it, girl, I thought to myself as I looked around. The start of a new life, a chance to move on from the past and build a new future together.

'Can we go round the house and look round once more before we go, Mummy?' Jade said as she came rushing into the room which just a few hours before had been filled to bursting with the neatly labelled boxes I'd spent days organising.

'We'll just have a quick look because we need to get going,' I told her. 'Stephen's left and we've got to keep up with him.'

Jade disappeared from the room with the puppy at her heels. She and Shadow had become firm friends and his arrival had been an important step towards normal family life for us.

The move was another. In the four months since my release I'd

269

become more and more convinced that if Terry and I didn't leave Salisbury we would never survive. The city that had once felt like home now seemed like a prison of a different kind as I walked the streets. I still felt uncertain among people, as if I would never know who was friend or foe, and there were constant echoes of the past – the magistrates court in the middle of the city centre, the sign for the A&E department of the hospital when I went for a check-up on my Bell's Palsy, the police station at the end of the road where Claire lived – buildings once part of the safe life we'd had before losing Matthew were now almost threatening. Sometimes it felt like we would never be able to move on – particularly on days like the one soon after the appeal judgement when Rob Findlay had dropped round to our house to return the property the police had taken for the investigation.

Terry was out when he arrived and handed me a plastic crate and four black bin liners – each bearing a tag explaining what it was, who had 'seized' it and on what date. Those bags contained everything from a half-full bottle of medicine to a roll of cling film, thermometers and rubbish from our kitchen bin. He also brought Matthew's dismantled cot with him. Nausea washed over me when, more than four years after my son's death, I saw the mundane details of our life, which had been taken as evidence against me.

I'd thought constantly about Matthew since coming home. Every so often, as I did the housework or walked to pick up Jade from school, I'd think back to our home in Waterloo Road and wonder what life would have been like if we were still there, the four of us. Our son would have been approaching five, and sadness filled me that he wasn't with us and Jade was on her own. At times thoughts flitted across my mind about having another baby – but I knew it was my heart talking, not my head. Even if Terry agreed to try for another child, I had been sterilised.

'Will you be all right with this on your own?' Rob Findlay asked as I signed for the property and fought the urge to scream.

'I'll be fine,' I said coldly. 'Did you find any evidence in all of that?'

He said nothing as he walked away.

Even after my name had been cleared by the Court of Appeal, the police had stuck to the rules. It sickened me that they hadn't bothered to ask me whether I might want these things returned. Four years on, would any mother want to pull her dead child's dirty nappies out of a bag?

The situation with friends and family was another reason why I wanted to leave Salisbury. I had been aware of tensions throughout my time in prison but it was only when I got out that I realised how strained some relationships had become and how let down Terry felt by many people.

'The day you were convicted the world and its mother descended on my house – family, friends and everybody,' he'd told me. 'But soon after that no one knocked on the door and the phone didn't ring. Gradually everyone left us behind. There were days when I didn't even speak to an adult and I'd find myself going up to the school early hoping to bump into one of the mums just for a chat. It was as if people didn't know how to react to us or what to do with us.

'Family would go and see you miles away in prison but they wouldn't nip round here. People we've known for years never came near me if I saw them in town.'

Although I realised that everyone had done their best to help, I too felt let down by what had happened. Desperate to support Terry, we had agreed we should have some time alone when I was released. After seeing most of my family over Christmas or into the New Year, I'd rung people to ask for some space to readjust. But I felt increasingly stuck in the middle of all the bad feeling. Terry still wanted to see the people he believed had been loyal to him, but made his feelings clear about those he felt had abandoned him. Looking back, I know some of those close to me felt hurt that I withdrew from them after all they'd done and the pain they themselves had suffered. It wasn't just me who had endured a terrible ordeal and after all their support I fear they felt rejected. Some say now it was as if I was still in prison because they saw so little of me. But all I can say in my defence is that I was trying to negotiate a new world in which there were no rules and mistakes were made on both sides. In time I hope we will repair them.

Some people, though, like my father, made their anger very clear and I had received a letter from him in late January saying that he wished to cut off all contact with me because I had not been in touch enough. We had had our rucks in the past but that letter felt like a knife through my heart. My relationship with him has yet to be repaired.

Terry also wanted to leave Salisbury, and had decided as much while I was in prison, so it was never a question of if, but where we would go. Using the money we had earned from the interview after my release, we had been to the Midlands before looking west. We'd been on holiday to Devon and Cornwall in the past and had some good friends living in Saltash, just inside the Cornish border, where we'd found a three-bedroom semi-detached house on a small estate. Terry and I were still unable to think about returning to work and money was something he worried about constantly. The three of us were living on £614 a month income support and didn't have another penny to our names. After using the interview money to put down a deposit, our small mortgage was going to be paid by our benefits. We both still struggled with living off the state but told ourselves we'd worked all our lives and needed time to recover before going back.

The only real worry I'd had about the move had been Jade. But I had underestimated both her sunny nature and the fact that she could be wise beyond her years.

'How would you feel if we moved house?' I had asked her one night as I lay with her while settling her down to sleep.

'Mummy, you've never lived in this house and I think it would be good if we went together, the three of us. This has been a sad house for us.'

And so we'd packed up all our belongings, had a good-luck drink with Mum and Brian the night before, and were now heading off. A rush of nerves washed over me as I pulled the door closed for the final time and turned to see our neighbours coming out to wish us well.

'We'll miss you, you've been a credit to this road,' they told us as I said goodbye and squeezed into the front seat between buckets and brushes.

'Are we ready then?' Terry asked as he started up the engine and we moved off. I looked at the sunny road ahead and felt hope burst inside me about the future lying in front of us.

It got hotter and hotter as we sped westwards.

'I can't believe this weather – it's only April,' Terry said as he wiped his forehead.

'Why's it so hot?' Jade called from the back seat where she sat with Shadow.

'Well, they have different weather in Cornwall,' Terry said solemnly.

'Really, Daddy?' Jade replied, her voice rising in excitement.

'Yes,' he grinned. 'We're getting closer now. Can't you feel it getting hotter?'

I smiled at them both – Jade convinced she was moving to a different country and Terry gently teasing her. The move was like an adventure to her and I hoped we'd have many more moments of fun. But as I looked at Terry staring at the road, I thought about how changed he was from the man I'd fallen in love with all those years before. While I'd known he was finding it difficult to cope when I was in prison, it wasn't until I was living with him again that I realised the extent of his problems. Four months on from being released, things were still far from easy between us.

Gradually I had realised how naïve I'd been about what would greet me when I came out. Terry was no longer the confident, smiling, generous, hard-working people-pleaser I'd known. He had been replaced by a shadow – nervous, preoccupied with his anger and so obviously vulnerable it saddened me deeply.

I clung onto the warmth between him and me on the night of my release – it had been real enough – and of course all the happy years we had had before Matthew's death. But it was hard at times because Terry seemed so uneasy, and while I desperately wanted to get back to normal life, there were moments when I felt scared we never would – where was our

273

familiar closeness, the jokes we once shared, our physical ease with each other? Terry may have come off the antidepressants in summer 2002 but I felt sure he was still in the grip of that awful illness.

My first trip to see Rose at Bullwood Hall had been a stark step towards understanding just what life had been like for him and Jade while I was away. Waiting to receive the visiting order in the post, the six-hour return car journey, the hut in the prison grounds where relatives were herded, the body searches and checks by sniffer dogs, the lockers where we put our belongings – it was a daunting process. As we waited I realised that lots of relatives seemed completely unfazed by the cold atmosphere, barbed wire and dogs, because prison was part of their family existence. But my relatives had never known anything like it and it must have been shocking for them.

Getting into the prison was only the beginning because you then had to contend with all the feelings that rushed over you as you saw the person you loved. Guilt, awkwardness, sadness, anger, concern – I felt them all during that visit with Rose.

I'd worried about her ever since my release and was so relieved to see her. But just as I had been while I was the one on the inside, I was all too aware of how short our time was together – and this time I would be the one leaving. As much as I wanted to make the most of every minute, it was hard as kindly officers kept coming up to congratulate me and the girls behind the servery hatch screamed with excitement when they saw me. It was good though to see Terry and Rose meet properly at last and, after the first hour, he left us together.

'So that jacket did end up being lucky in the end,' she smiled before launching into a stream of questions. 'What's it like at home? How are things? How are you coping? How is Jade?'

'Oh you know, we're taking it a day at a time,' I replied. 'So how are you, Rose?'

She paused, before looking at me sadly. 'I am struggling a bit without you,' she said. 'It's hard.'

'But I'll still be there for you – we can talk on the phone and I'll visit as much as I can,' I told her as we hugged each other.

But I could see that my words had done nothing to ease the pain on her face as we stood up to leave. I forced myself to keep smiling, knowing only too well that in a few minutes Rose would walk back to her cell feeling utterly alone. She didn't need me making it worse with tears. But I couldn't stop them as I walked out of the visiting hall and guilt filled me that I was abandoning her.

And it was then, as I stood waiting to leave that I realised for the first time how Terry and Jade – and all my family and friends – must have felt. They might have been on the outside but they were in their own kind of prison without me.

We arrived in Saltash at about 2 p.m. We'd felt immediately at home in the small town when we'd looked at houses there. The one we had finally bought though was more of an unknown quantity because we'd spent just twenty minutes looking at it in the semi-darkness. But it ticked all the right boxes – there were two decent bedrooms, a bathroom and a tiny third bedroom, while downstairs was a dining and living room in one, with a kitchen running off it. It was small but at least it would be ours. What had convinced us was a balcony at the back of the house overlooking a wooded hill with a small castle perched on top. After being locked in for so long, I only had to walk out onto it and look at the space to feel reassured that it was all real, that I was free.

Now we were back again – but this time the house was our home. Terry slipped the key into the lock before pushing open the front door and walking inside.

'Look at how they've left it,' he exclaimed as he walked into the living room. The house was spotless, the people who had moved out must have spent a week cleaning it.

'I'll start unloading the van with Stephen,' he said as he walked back outside and up the grass slope that led down to our front door.

Alone inside the house, I looked around. I could hardly believe we were really here, that we'd left Salisbury behind, and cautious excitement filled me about what our future held. I didn't think the damage would be repaired overnight but this was a new start for us, a chance to recapture the happy life that had once been ours before the damage wreaked by the authorities.

They're not going to beat us, I thought as I climbed the stairs. Think of all those other families out there who'll never get the chance we have now – who'll never be back together. We can't wallow in what's happened to us. It's affected us all in different ways but we'll get there.

Terry seemed to share my determination – he'd stopped drinking at the end of January and had been looking forward to the move.

'It will be a way of leaving the sadness behind,' he'd said. 'It will be a good move for us.'

Now I stood in the living room unpacking boxes.

'Mummy, can I go outside and play?' Jade said breathlessly as she ran into the room. 'Some of the children from the other houses are out there.'

'Of course you can,' I said as she ran out.

I smiled as I watched her go and felt hope burst inside me that for her sake too we would be able to repair all the damage in time. The distance I had felt with Jade almost as soon as I left prison was still there – it had taken until March for her to finally let me take her to school without Terry and she still ran into his arms when she wanted comfort. He too was physically distant from me – after our first night together he seemed to find it hard to touch me and I felt so emotionally separated from them both in a way – as if I had been suspended in aspic all the time I was in prison dreaming of them, while they had been living their lives and moving on without me. But now we could begin again.

'Just look at that view, Ange,' Terry said later as we stood in the fading sun on the balcony.

'It's fantastic,' I told him as I stared out at the fields – freedom was surrounding us.

*

276

'Come on, Jade,' I shouted. 'We're going to miss the bus if you don't hurry up.'

It was 22 May – my forty-first birthday – and I was taking Jade and her friend Jamie into Plymouth for the afternoon.

I was so looking forward to it. We'd been in Saltash a month and Jade seemed to have settled in well. She'd made friends, started at school and that tiny bit of normality was holding life together for us day by day. We were still feeling our way, getting to know the area and meeting people, but I relished walking Jade to and from school each day with Shadow at my side as she chatted about what she'd done.

I was also increasingly aware, though, of problems we had not left behind in Salisbury. What I had seen in the first six months of freedom had frightened me and it was only now beginning to dawn on me just how much work was needed to repair my relationship with my husband and daughter.

In those first few weeks after my release Jade had seemed overjoyed that I was back but, as she got more used to me being home, tiny things had begun to hint at far deeper troubles.

After 7 p.m. at night it would seem as if I almost didn't exist when Jade, tired and vulnerable, would always turn to Terry. She also wanted constant attention and often came into our bed after one of us had taken her up to settle her down to sleep in her own because she couldn't drop off alone. For the first two weeks we'd been in Saltash she had refused to go into her bedroom at all.

'I can't go in there. I just don't want to go in there,' was all she would tell me.

'Why, Jade?' I asked. 'That's your bedroom. It's your room now. That's why we came, so that you could have a bigger room.'

But she would fall silent – unable to explain why she couldn't be apart from us.

There were other things too. While Jade could be uninterested in me at times, she could also be anything from clingy to argumentatively aggressive like a teenager.

'Should you really be putting that on?' I would ask as she got ready to go out to play with friends at the weekend and put on a bit of make-up.

'Course, Mum,' she'd reply angrily. 'Everyone else wears it.'

She was right, her other friends did wear make-up, but in Salisbury Jade had mixed with girls at least two, if not three, years older than her. She might have still played with dolls but she also put nail varnish on at times and would refuse to take it off on a Sunday night when I asked her to because school started the next day. I thought she was too young for these things but it was difficult to tell her no when she'd been allowed to do it during all the time I'd been away. I told myself that I must just go with the flow for a while and accept that things wouldn't change overnight.

Once she did start sleeping in her bedroom, which didn't happen every night by any means, I had also noticed that everything had to be exactly in its place – woe betide me if I went in to clean while she was at school and moved anything.

'You've been in my room,' Jade would say accusingly. 'You've moved Rosie and Jim from my bed.'

'Well, I had to move the dollies when I went in to change the bed,' I'd tell her. 'That's what mummies do.'

'But you didn't put them back in the right place, Mum,' she'd reply. 'That's where I put them and that's where they've got to be.'

I found it unnerving – how exact she was about her room, and still is today – but the issue of my care for her and our home was becoming more and more of a battleground. It was as if she felt that I was moving in on her space. She wanted to cook, dust, hoover, wash up and even iron.

'Jade, you don't need to do that,' I said one day as she got the hoover out. 'It's lovely that you want to help out but I can do it while you're at school.'

'But I always did it when I was with Daddy,' she told me, annoyance plain in her voice.

'Well, honey, it was very good what you did do but now I am home and this is what mummies do. And some things mummies do so that children don't have to.'

I was trying to reassure her, to convince her to become a child again and leave adult things behind, but every time I did it just seemed to put up another barrier between us.

I often had the same feeling with Terry – that I had moved in on his space and he almost resented my presence.

'I don't like her doing all these things,' I told him one night. 'Apart from anything else, there's a safety element to it. She's only eight. She shouldn't be ironing or making cups of tea. It's like when they're little and you put things out of reach.'

'It makes her happy,' he replied. 'It's what she's got used to. Let her do a bit, Ange. Look at all she's been through. She's different from other kids.'

So part of me hung back – as much to meet my own needs as Jade's. At the beginning for instance, I found having her in our bed comforting and I was happy to go along with it. Every night I'd spent away had been filled with longing for Terry and Jade and now, selfishly, I wanted to know they were both there beside me. Sometimes I would wake up early and watch them asleep, drinking the moment in – Jade, pretty as a picture in her pyjamas as she lay sprawled across the bed, her face soft with sleep, her father on the other side – a strong, solid presence protecting us all.

But as time wore on it worried me more and more and, as we got to know each other again – Jade's shoe size, the fact that she didn't like Penguin chocolate biscuits, the names of her school friends – her obvious confusion about the situation became more and more apparent.

'I have this big knot inside me,' she told me one day.

'Well, I'm here now to help you untie it,' I replied. 'I was in prison for so long and I wanted to be with you every minute. But now I'm home.'

'I know, Mummy, and I missed you too and I do want you here.'

But no sooner had we had the conversation than something else would happen to push us apart again. Looking back, I wonder if I tried too hard to treat Jade as an eight-year-old and forgot the four years with me she'd lost. I found her childish traits, such as her use of the dummy, hard to deal with – especially when it contrasted with behaviour that made her seem old before her time.

I struggled to know how to deal with it but I too was divided. While part of me felt guilty about the effects of the past four years on Jade and I had to stop myself from stifling her with love, I was also strict with her. I'd been brought up to respect certain values and felt I had done a good job with her until we were parted. But there were aspects of her behaviour, such as shouting and a couple of occasions when she'd hit me, which I found very difficult to cope with. I'd been brought up not to backchat my parents and I found her aggression shocking. As time wore on, I realised just how angry an eight-year-old can be.

'You ugly pig, you're horrible to me, you shout all the time,' she would scream if I even slightly raised my voice.

It was as if Jade had lost a piece of herself and was blaming me. But while I tried to remain calm, there were times when I shouted back. I didn't expect things to be perfect but as the months passed she seemed more and more like a coiled spring – ready to leap at me with the slightest provocation. Sunny one minute and aggressive the next, Jade could sound far more mature than her eight years and I think I forgot at times that she was just a child.

The sun shone as we made our way towards Plymouth market. It was about 4.30 p.m. and we'd been shopping and had a burger. Now all we had to do was find something for Jamie to spend his last pound on before getting back on the bus home.

But I could see Jade was getting increasingly impatient as we waited in the sun while he found a joke stall and started inspecting it.

'How long is he going to be?' she suddenly whined. 'I want to go home now.'

'I know,' I replied. 'But Jamie just wants to spend his last bit of money and then we can get on the bus. You know what boys are like, Jadey.'

'Well, I wish he'd hurry up.'

Jamie looked round, his face concerned, as he heard Jade's complaints.

'Don't worry about it, love,' I said to him. 'You carry on.'

Jade fell silent for a moment before piping up again. 'I want to go now,' she said, her voice rising and hardening with anger. 'And I want Daddy. I want him now.'

'Well to get to him we need to get on the bus,' I replied. 'It won't be a minute before we go.'

But as we stood and waited, I could see her getting angrier and angrier.

'I want to go now,' she shouted as people started staring at us.

'Don't do this to me, Jade,' I snapped at her. 'Not in front of everyone. Calm down. We'll go in a minute. You've just got to wait for Jamie.'

'Well, can't he hurry up?'

Aware of Jade's rage, Jamie quickly bought something and we started to walk to the bus. But by now she was in a complete state – moaning and whining at me more and more loudly as I felt my embarrassment rise at her bad behaviour.

'I'm so hot, Mum, and I'm tired and I want to get on the bus.'

'Well to get to the bus we've got to walk there,' I replied in a low voice.

Her behaviour ran counter to every lesson I had been taught as a child – respect for your elders, good behaviour in public, don't let the side down in front of strangers. I couldn't believe she was throwing such a tantrum.

I turned to Jamie and tried to ignore Jade as she trailed behind us.

'So what did you get in the end?' I asked him, trying to keep my voice light before adding, 'Don't worry about Jade. She'll be okay.'

But I could see he was getting worried as her moans turned into shouts.

Suddenly Jade appeared at my side as we walked onto a road crossing and dug her fingers into my arms as she hung onto me. I struggled to keep hold of several shopping bags as she was dragged behind me.

'Stop ignoring me, Mummy, stop ignoring me,' she screamed. 'You're just taking Jamie's side.'

'I am not, Jade,' I told her. 'I am trying to get us to the bus and I want you to calm down.'

I carried on walking. I had never been in a situation like that before and had no idea how to react. Desperate to avoid an argument in public, I decided not to annoy Jade even more by responding. But her fingers dug deeper into my arm as she started crying and shrieking, before her hand flew up and caught me in the mouth as she hit me.

'Jade,' I hissed. 'That really hurt. Whatever the problem is we can sort it out when we get home. Don't worry. We'll be there soon and we can talk about it then.'

Anger jostled with upset inside me. I could see what a state she was in but didn't know what to do. As tears streamed down Jade's face we carried on walking and, by the time we reached the bus stop, she was oblivious to everybody. It was as if a red mist had descended on her and she was unaware of anything else. Shouting and crying, she grabbed at the bags I was carrying.

'You're being nasty to me, you're being horrible to me,' she screamed. 'I want Daddy.'

'Jade, please not now,' I said in a low voice. 'Everyone is looking at us.'

'Is she all right?' a woman I did not know asked me.

'Yeah,' I said. 'She's just having a bad day.'

But even the arrival of the bus did nothing to calm Jade down and she carried on crying as we got on.

'I want Daddy,' she sobbed as everyone looked at her.

Sadness welled up inside me to see her so distraught and I wondered desperately what I could do to soothe her pain. Tentatively, I put my arm around her. As if by magic, she cuddled into me and the spell seemed to be broken.

'I'm so sorry, Mummy,' she said. 'I'm really sorry.'

I didn't know what to say. Part of me couldn't believe that Jade was eight and had just behaved so badly, while another piece of me wanted to cry at the rage and pain pouring out of her. I felt torn between reassuring her and the sense that I might then indulge her bad behaviour.

'It's okay,' I said as I hugged her.

When the bus drew to a stop, Jade ran off it and into the house without a backward glance.

'Are you all right?' I asked Jamie as we stood on the pavement.

'Yes,' he said quietly before turning to go back home.

I walked into the house to find Jade, face tear-stained and red, sitting with Terry. Sighing, I sat down in front of them and started to tell him about what had happened – showing him the bruises on my arm and the lump on my lip where I'd been hit. Tears started sliding down my face as I spoke. I couldn't contain them any more, I felt heartbroken at seeing how upset Jade was, shocked at her bad behaviour and ashamed of my confusion about how to deal with it. Five months after coming out of prison I felt almost defeated by her behaviour that day. It seemed as if she hated me, that I could do nothing to soothe her distress and I wondered if we would ever climb the mountain between us.

'I'm so sorry, Mummy,' Jade said as she saw my tears and rushed towards me. 'I didn't mean to do it.'

Of course you'll get there, I scolded myself silently as she hugged me. Give it time. Just be patient.

Throughout the months that we started trying to build an ordinary family life together there was one extraordinary aspect to it that I had been unprepared for. The media attention my case had attracted was ferocious and I had a clear choice – whether to retreat into silence or cooperate with it. I chose the latter. As the months of 2004 rolled by the case review which had followed my appeal judgement garnered headline after headline and I was often asked to do interviews. Just as Terry had been before me, I gradually became the public face of a problem that had long lain hidden in the family courts and I felt duty bound to do what I could to help. Interviews with radio, television, newspapers and magazines became a regular part of life and, while I found it daunting at first, I slowly began to gain confidence. I know some people thought I should have stayed quiet and disappeared. But both Terry and I felt a wrong had been done and, while we had the platform to campaign, we should do it.

I had had little understanding of what other parents accused of abuse had been through in the family courts when I was first released. But gradually, with Terry's help, I had learned more about it and was appalled by what I discovered. I joined others at a demonstration outside the High Court when two families tried – and failed – to overturn family court judgements which had taken their children from them, and I did whatever I could to highlight the hidden problem. I felt passionately about it. Of course there were, and are, many parents who abuse their children. I have never sought to deny that. But I met family after family whose rage at the injustice done to them burned out of them and I realised there were others who had had their children taken from them with little other evidence than the 'think dirty' theories that had been used against me. It's hard to put into words but having met many mothers and fathers and heard stories so similar to ours, I became increasingly familiar with the pain etched onto their features, which echoed ours.

It was a battle being fought in the highest corridors of power and I often wondered what I, a Tesco girl and mother, could do to help. As the year went on both sides in the argument became increasingly entrenched. While campaigners argued the biggest miscarriage of justice of all time was being brushed under the carpet, the medical profession warned the pendulum might swing too far – that children at risk of abuse would not be protected because medics were too fearful of reporting concerns after the media witch-hunt focused on Professor Meadow. Doctors wrote blistering attacks on the media coverage while others warned abusive parents might go unpunished. At times it seemed as if there was a real reluctance to admit there might have been a problem with wrongful accusations. A BBC report revealed that 74 per cent of local authorities they'd surveyed would not be reopening any family court cases after the review ordered by Harriet Harman.

'We must do what we can to help,' Terry told me when it all felt like too much. 'I've met grannies, mums and dads, seen pain on their faces, and I feel it is our duty to help people who can't speak for themselves. They haven't got a voice. We could so easily have been dragged into the family court, lost Jade and we wouldn't have had one. But we have and we can use it to highlight the problem. I am not judge and jury when I meet these people, but I've met enough to know many are sad and many are truthful.'

The media were nothing but supportive of us. Terry had built relationships with many journalists while I was in prison and gradually I began to as well. I can honestly say every one was kind and supportive and at a time when the press is so often criticised, I can safely say that I have only had good experiences.

Over the past two years we've been interviewed by Richard and Judy, John Humphrys for Radio 4's *On the Ropes*, Jenni Murray for *Woman's Hour*, John Suchet for ITN, the *Sun*, the *Daily Mail*, the *Daily Mirror*, the *Sunday Times*, the *Sunday Telegraph*, the *Observer*, *Marie Claire*, *Closer*, *Best* and been on the GMTV sofa numerous times.

But in some ways the media attention drove another wedge between Terry and me. Where once media work had been a big part of his life and journalists had rung to speak to him, they now said a quick hello before asking for me. The one project we were both committed to was working with the BBC on a drama about our story. Terry had first been approached while I was still in prison but we met the producers and writer together in February 2004 and their empathy for our story touched us both. They were not just interested in the headlines but what events had done to us as a family, and I was pleased that at last Jade and Terry's story would also be told. Sarah Lancashire was going to play me and Timothy Spall was to 'be' Terry in the drama entitled *Cherished* – a reference to what Justice Hallett had said when she sentenced me. It felt strange that our lives were going to be dramatised on screen.

'Shadow,' I shouted as he streaked off down the hill.

It was late September 2004 and I was walking in the

Churchtown nature reserve a couple of miles from our house – a place that had become a sanctuary for me. I went there nearly every day, still relishing the joys of freedom. However heavy the rain, or strong the wind, I would take the dog for a walk and lose myself in the freedom of the countryside. It was so quiet and peaceful as I stared out across the river at the hills beyond, caught a glimpse of birds and cattle, and breathed in lungfuls of fresh, clean air as I tried to readjust to being free again. It is hard to explain how it felt. I had spent every minute of every day in prison forcing myself to accept that I would be incarcerated for up to fifteen years and now it was taking a long time to convince myself I was really free.

Prison wasn't with me every waking minute and I didn't talk about it a lot for fear it would bring all those feelings back out into the open and remind me of how fearful I had been. It was still there but I just wanted to concentrate on getting back on track with Terry and Jade after seeing so much that frightened me. After all, I had done so much crying in prison I felt all cried out.

But tiny things would remind me, like a new series of a programme I had watched in my cell, and I found it hard to give up some habits, like rolling super-skinny cigarettes to try and make the most of my tobacco. Steve Crouch had come to stay in the summer and I'd felt a cold rush of panic as he laughingly shouted, 'You nonce!' at a jockey he and Terry were watching on a television horse race.

'Please don't say that,' I asked him.

'What?' he said as he looked at me in confusion.

'Nonce,' I replied, feeling almost panicked as I uttered the word that had haunted me.

'Oh, Angela,' he said. 'I'm so sorry. I didn't even think.'

I knew Terry thought prison had created a new hardness in me. He told me I'd changed, my fuse was shorter and my aggression quicker to show itself. But it angered me when he talked that way. I'd spent four years away from him and Jade, two years locked up with arsonists and murderers, so was it really surprising I was different? I did not feel I was more aggressive, but he remembered the laughing girl he had once known – the Angela with a quick, dry sense of humour who had danced on tables and enjoyed life. But first the Bell's Palsy had drained me of confidence, setting my features into stone when I was just thirty-six, and then prison had destroyed my ability to have easy fun.

He also missed the softness I'd once shown and believed I was hiding my feelings. Before prison I used to cry as I sorted through the boxes I had made for each one of my lost children containing mementoes like a silver cutlery set Claire had given Matthew, a porcelain shoe bearing the words 'Baby's First Christmas' we'd bought for Jason and a red rattle I'd got for Gemma. But while I still quietly looked at those things after my release, I no longer cried when I opened them. Terry says he saw so much sadness in me that I never expressed but, just as before and since, there wasn't a day when I didn't think of my babies. I simply forced myself not to dwell on the past because I was emotionally exhausted, I felt washed out, drained. Yes, I was indeed a different person from the one he knew and loved, but I felt sure that, however battered and bruised, I was still the same at heart.

His concern for me, though, was mirrored by mine for him and I thought constantly about how I could help him past his pain and into the future as I walked across the fields.

'Next year I'll be nine and I'll be in year four at school,' Jade would say.

'Well, you will be if we're still here,' he'd reply.

The uncertainty about our future and whether we would stay in Saltash worried me.

'Why are you saying that to her, Terry?' I would challenge him. 'We've only just moved here. Jade needs to feel settled and we can't up sticks and move again.'

But Terry, who had been crippled by homesickness for his parents and Stephen after we'd moved, just didn't seem to want to commit to our new life. He still wasn't drinking or smoking, but without those crutches it was as if he didn't see any point to life and he'd started going to bed by about 9 p.m. each evening, leaving me alone downstairs, wondering how I could break through his silence.

We didn't argue. Instead we were like a brother and sister who chatted about day-to-day things but never went below the surface. We never touched, and where before Matthew's death I'd known how deeply Terry loved me, I now felt vulnerable. Time after time I'd try to talk to him and we'd come back to the same thing.

'I can feel myself going back to that morning you found me lying on the carpet, Ange – to the day when I thought I might kill myself,' he would say. 'Before all this I was a fortunate guy. I'd always had my mum and dad, I was married the first time at seventeen and then I had you, Ange, and I worked sixty hours a week.

'Then everything I took for granted for thirty years – work, coming home at the end of the day, you, my daughter, my house, my family, my wage packet – was taken away. I felt like all I had left to control was being clean, Jade being clean, Jade being fed, everything that a woman does, while everything manly – working, dealing with staff, running our money – was gone. Now you're home and I can't even make love to you properly. Look at the way we were before this. I couldn't get enough of you and look at me. Bar sticking a knife in me there is nothing left of me as a man.

'I couldn't deal with so many things when you left – the loneliness, the not working, having depression. I felt like a failure that I wasn't getting up and doing a twelve-hour day when I'd done it for thirty years, that I was buying a packet of fags using benefits and not money I'd earned. Everything I knew fell apart. My wife wasn't allowed to be with me, I had to look after Jade, I had to run a house and I couldn't work. You just don't realise what it was like for me out on my own. The one left behind.

'What you're seeing with Jade now, I had to deal with alone. All the time you were inside I felt like you didn't believe me and the world thinks this is about Angela Cannings, but it's about Angela, Terry and Jade. We've all been hurt by this but sometimes I feel like I've been forgotten. I've lost all faith in the majority of human beings, I don't trust anyone any more, and once I only ever saw the good in people. But I feel so angry at what happened to us, at the authorities and the fact that there were a lot of people trying to break us up.

'I'm not controlling myself any more, Ange. Something's controlling me and it has been for a very long time. I can't make it go away and you've got to accept that this is the way it is.'

It became harder and harder to know how to comfort Terry as the months went by and we had the same conversation again and again. But where people had once swooped into our lives to rip it apart, no one came forward to help us put it back together. The phone never once rang with offers of support or assistance after I was released – social services, GPs, everyone stayed away – and it was hard to know how best to help him.

All I could do was hope that by weathering the storm, by listening when Terry wanted to talk and showing Jade I was here to stay, we would come together once again as a family.

'I can't go into school, Mum,' Jade said as tears started to roll down her cheeks.

'Why not, darling?' I asked as we stood in her bedroom.

'I just can't. I don't want to go, Mum. I've got a fuzzy head.'

'But you've got to go, Jade. All your friends are there. You need to be in school.'

Jade started to sob uncontrollably as she sat down on her bed. It was the end of the October half-term and there had been signs in the previous few weeks that she was struggling with school – she didn't want Terry to leave her when he took her in and she refused to mix with the other children. But I didn't know what to do on that first morning when my eight-year-old daughter simply refused to go out of the front door. It wasn't like dealing with a toddler. I couldn't just pick her up and carry her where I wanted her to go.

'What is it you don't like, Jadey?' I asked her. 'Have you been bullied?'

'No.'

'Well, has something else happened to upset you?'

'No.'

'But what is it then?'

'I don't know. I just can't go into school, Mummy.'

'Well okay then, but you'll have to give it a try tomorrow, Jade.'

But she simply wouldn't and, as the days rolled into weeks, she continued to refuse to go back to school. I became increasingly concerned and confused. I knew she was struggling and didn't want to force her but, on the other hand, I felt it was part of normal life and she should be encouraged to go. But whatever I did or said, Jade would neither leave the house nor explain why. She became anxious, unable to sleep and soon she had started going off her food.

It hit me like a truck. I had no idea what to do. I'd always attended school and so had Jade while I was away. But even as I struggled to understand what was happening to her, Terry – like Jade – stopped coping. Within weeks of her starting to refuse school, he had started drinking again. He insists to this day it was nothing to do with Jade but I believe it was. That thread of normality she had provided us with snapped when she finally reacted to all that had happened and her father also let go of the dream that we were coping.

I felt shell-shocked. We had moved to Saltash and it had been a hard summer but I'd really believed we'd get through it. There were problems with Jade but she had seemed to be settling in and Terry, I thought, simply needed time to sort himself out. But now, in the space of just a few weeks, things had completely fallen apart. Even the tiny bits of normal life I'd been clinging onto had gone and we seemed totally lost.

Why is this happening? I thought to myself night after night as I lay in bed. I'm out, I'm home. So why aren't we happy?

But my questions were never answered and, as 2004 drew to a close, I was forced to admit that nearly a year on from my release things had got worse not better. As I lay in the dark, listening to Terry padding about downstairs as he poured himself another brandy in the search for sleep, I realised I had another fight on my hands. But this time it wasn't about convincing the jury of my innocence or getting out of prison. Instead it was the most serious battle I would ever face – because if I lost it I would lose my family for ever.

CHAPTER SEVENTEEN

'Do you mind if I swap seats with you?' Jade asked her friend anxiously. 'I can't see properly from here and I don't like it and because you're taller than me you should be able to see better than me.'

I watched silently as Jade and her friend changed places. It was January 2005 and we were at the Theatre Royal in Plymouth to see *Cinderella* for her ninth birthday treat. The air around us hummed with chatter as parents handed bags of sweets down rows full of excited children.

But while they talked, relaxed and happy as they waited for the curtain to go up, Jade couldn't settle. She'd got more and more worked up on the way into town earlier that afternoon and now, as we sat waiting for the performance to start, was consumed with questions. What time would it start? How long would it last? Who was going to be in it? How much did the tickets cost?

Try as I might to answer her questions, nothing seemed to calm Jade down. Her nervousness had rubbed off on Terry, who also looked uncomfortable. As we'd walked into the theatre earlier, I had seen the look of confusion on his face and the sweat covering it. I knew he was finding the crowd difficult to deal with – a problem he'd had ever since Matthew's death when he'd gone to watch Southampton play and felt frightened by all the fans surrounding him. It had got so bad that he'd given up going to matches after thirty-six years.

'Jadey,' I told her gently. 'Settle down, love. There's nothing to worry about. Just calm down and enjoy yourself.'

'But how long will it last?' she replied. 'Do you think we should go to the toilet again before it starts?'

Her questions were finally hushed when the lights went down and Cinderella appeared on stage. I looked at Jade's face bathed in the golden glow of the theatre lights and wondered if we would ever get her back on track. Things had got worse in the three months since she'd started refusing to go to school – she had refused to take part in any Christmas activities, was still off her food and having difficulty sleeping, not getting off until 1 a.m. on some evenings and often sleeping in our bed.

She had also withdrawn even further from me. Where in the first year after my release there had been moments when she seemed prepared to let me in, it now seemed as if she felt she could only trust Terry – the person who'd always been there. Their closeness was making me feel increasingly pushed out, and try as I might to make things better I could not seem to help either of them.

But at least Jade had asked for help. Aware that Terry and I had started counselling after going to see our GP, she'd told me she wanted to see someone. We had been referred to a paediatrician by our GP after going to see her about Jade's appetite loss, and the specialist had referred us to a centre in Plymouth. Jade was due to start weekly play therapy at the end of January. I hoped it would unlock some of the secrets she was still carrying inside her, because I'd had no luck in finding out what she was thinking.

'I have a fuzzy head,' was all she could tell me.

'What's in there, Jade?' I'd ask. 'Can you tell me?'

'No I can't, Mum. I can't tell you.'

Time and again she would start to sob uncontrollably before shrieking for Terry's mum.

'I want Granny, I want Granny,' she'd shout until we handed her the phone and her grandmother would calm her down.

At other times she would call for her lost brother.

'I want Matthew,' she would cry.

'Sweetheart, Mummy wants Matthew as well and so does

Daddy. We all miss him very much. But he's looking down on us and he wouldn't want you to be unhappy. We are here all the time to look after you and you must tell us if you have a problem because if you don't we won't be able to help you. Even if you feel as if you have done something naughty it doesn't matter because you have to tell us everything that has happened.'

But my encouragement did little to help Jade explain her distress and the situation was putting an increasing strain on Terry and me as our differences in dealing with it became apparent. Where he seemed incapable of seeing Jade distressed and gave in to her pleas, I felt that however much she cried we should encourage her to cling onto some part of real life. It meant I was the one who questioned her more about why she wasn't going to school and so got shouted at. At times she would turn into someone I hardly recognised as anger and hurt filled her.

'I can't do it, Mum, I can't go to school.'

'But you've really got to try.'

'I can't do it, Mummy, you're harsh you are. I can't go.'

'Jade,' I would reply, my voice raised in frustration. 'It's been nearly four months now, you have to give it a go. I know you're suffering but you've got to try.'

'Get away, you ugly pig. Leave me alone. Don't make me.'

I had no idea what to do. Pain at seeing how she was and hurt at her rejection both rose up inside me. It was the most awful situation I could have imagined – I had longed to be Jade's mother again but it seemed I could do nothing right. Just as it had with Gemma, Jason and Matthew, it cut me deeply that I couldn't protect her from hurt. It was as if something was weighing Jade down which she couldn't push away, and whatever I did it didn't seem to make a difference.

Her school was very supportive and Jade was due to start home-tutoring at the end of February because in the run-up to Christmas she hadn't gone to school at all.

As the lights went up at the end of the performance, she turned to me.

'How did the Ugly Sisters know it was my birthday when they read out the children's names?' she asked.

'I don't know, darling,' I told her. 'Maybe your Fairy Godmother told them.'

'It was you, wasn't it?' she replied.

'Maybe.'

'Thanks, Mum. I really enjoyed myself.'

'Well, I'm glad you did,' I said, filled with happiness at that moment of peace with my daughter. 'Now let's go and get a burger.'

But as we walked out into the cold darkness, chatting about the panto, and went over a pedestrian crossing, a car came speeding round the corner towards us.

'No,' I shouted in panic and I pushed the girls onto the pavement on the other side.

Jade's friends took it in their stride – just a fleeting moment of fear which disappeared in the excitement of being out and about. But she immediately dissolved into tears, shaking and shouting and starting to scream.

'I thought we were going to get run over,' she sobbed. 'I thought the car was going to hit us. It was so close to us. I didn't think we would get out the way.'

'You're all right,' I said as I knelt down to hug her. 'I got you across the road, I made sure you were fine.'

'But it was coming so fast, I was so scared.'

'Jade, you're fine, love. We're all fine.'

I looked around for Terry, who was walking towards us across the road, completely unaware of what had happened.

'Are you all right?' he asked Jade as he walked over to join us.

'A car came round the corner and nearly had us,' I said, annoyance rising up in me. 'Didn't you see?'

But he hadn't. He was too cut off from it all to notice.

It was Jade's friends who got me through that day – two smiling nine-year-olds who enjoyed their trip out, while Jade and Terry seemed paralysed by anxiety because of it. When we finally got home that evening, all I could feel was relief. The day hadn't been a happy one, it had been more of a battle. I felt increasingly that I was on the opposing side to my husband and daughter, as if I was the only person in our family trying to hold together the threads of our life, which they seemed happy to let go.

Each morning as spring got under way, I got up early and sat on the balcony after letting out Shadow and the new addition to our household, a springer spaniel called Chewitt. All around me were homes where parents got up together, children sneaked a look at the television before breakfast and then got ready for school. But in my house, no one stirred apart from me. Terry was often not out of bed until 11 a.m. while Jade was still struggling with school.

A home tutor had been visiting her for an hour each morning four days a week since late February and Jade had instantly bonded with the kindly woman. A month later we started edging towards getting her back into school for at least some of the time – an hour here, a morning there – and while it was hit and miss, at least it was progress. But as the clock ticked nearer to the time when we'd have to leave the house, Jade would become increasingly unsettled, worrying about putting her uniform on and getting angry with me. Terry had started doing voluntary work with special-needs adults at a farm three times a week as a way of starting to move back towards working again, which left Jade and me alone in the house together as the battle raged.

'Come home, Daddy,' she would scream after running to the phone and ringing him. 'Mummy is hitting me.'

I wasn't, of course, but Terry would rush home to try and sort us out and eventually stopped doing the voluntary work because it was just too much for him. On one occasion I had left the house with Jade and, as I walked up the drive, she had run back to the front door and clawed at it, begging him to let her back in. But where he seemed to crumble in the face of her emotional pain, would do anything to calm her sobs and screams, I felt that however much it hurt me to do it, we had to try and get Jade back to school. The problem had been going on for months, and the longer it went on, the further she would retreat from real life and the farther she would fall behind. I believed she was having a delayed reaction to all that had happened but that she couldn't be allowed to give up on normal life.

At the beginning of the year, she had also started telling me she was scared to go to school because she feared I might not be at home when she got back. Once again I could have wept when I realised she still couldn't trust that I was really home, and I did all I could to reassure her. She'd even got a letter from the Attorney General after I met him in January to discuss my case and others like it in the family courts. I'd told him about Jade and he'd sent her a letter explaining that Mummy wouldn't be going back to prison.

'Your mummy has told me that you are frightened that she might be taken away again,' it read. 'I am writing to tell you that those days are all over now. Your mummy is back with you to stay. Do not be afraid. She is there to look after you and to love you.

'I hope that you enjoy your new home with your mummy and daddy. Cornwall is a lovely place to be. Continue to be a brave girl because your mummy needs you to be.'

I was touched by the kindness of such an important man.

But nothing seemed to sink in and Jade continued to swing between clinging onto me in odd moments and spitting aggression at me during many more. 'Daddy was always there for me and you weren't,' she would scream.

'Jade, I'm home now and I'm trying to help you but I feel like the big bad momma here just because I'm trying to do things with you,' I'd reply.

'I do love you, Mummy,' she'd almost plead.

'But do you, Jade?' I snapped, as frustration and hurt rose up in me.

'Yes, I do.'

'Well, it really upsets me when you are nasty to me. It wasn't my fault that I was taken away from you. Other people said I had to be away from you and Daddy. Why are you like this with me?'

'I don't know, Mummy.'

Guilt flooded over me each time I said such things to my daughter but I found it hard to be patient at times. I am not a perfect parent, I made many mistakes with Jade as we tried to get to know each other again and I regret them all. I had been out of prison for fifteen months and found it draining to withstand her anger hour after hour, day after day. I kept trying to build bridges and repair our relationship, but felt like a failure in a world where perfect parents seemed to stare out of every television screen and magazine. On particularly bad days I would retreat to bed by 7 p.m.

I'd had four children but I was increasingly aware that I had only cared for babies and for Jade full-time until she was three and a half. I knew nothing about coping with a nine-year-old full of confusion and anger, and struggled continually with what to do for the best. During talks with other mums, I realised I was over-reacting at times – that all children could behave badly – but it was confusing. All I had wished for in prison was to see my daughter. Now part of me had almost begun to resent her because she was refusing school and constantly with us in our tiny home. With all the help and support she was getting – from Terry and me, other family, her home tutor, her school teachers – Jade didn't seem to even want to try and get back to normal life. Instead she was as demanding of our attention as ever and, as awful as it sounds, I felt worn down by being with her twenty-four hours a day.

'What can I do, Mummy?' she would ask as she came down-stairs.

'Jade, you've got dollies, you've got games, you've got a video player.'

'But I don't want to do all that.'

'Well, I've got to do some housework and I'll play with you later on.'

'I want to use the kitchen for a game.'

'You have your bedroom, the spare bedroom, even Mummy and Daddy's room and you can't use the kitchen because I need to use it. If you can't go to school and meet us halfway, then you'll have to go to your room.'

'You're harsh, Mummy. I don't want to stay there all day.'

'Well, if you're not going to school then you'll have to stay up there.'

Sometimes she would dissolve into tears, which Terry invariably gave in to, at other times she would shout back – as if trying to push me as hard as she could for a reaction. I found it more and more difficult.

'Mum, Mum, I'm really sorry,' she would say after screaming at me.

'But it's too late, Jade. You've done it.'

'You're not going to forgive me, are you?'

'Of course I am but it's over now. Just calm down and let's leave it.'

'You don't mean that. You hate me now.'

'Of course I don't, and I do mean it, Jade, but let's move on now.'

In those moments of anger and hurt, I wanted her to know she had upset me – to understand that behaviour had consequences – and Terry would criticise me for my coldness. But it was hard to be consistently kind when Jade was testing me all the time – aggressive one minute and needy the next; like a teenager one minute and a toddler pushing the boundaries the next. But where you can look at a three-year-old and tell yourself they are too young to understand their behaviour, I struggled with the fact that Jade was nine and could see the damage she caused at times.

As I struggled with her and all the difficult emotions our relationship sparked in me – guilt, anger, rejection, impatience, hurt – I was also wrestling with other feelings. In the year since we'd moved to Saltash, most of my family had come to visit, but I knew there was distance between us. Terry still felt raw about what had happened while I was in prison and, anxious to support him, I remained stuck in the middle. I was also so wrapped up in him and Jade that I made little effort elsewhere. My relationship with them was so consuming I hardly had the energy to pursue others. I missed my family and friends but was reluctant to spend too much time in Salisbury because of how uncomfortable I felt there. Over time, the phone calls got less and less frequent.

I also felt filled with rage that so much damage had been done to my family and it was worsened by the fact that no one seemed to want to hold their hands up and take the blame for all that had gone wrong. We'd been told in December that a compensation application had been turned down by the Home Office because I didn't fulfil the criteria for automatic payment. Victims are only entitled to money if new facts show beyond reasonable doubt there has been a miscarriage of justice. According to Home Office officials, the Court of Appeal had decided my conviction was unsafe 'in the absence of any conclusive proof that there had been abuse' and the Home Secretary, who was able to make discretionary payments in 'exceptional circumstances', had decided not to. Yet again it felt as if the mystery surrounding my babies' deaths had been used to cast a shadow – this time over my freedom. Terry was outraged.

'They've taken the past, the present and now they want the future from me,' he'd said. 'I worked all those years, they did this to us and now they won't make amends. I battle every day with income support, it's not what I want and that money would have helped us get off it.'

I felt disgusted that yet another authority was letting us down, and when the story broke in the *Daily Mirror* it seemed ordinary people up and down the country agreed with me. Bill and Jacqui decided they were going to go to the High Court to try and get the decision judicially reviewed.

The General Medical Council had also turned down my complaint against Professor Meadow after a panel decided there was no case to answer. I had received a letter telling me no further action would be taken because the Court of Appeal had not directly criticised the paediatrician, other experts had expressed similar opinions during my trial and my conviction had been quashed due to new evidence. It was yet another interpretation of the judgement in my case and I was shocked and saddened by the decision.

On the other side of the coin, Professor Carpenter's research into the deaths of 6,373 babies using information gathered by the CONI scheme found 87 per cent of deaths in families who had lost two babies were from natural causes – another resounding blow to the automatic assumption of guilt in cases like mine. *Cherished*, the BBC drama about our story, was also shown in

February and some eight million people tuned in. I'd had to smile when I heard the cast's broad Wiltshire accents and saw pictures of Salisbury Cathedral screened to a backdrop of Meat Loaf music. But I couldn't fault the film and felt that for the first time people had seen what had really happened to us as a family. For both Terry and me it was a huge relief that justice had finally been done to our story. In April, Donna Anthony, who I had met in Durham prison, was freed after her conviction was also quashed.

Meanwhile I forced myself to keep going with Jade. Just as I had done with Stephen, I mothered her in very practical ways as I tried to re-educate her about family life – three meals a day, regular bedtimes – all the things that had gone out of the window when she was at home with Terry. And I made myself hold on to tiny moments – the way she ran to me and gave me a hug when she came out of school on the days she went; the times we went into Plymouth to shop together and have a look round; the soft, relaxed slump of her body as she drifted off to sleep on a lavender pillow I had bought her because of its calming smell, and the delight on her face when she squealed with excitement on a ride at a leisure park. There were also quiet, private times when we were alone together that I cherished because tiny hints of the intimacies of a mother-daughter relationship began to reveal themselves.

Sometimes I would be drying myself off after a shower and Jade would look at my caesarean scar and ask if it hurt, or pat my 'wobbly' tummy, or ask why I had to shave my legs – I loved her questions, her interest. I'd also often talk to her about when she was a baby – filling in the gaps of our past together and trying to remind her that, even though she couldn't remember, I had been around for her.

'What did I eat as a baby, Mummy?' she'd ask.

'Well, you used to eat carrots, swede, potato, broccoli – every vegetable there was going. Not like now, Jadey.'

'Errrr,' she would shriek with laughter. 'I didn't eat all those. I don't like them.'

'Oh yes you did,' I'd reply.

I would flourish on those conversations – moments of happiness which spurred me on to try and give my daughter more.

But even so it felt like the darkest of times on those spring mornings when I sat on the balcony and watched the morning light flood over the hill behind us because I was forced to admit to myself that the life I was living was in some ways worse than prison. The situation with Jade was one thing, but the loneliness I felt because of my distance from Terry was what threatened to break me. Whereas in prison I had had Rose, who I continued to speak to at least once a week, it now felt as if there was no one on my side. Terry was still drinking every night – he started at 7 p.m. on the dot – and as I withdrew from him, he found it hard to cope with the fact I still had such a deep bond with Rose while there was only increasing coldness between us. Jade was aware of the distance between us.

'I wish you were like my friends' mums and dads,' she'd say.

'What do you mean?' I would ask.

'Well, they sit together and they cuddle each other and if they're in the kitchen they put their arms around each other. That is what mummies and daddies do and I'd like you and Daddy to do it because then we'd be like a family again.'

'But we are, Jade,' I tried to reassure her. 'It's just that sometimes Mummy and Daddy don't do that, but we do love each other.'

'Well, I worry that you and Daddy are going to split.'

'No, Jade. We'll be all right.'

Day after day I got up and forced myself to be practical. But when Jade started screaming, I would look at Terry sitting in his chair, watching television and reluctant to get involved, and the voices deep inside me would whisper at my unhappiness.

You've got your freedom back – think about where you're living, all the good things you've got, a voice would say as guilt washed over me at my 'bad' thoughts.

But you're not happy, another replied. Stop kidding yourself. You feel miserable.

I felt so incredibly sad. I hadn't expected miracles but I felt more and more desperate as things got worse. I tried to go to bed each night, get over a bad day and pray the following one would be better. But the next morning I would get up, see Terry as withdrawn as ever, Jade not going to school and wonder how I would deal with it.

The sense that I could do nothing to help the people I loved was almost as painful as seeing how damaged they were. Sometimes I would lie in bed at night and cry silently with Terry next to me, unable to push the sadness away. But I also felt angry at times. I hadn't gone through all I had to be rejected like this and it cut me deeply that it was happening. It almost felt as if there was no space for my feelings – I couldn't have fallen apart even if I'd wanted to. Part of me felt almost resentful that I was looking after Terry but getting nothing back and didn't have the time or the space to show my sadness – however much he said I needed to. I think many wives and mothers can find themselves in that situation and I absorbed myself in housework as I tried to keep busy.

As the months had passed, though, the feeling that I was the only one who cared if we stayed together as a family only intensified. At times it seemed as if Terry and Jade almost didn't want me home at all, as if I was somehow an obstacle to their retreat from life – Terry behind the television screen and Jade to her room – both unresponsive and unknowingly shutting me out because of their natural bond. They laughed at jokes together, hugged each other, chatted to each other and I got none of that. Jade would crawl onto her dad's lap in the evenings as they watched television while I would sit on another sofa, desperate for some of the love and affection they so obviously shared.

Emotionally they almost seemed to mirror each other. Jade was anxious like her father was, angry like he was and shared his sense of being let down by life. She also constantly worried about him. If Terry coughed the wrong way she would run up, terror written across her face and cling to him. As I watched them together it seemed to me that Jade was like a mini adult – worrying about issues like health, parking spaces and punctuality that most nine-year-olds never thought about – and instead of us being a family unit with parents and a child, we were like three adults with Jade in control for much of the time.

I tried to broach the subject, to talk about my increasing sense of isolation, but Terry did not seem to want to listen. Seeing Jade go through so much pain while I was inside prison had made him unable to stand seeing even the slightest hint of it again. He also felt that I was too aggressive with her, too hard, and I knew I was at times. But there was also a point hidden in my increasing anger which he didn't want to accept. I was being forced to play the bad cop to his good. I was the one trying to instil the boundaries which had been lost when I was away, while Terry was still cuddly daddy.

Stop thinking like this, I'd scold myself when it all felt like it was getting too much. Someone's got to keep us going. It will all come right in the end.

But it got harder and harder to cope with as our days drifted into one another following the same routine – Terry would lie in, get up and watch some television, go into town to put his bets on, come back and watch television again, walk the dogs, make his daily phone calls, before settling back down in front of the television to watch the soaps.

Where before Matthew's death, and even after to an extent, we had always made sure we had time together, he now seemed to make efforts to avoid me. I got on with my things – taking Jade to and from school, doing the housework – but it wasn't enough and when I tried to suggest doing something he always seemed reluctant. Jade could sometimes pierce the shield Terry had built around himself, but I couldn't. In March he went back onto anti-depressants. Blackness had overwhelmed him once again.

What I know now was that Terry too felt life had got worse after my release from prison. Aware of my increasing withdrawal and dragged down by the arguments between Jade and me, he was torn between who to support. He could see Jade was being difficult but felt I was too strict with her. She was his priority, not me, and he was highly aware of how much she had been through.

'Jade knows how far she can push me, Ange,' he would tell me when I challenged him to discipline her. 'But look at all she's been through. We mustn't push her. Things will happen in their own time. You go at her too much. Just leave her be a bit more.'

Terry hadn't simply given up – he was trying to deal with the loss of yet another role. After my arrest and the destruction of everything he knew when the authorities took over our lives, he had clung onto the job of being Jade's sole carer and had fought hard to learn how to do it. But my return meant he'd lost even that – I had stepped back into the practical shoes and Terry found it difficult to let go of the one piece of stability he had carved out for himself. He had clothed Jade, washed her, fed her, loved her, and now he had to share again with me. He says now it took him back to that day in 1999 when everything was ripped away.

Initially when I scratched at the surface of the problem, it almost annoyed me.

I know I've been away but I did it all for twenty-odd years before that, I'd think to myself. It feels like he thinks I haven't come home, I've taken over.

Then, after all the months of trying to understand and build bridges, I began to lose patience.

'Time is moving on,' I said to him one day.

I had been preparing myself for our conversation, knowing that if I didn't say something I would fall apart. But it scared me to think of Terry's reaction and how defensive he would become if I tried to rock the boat.

'I've got to talk to you about how I feel. I know you have a problem struggling with life and Jade does too – so do I – but I can't bring it to the surface because I have to cope for you two. If this life continues with no thought for the future, we won't be a family unit. We won't survive. You don't seem to be able to move on at all. I don't mean that nastily but when will be the time that you can start to think about it? It's been more than a year now and I am physically and mentally shattered because I don't know where I go with all this.'

'I feel as I feel,' Terry said simply. 'You can't force it to go away with a click of your fingers. It's got to take its own time. I don't choose to feel this way but I can't do anything about it, and if you can't accept that, I understand you might want to go. I've lived with this for five years and I can't defend myself so I might have to let you go.'

'For goodness sake, Terry,' I said, fear and anger rising up in me. 'What do you think I am? Do you think I will up and leave? I haven't spent two years in prison and two years before that having visits with Jade to lose you both. But can't you see? We've got to do something to move forward. I'm trying to understand but you don't seem to want to do anything to improve things. They are just getting worse. Those judges gave me my life back but I feel as if we're wasting it and I'm worried. After all this time I don't know what the answer is any more.'

'Don't be so aggressive with me,' Terry snapped. 'I can't cope with it when you go at me. If you don't understand how I feel or go halfway there then I'm going to put my guard up. It's not a cut leg or a broken arm and it frustrates me that I can't explain. But do you know what it's like to be in between you and Jade sometimes? I'm piggy in the middle. Now you know what it was like for me. I had it for four years all on my own.'

'Well, what do you think I was doing?' I shouted. 'Do you think I was enjoying life in prison?'

'But you had people and a structure, Ange. I had nothing.'

'Oh but Terry, you did,' I snapped. 'I've heard it all before. You're pulling me down to your level and I'm not going there because one of us has got to keep this together. I know you feel bad but you've got to try and be positive.'

He looked at me coldly. 'If you're going to get aggressive and angry then I'm going out,' he said before grabbing his coat and walking out the door.

I sat and fought back the angry tears that rose up inside me. We weren't living, we were just surviving, and I felt like a stranger in my family. Pain rose up inside me. I couldn't understand why I was slowly being pushed out of the equation. It was worse than anything that had gone before. Strangers had turned on me during my arrest, conviction and imprisonment. But now the two people I loved, who had kept me going through everything, didn't seem to want anything to do with me. I felt almost dirty again because their anger and resentment reminded me of what I had faced in prison. I understood Jade was just a child but Terry almost seemed to be holding the fact that I was surviving against me.

He wants me gone because I'm a constant reminder that he's not coping, I thought to myself.

And in that moment I felt totally hopeless.

Nerves washed over me as I walked into the modern meeting room where Professor Meadow would face the General Medical Council's disciplinary panel. It was June 2005 and the start of a hearing about the statistical evidence he had given at Sally Clark's trial. I had travelled to London for the first day of the hearing and it was the first time I had seen him since he went into the witness box against me. It felt strange that now he was on trial instead of me.

Now you know how it feels, I thought to myself.

It was a long room and Professor Meadow was sitting to one side of a U-shaped table, flanked by his lawyers. A slight sense of embarrassment filled me. I had shouted at him minutes earlier as he walked into the GMC building and I stood being interviewed by a camera crew.

'Can we have an apology for the families whose lives have been destroyed?' I had called but he'd taken no notice.

I knew I should not have heckled him in public and that I'd let myself down by doing so. But I felt overwhelmed by anger when I saw him for the first time in three years.

Now, as I sat waiting for the hearing to start, I felt almost frustrated that my complaint wasn't being heard.

Professor Meadow looked very uncomfortable as a barrister started addressing the panel and accused him of giving seriously misleading and flawed evidence.

'When doctors offer themselves as forensic medical experts, increasingly a feature of consultant practice, they must be scrupulously fair,' the barrister said. 'They are not hired guns. They are not advancing their own pet theories.'

Four weeks later, after a long and complex hearing about statistical data, I was deluged by media phone calls when Professor Meadow was found guilty of serious professional misconduct and struck off the medical register. The GMC panel had decided he had 'abused his position as a doctor' by giving 'erroneous and misleading' evidence at Sally Clark's trial. The phone was red-hot all day as journalists rang for my reaction. But I had mixed feelings – sadness that my complaint had been ignored and cynicism that it was too little too late.

Days later, Terry and I received a letter telling us the Home Secretary had reversed his decision about compensation. We were going to be given it. Terry was overjoyed but I found it hard to feel anything much after the fight we'd had to get them to agree. Dully, I wondered to myself why the Home Office had done a U-turn.

The sunlight cast a green glow on Jade's face as it streamed through the side of the tent. We were camping on the small patch of grass in front of our house and I lay gazing at her as she slept.

It had been a summer holiday full of ups and downs. Stephen had bought us a blow-up pool when he'd come to visit and we'd kept it up in the back garden for weeks. Terry had taken to it amazingly well. He spent most of his time in there on sunny days, listening to the radio and lying in the cool water, and he was very particular about cleaning it out and repairing any punctures. Jade, though, had found it difficult to be so keen and would leap in for a few minutes before jumping out again.

Stephen had left his daughters, three-year-old Shauna-Esme and Shayleigh, four, with us for a week in June and it had started off happily. Terry loved seeing them and Jade enjoyed being in charge. But as the week progressed she'd become more and more possessive over Shauna-Esme, wanting to treat her like a baby and pushing Shayleigh away. The little girls had noticed and withdrawn from her and there had been shouting matches when I'd tried to talk to Jade about her behaviour.

Another flashpoint had been the amount of time she spent with a pregnant neighbour of ours. I had been fine about it at first because I told myself it comforted her. Jade was deeply interested in babies and pregnant women, and although she couldn't really remember Matthew, I believed she was deeply aware of his loss. She had also started to call one of her dolls by his name.

'Why have you called him Matthew, darling?' I asked her one evening.

'Because it reminds me of him,' she replied. 'It feels like he's here with me. I love him lots and I miss him.'

But as the weeks passed, Jade spent more and more time away from home and I began to suspect she was avoiding us. She was up and out the door as soon as she'd eaten breakfast or she'd rush out as soon as we got home from a trip.

I struggled with my feelings of rejection. Terry had told me she had sought out the same kind of female contact while I was in prison, that I should let Jade be because she was happy. But I felt so rejected. I was home and she didn't seem to want to know. I also felt hurt as I wondered if she was angry with me because she knew I would not have another baby. I had told her when I returned home that I had had an operation that meant I couldn't.

'I think you might be spending a little too much time around at Donna's,' I said to Jade one night after I'd decided to try and talk to her.

'But I like talking to Donna, Mum, and she's having a baby,' Jade replied. 'I like that because there will be a baby there who will remind me of Matthew a little bit. And my head will feel less fuzzier.'

'But I think it might be good if you spent a little bit more time at home, Jade,' I said gently.

'What are you trying to say? That Donna doesn't like me any more?'

'Course not. It's just that you're there a lot.'

'You don't want me to go round there any more,' Jade started to shout. 'Well, I don't care. I'm going to go round there.'

'It's not about that. It's about giving them time alone as a family.'

'But Donna hasn't told me she doesn't want me round there.'

'Of course she hasn't because she likes having you but you're going round a lot and I would like to see more of you.'

Jade stormed out – furious at my interference – and I felt heart-broken.

But things were more peaceful now that we were lying in the

tent together after sleeping in it overnight. We'd found it as we left the supermarket one day and saw it lined up outside with lots of others. A two-man tent was only £7 and I thought back to my summers of fun as a child.

'What do you reckon, Jadey?' I'd asked her. 'I think I might get one and we can put it up in the garden.'

'But I don't know if I could sleep out there, Mum,' she anxiously replied.

'Well, let's give it a try. We can put it up and see how you feel.'

We'd spent the afternoon setting the tent up and as the hours passed I could see some excitement rising in Jade.

'So are we going to sleep out in it then?' I'd asked her as we stared at the tent.

'I don't know if I can, Mum,' she said nervously.

'Well, shall we give it a go? If you don't like it you don't have to stay in there.'

'Okay then.'

We trooped outside for the night at about 9.30 p.m. carrying sleeping bags, quilts, pillows, a torch, a mobile phone and front door keys. I'd also taken sweets, crisps and a small radio.

'We can have a midnight feast,' I told Jade as we climbed in and zipped ourselves up. 'This reminds me of being in the St John Ambulance when I was a teenager and we went on camping trips. The tent was huge. There must have been twenty or more of us in there. I was about thirteen and we had the best time. And now we can try this together; it is something we can explore together and have some fun.'

'But, Mum, nothing will come in, will it?'

'No, sweetheart. We're all zipped in from the inside. We've got keys, we've got the mobile and nothing will happen because we're in the front garden.'

Now in the morning light, I lay looking at Jade asleep. It was so good to see her looking so peaceful.

'You did it – you slept in the tent,' I told her as she opened her eyes.

'It was all right, wasn't it?' she replied.

'Well, I thought it was pretty good fun.'

'Can we do it again tonight, please?'

'Of course we can, my love.'

We spent the next four nights in the tent and even Terry slept out there a couple of times in the end. I felt so pleased. It might have been a tiny step but to me it felt like a mile. I'd introduced Jade to something she had never done before, she'd overcome her fear, we'd had fun together and she was enjoying herself. At last I was beginning to do what any mother would do and it felt fantastic.

CHAPTER EIGHTEEN

'How are you feeling, Angela?' the therapist asked.
Terry and I were in our third counselling session together after it was suggested by staff at the centre where Jade had play therapy. We'd taken them up on the offer but I'd said little in the first couple of sessions as Terry poured his heart out.

Now it was my turn to speak.

'I feel like a failure and I'm trying to hold on but I don't know if I can,' I said in a rush. 'I feel as if I'm trying to climb a mountain but I'm being knocked back at every turn.'

I felt the anger rising in me as I started to speak but knew I had to get it all out before I started crying. Terry had spoken a lot in the first two sessions and I'd told myself I had to tell him how I felt. It was the beginning of September and Jade was due back at school the following week. I knew we had to get some things out into the open if we were ever to work together as a team with her. My relationship with her continued to show small signs of improvement – a shared joke, a request for help with something she was doing, more talking and less shouting, the odd moment of affection – but things with Terry did not.

'I've taken a few steps forward with Jade but I still feel like a spare part in our family unit and I don't know how to deal with it. I feel as if I don't know how to look forward any more and I've always been able to do that. I know Terry is struggling and we've sat and talked about it enough times. There have been moments where we've got heated but we've still been able to talk, which is a good thing. But it's an uphill struggle and I don't know how much longer I can hang on. He doesn't seem to want to change.'

The words came out in a rush and the tears followed.

'So how are you feeling, Terry?' the therapist asked.

'I've got a problem with life,' he replied. 'Ange has said what she needed to say and it is good to hear her open up. We all know my thoughts and feelings.'

'But what is it that you would like to see in your life, Terry?'

'To feel better than I do now.'

There was a short silence before the counsellor turned to him again.

'And do you want your relationship with Angela to flourish and become closer?'

'Yes, I do want that.'

I looked at him with only one thought rushing through my head: But you don't want that. You do nothing to get it. You're not being honest with me.

I kept silent.

'Why do you think you're struggling, Terry?'

'It's hard to explain,' he replied. 'Since Angela has come home I've had to try and get used to the fact that we are all back together. When she was away from me and given a life sentence, which we understood was going to be for years, I got it into my head she wouldn't be coming out until I was well into my sixties. I had to learn how to live with it and I forced myself to. Now I can't get past that. What I have done is emotionally detach myself from her. That is how I feel today.'

At last Terry had admitted what had lain unspoken between us for so many months. He had emotionally cut off from me. Now at least he had spoken the words, said something we could hold onto and discuss. It felt as if the thunderstorm had finally broken after the tense stillness of a heavy summer's evening and, strange as it sounds, it was a relief.

'So what can we do to improve this?' the therapist asked us.

'I can't change the way I am and this is the way I am at the moment,' Terry said.

There was nothing I could say.

I couldn't contain my anger. Terry and I were sitting in our lounge and Jade was upstairs. I'd just got back from a couple of nights away and discovered she had not been to school. Apart from missing just one day, she'd spent the previous three full weeks at school and I had felt so happy. We'd grown closer at the end of the summer holidays and her progress at school had made me feel that we were finally moving forward.

But rage now filled me that the moment I had left the house she had played on her father's soft spot and he had not been firm with her.

'I am back in this house, Terry, I am Jade's mum, I'm different to you and I'm sorry about that,' I said to him, annoyance making my voice hard. 'But we are going to have major problems if we don't start instilling values into her and encouraging her with discipline. If this continues we won't have a family unit because she will be doing what she wants when she wants. You have to back me up. We have to work together on this.'

'I know, Ange, but I just don't agree with your colonel approach at times. I think you over-react with her and she has to defend herself in a way she has never had to with me. Jade knows how far she can take things with me before she gets told off and I'm sorry she didn't go to school while you were away but I could not get her to go.'

'Okay fine,' I spat. 'I agree I'm too strict at times. But because you don't back me up she will continue to twist things to her advantage. We need to be together on this. I know she's been through a lot but we have to help her.'

'But it's hard to be together when I feel like you're being too harsh. There's no need for it all,' Terry replied. 'I think sometimes you take a sledgehammer to crack a walnut. We just aren't emotionally strong enough to deal with it, to get her into school. What could I do? I can't drag her out the door.'

'But we just aren't moving on, Terry,' I hissed. 'There's no effort being made here. And if we don't start coming together and being a bit firmer with her she will continue to rule the roost and I cannot see us progressing as a family.'

'But you're trying to run and I'm trying to walk with no legs, Angela,' Terry said. 'If you love me why can't you be patient? When we lost Gemma, we lost our daughter, when we lost Jason, we lost our son but when we lost Matthew, we didn't just lose our child, we lost everything. All I can feel is anger from you. You've withdrawn from me, you've withdrawn from your family and friends. I'd love to see you chatting to them more but you just don't. It was such a relief in that session we had a few weeks ago that you actually opened up a bit. But you've shut down again.'

'What am I supposed to do, Terry? The moment I go away, Jade stops going to school and we're back to square one. I've spent months trying to move us forward and I'm sorry I'm distant but I'm getting to the end of my tether.'

We both fell silent – aware the argument could go on for ever. Terry and I were on opposite sides of a gulf there seemed no way of bridging. I was filled with concern. I was his wife and where once I had believed my role was to help him, I wasn't so sure any more. I felt scared and unconfident after all the knock-backs – I wasn't a real mum or wife and I knew Terry was right. I had distanced myself from so many people. But feeling so alone had begun to grind me down and at just forty-two I'd lost all interest in looking after myself. I looked dowdy and my physical appearance mirrored what was happening inside. Because the more I grappled with doubts about whether we would be able to stay together as a family, the more I withdrew into myself.

In the weeks that followed it was hit and miss whether Jade went into school or not. Sometimes she did and I held my breath that we'd finally turned a corner but after a day or two she'd refuse again. The delicate closeness that had started to bud between us was threatened by the tension her behaviour sparked. Both Jade and I are bad in the mornings and it was the most risky time of day for us. We'd begin arguing when I tried to persuade her into school and she would cry, shout and beg not to go until she turned on me, I snapped and the screaming would start.

By the beginning of November there had been a change in me. I felt utterly hopeless and instead of nipping at Terry and Jade's heels continuously, I almost gave up. For the first time I didn't have the energy to push any more and I fell silent. Terry noticed the change in me as I spent hours walking the dogs, trying to calm the frustration that I knew was making me tense and snappy much of the time. But I just couldn't seem to and I remained subdued – too tired to carry on the fight.

One day I left the house for about five hours, walked myself into the ground and returned home quiet again. As I lay in bed that night I felt an arm slip round my waist.

'What are you doing?' I asked in surprise. Terry and I hadn't touched each other in months.

'I need a cuddle, Ange,' he replied.

For a moment I almost didn't know what to do but the feeling quickly disappeared. Terry had reached out to me and I couldn't reject him.

As we lay in the dark, he started speaking. I don't know what made him do it but the tentative physical affection between us, and the darkness surrounding us, seemed to ease away the tension you could almost touch between us during the day.

'I'm sorry for the way I've been from the day that Matthew died,' he told me. 'That was the moment when I started to feel scared of losing you, but I didn't treat you in the way you deserve to be treated, I cut off emotionally because I thought you'd be gone for years. I couldn't deal with it and I've questioned myself about it again and again. I didn't stop loving you, Ange, and the times before Matthew's death drove me on, but it became increasingly difficult to visualise carrying on with you in prison for fifteen years. I knew I loved you but I didn't know how I was going to love you if you were away from me and the only way I could deal with that was to distance myself. I've continued doing it since you came home. I find the way you've become very hard to deal with – there is a shell wrapped round you and you're not the woman you were prior to Matthew's death. But I love you and I hate things how they are.'

Memories of all those years ago, when we'd spent hours talking to each other as we lay in bed waiting to fall asleep, came rushing back. In that moment I felt appreciated for the first time in so long.

'I know I've changed as a person, I'm not who I was six years ago,' I told him. 'I went to sleep every night in a prison cell, I can't explain how awful it felt. When you're in an environment where you're being name-called and every conversation you hear is full of nasty words and threats, is it any wonder you come out changed? You can't ignore it because you live in it every day and I'm sorry if I'm aggressive but I don't think I am. I'm just frustrated because I'm trying to hold us together and if I didn't we would not be a family now because Jade would have been taken from us.

'I've come home and I never expected it to be a bed of roses but I feel my role in this house is just to exist. I don't feel like a wife to you. I'm making progress with Jade but I'm not with you. I worry about your health, your weight, your drinking, the way you are, and when I do try to suggest something you say you'll do it your way. But how long am I supposed to sit in the background and watch you suffer? How do you think it makes me feel to see my husband living like a shadow? It hurts deeply that we can't seem to move on a bit.'

We talked for hours that night as we held onto each other and opened up for the first time in months. We weren't arguing or competing over our pain, we were simply telling each other how we felt. Like that last Saturday night we spent together before I was convicted, we were able to reconnect with all those years of love and friendship between us.

'I love you so much, Ange,' Terry told me as we drifted towards sleep.

'I love you too,' I replied softly.

Kellie immediately noticed the spring in my step when she and Stephen arrived with the kids to spend the weekend a few days later.

317

'I think we might be getting somewhere,' I'd told her as she asked about the sparkle in my eyes.

I felt so hopeful. Somehow Terry and I had got back some of what we once had been and I could feel it there in the tiniest gestures – the odd hug, a shared joke. We felt like a team again.

'That's enough,' he would say when Jade shouted at me as we argued over school. 'Don't talk like that to Mummy.'

'Oh you're sticking up for her now, are you?'

'Don't be so silly. You just mustn't talk like that.'

Jade said she was pleased we were happy and the half-term week was fun. But she refused to go back to school on the first Monday morning and as the days passed it became obvious she was not going to go at all.

I was completely confused but as the time passed I began to suspect she felt almost threatened by the new closeness between Terry and me and eventually she said as much when she confessed she was scared that if she went to school she would be left out.

'But that is what happens. Look at your friends, their mummies and daddies do things together,' I told her. 'It's not about you being left out, but you have to go to school from 9 a.m. to 3.15 p.m. and you'll have to go until you're sixteen. You need to go, you need to learn things and make friends. Daddy and I love you, we won't leave you. But it's normal life, honey, and we've got to live it.'

It was almost as if Jade didn't know what to do – caught between moving on and staying hidden in her room, she felt threatened by the fragile changes in our family.

'I think you and Daddy are going to leave me out because you are sticking up for each other.'

'Darling, mummies and daddies do cuddle each other, go out and do things together and that is what happens. You wanted Daddy and me to be closer but now it seems as if you don't like it.'

'But I feel as if you're going to leave me out.'

'How could we? You are our daughter, we could never leave you out.'

I could sense her confusion. Unsettled at the dismantling of the safe world she and Terry had built around themselves, she didn't know whether to venture out or retreat again, and my reassurances didn't seem to make a difference. The situation soon brought the tension between Terry and me back to the surface. The brief moment of connection between us was too weak to withstand such pressure as yet again we clashed over how to get Jade back to school. I was insistent that if she refused to go she must spend the day in her room but he didn't always agree. If she became upset he would allow her downstairs and the anger between us would start. I pushed my hurt down as I realised the moment of closeness was gone. We were as distant as we ever had been.

In early December we were visited by a school welfare officer who talked to us about the problems with Jade. He was very kind and listened to our story but I was worried that the authorities seemed to be on the verge of becoming involved in our lives again. I was determined we must get Jade back to school. I'm sure parents who've never encountered such behaviour must think it would be easy to get a child to go – you simply put your foot down. But it is not as easy as that – Jade's distress about going back made it hard to force her and she, like her mother, had an incredibly strong will. But she was also still showing signs of trying to move closer to me, and I felt school, and the normality it would bring, would only help.

'If we continue like this it will be taken out of our hands, Terry – people will be coming in to tell us what to do and I didn't go through all I did to come home and have my daughter taken from me,' I told him. 'Can't you see what is happening? She is not at school, she's missing out on schoolwork, friends, her own life away from us. And if this goes on we will have no control over her at all when she hits her teens.'

'I've dealt with three children, Angela, and I'm not seeing what you're seeing,' Terry replied. 'I don't feel there is a problem with boundaries and discipline.'

'You don't stand up to her,' I said, my voice raised in anger. 'I'm the one who has to when she screams at me.'

'But by the time you get to that point you're both so wound up you don't know what she's saying,' he told me. 'I keep telling you not to provoke her, to just walk away, and I get fed up with telling you both to back off.'

'But there is no support for me as a woman, Terry. It hurts me and for my sake, as well as Jade's, you need to show her that we're together. There are two adults in this house and a child and she must understand that. And I need to understand that.'

'Are you jealous of Jade?'

'No, of course I'm not – she's my daughter. But I do believe that for all our sakes she has to understand we are a team. At the moment it feels like you two are, instead of you and I.'

Terry looked at me. 'I love you, Ange. You must know that. Whatever is happening, I can't see a future without you and I want this to work.' He paused for a moment. 'Do you love me?' he asked.

I hesitated as I searched for what to say. 'I think it has got lost somewhere along the way,' I replied quietly.

'Oh God,' he said as he looked down at the floor.

'I'm sorry but I'm being honest. I do love you but for the last two years I don't feel as if I've been your wife and it seems your responsibility is to Jade and no one, including me, can get in the way of that. Words aren't enough, Terry. Even though you say it, I don't feel it.'

'Do you mean that you don't love me?'

'No,' I told him. 'I mean that I love you but it's got lost somewhere.'

Terry walked out of the room. I could see how hurt he was but I couldn't lie about how I felt. It was unimaginable – we'd been together for more than twenty years and now, when we were supposed to be happy again, things had reached rock bottom. It scared me that I was no longer sure about how I felt. Terry had been everything to me for so long but our life together after prison seemed to have slowly drained my feelings away.

How can this be happening? I thought to myself. We were the

320

ones people used to envy, they used to tell us how good we were together, but look at us now.

As I sat on my own I wondered if there was anything left to cling onto.

I felt desperate after my conversation with Terry and struggled through Christmas. Tears threatened to overwhelm me as we saw in the New Year with Stephen, Kellie and the children. We'd gone outside at midnight to stand on the balcony but I felt hopeless as fireworks zoomed into the night sky from gardens all around us. I was a failure – I had tried everything but I couldn't make things work and I almost didn't want to have to see in another year. But I forced myself to say something.

'Here's to 2006,' I said as I raised a glass. 'Let's hope it's a happy year and we'll all be together as a family.'

The words seemed almost hollow but I knew I had to keep going – I couldn't give up yet. My relationship with Jade showed real potential and Terry had promised me that one day things would get back to the way they had been between us.

I forced myself to focus on the beginning of the school term. The welfare officer had been to see us again at the beginning of the Christmas holiday to tell us other people would have to become involved if Jade didn't start back at school. He was not threatening in any way – but as parents we understood the authorities couldn't stand by and do nothing if a child didn't attend school. During his visit we wrote a strategy of how we were going to get Jade back to school on the first morning of term – a minute-by-minute timetable of what she did in the mornings with suggestions about what we could do differently.

'The main thing both of you must do is not engage in a conversation about school,' he told us. 'If Jade brings up the subject and tells you she can't go, just distract her. Don't get into a discussion, and make sure she sees her parents are together about getting her to school. If she refuses to leave the house then one of you must go out to the car while the other physically takes her out.'

'Hang on a minute,' said Terry. 'What about the neighbours?'

'You have to concentrate on getting Jade into school and if anyone did report you we would know what was happening. In my experience children who are taken into school against their wishes go back voluntarily within a couple of days because they are embarrassed by their behaviour. You will be upset at what is happening but children are resilient and Jade won't be half as worried as you think she will be. When you get to the school there will be a teacher there to meet you and they'll take over.'

We knew time was running out before someone else stepped in to resolve the situation. Terry was insistent we wouldn't physically force Jade to do anything but I felt if it came to it then we'd have to. I hoped it wouldn't. But the threat of outside intervention was enough to make us agree on one thing – Jade had to go back to school.

Unsurprisingly she got anxious on the first morning of the new term. It had been fourteen months since she'd last attended full-time and I knew it was going to be hard for her. She struggled with friendships, moved from one to another too easily, and I was aware her classmates might take some time to accept her back.

'You'll be fine,' I'd told her the night before. 'All the other children are going back too and you'll be okay.'

But the tears wouldn't stop as she pleaded not to go. My frustration and disappointment wrestled with sadness that she would not budge an inch. In the end Terry went in to her.

'If you don't go back to school the horrible people will come back into our life and start telling us what to do,' he said. 'You don't want that, do you?'

'No,' she whispered.

Silently I packed up the school clothes she'd ignored when she got up and put the bag by the front door for Terry to take with him. As I went back upstairs Jade ran into my room.

'You're being horrible, Mummy, you're making me go to school,' she shouted.

'No, we're not being horrible, Jade. You've just got to go.'

We walked downstairs as she continued crying and Terry grabbed the car keys.

'Bye, honey,' I said as she hugged me. 'Have a good day.'

'But I'm not staying all day. I'll be home soon.'

I said nothing as Jade tearfully walked out of the door and got into the car. Terry was upset when he arrived home because he'd left her cowering in a corner as a teacher came to pick her up. He felt he had been cruel to her. But minutes later, when he rang the school, they said she was fine.

At the time of writing, Jade has been back at school for three months. I don't know what it is that made her decide to go – maybe it was because Terry and I were in complete agreement about what had to be done, maybe she got bored of sitting in her bedroom and being cut off from the world. But something clicked and her confidence grew as the days and weeks passed. We praised her and congratulated her, but most importantly I could see she was proud of herself.

A couple of weeks into January we took her to see the pantomime again for her tenth birthday and the trip made me realise that we had in fact made progress. She was laughing, sitting comfortably – like any other child – and her father too was far more relaxed than he had been a year before. I could tell that this year he wanted to go – rather than felt obliged to – and he laughed his way through the performance. Terry, too, was moving on in some ways. Things between us were as distant as ever but at least Jade's return to school meant we finally had some normality in our lives and more time together. As she started to eat better, sleep more easily and enjoy school again, I could feel the pressure easing off us and I believed good would come of it eventually.

Maybe I just can't see the little ways in which things are getting better, I thought to myself and determined to keep a closer eye on the tiny steps forward we were making. Little by little we would get there.

Before I went into prison I was an ordinary person. I'd led a comfortable life and was naïve in so many ways about so many things. Now I know I will carry the label of being a baby-killer to my grave. There will always be those who doubt my innocence,

323

medical experts and the general public alike who think there is no smoke without fire. After all I am not innocent in the eyes of the law. I was guilty until my conviction was declared unsafe, but no one used the word 'innocent'. It is not a concept the law recognises when dealing with appeals. My greatest hope is that one day we will be given an explanation as to why our children died because until that day I fear we will never experience real peace. The not knowing haunts us but I cling to the idea that advances in the understanding of genetics and the mysterious mechanisms behind cot death might give us some release.

As any mother who has lost a child will tell you, grief is something that never goes away. It may change over time, become less piercing, less constant, but it is the one emotion that keeps its intensity. Happiness or joy are fleeting and fade. Grief does not. There are odd moments when I feel it as fresh as the day my children died. I almost want to suck my breath in as a sense of loss overwhelms me and the feeling of failure flickers inside – as a woman you should give birth to life, not death; as a mother you should protect your children and, however irrational, part of me feels I didn't.

I often think about my lost children – Gemma, who would be seventeen this year, Jason, who would now be fifteen, and Matthew, who would be nearly six – and it saddens me to think of the life I might have had. I also feel sorry that Jade doesn't know the joy, closeness and comfort of siblings. I am haunted by the relationship I should have had with my surviving daughter – she was almost four when I was taken from her and the bond that was close and natural between us was broken. I know it is not there any more and every day I find it hard to see that it is with her father. I am working hard to create it once again and I believe Jade is too. But I worry about the future. I have had four children and yet I wonder in years to come whether I will have an easy, close relationship with my surviving daughter or whether there will always be distance between us. I hope not.

At times I question how I have managed to get through all this. If I was an outsider looking in, I think I would be shocked that I have. But all I can say is that I had no choice, it was within my character to fight. Call it my mother's practicality or my father's stubbornness, but I believe I was born a survivor. I have sometimes wondered if I am hard, unemotional, and I think I have become more so since going into prison. But I don't feel strong in my private moments. I have simply had to carry on.

I have also locked many feelings away deep within me. Unlike for Gemma and Jason, both Terry and I have yet to grieve properly for Matthew and I am scared about what will happen when we do.

Emotion does overcome me at times – tears spring into my eyes when I watch a video of Jade walking into school on her first day or describe the moment when she first ran into my arms when I was freed. But I seldom weep when I talk about Gemma, Jason and Matthew and I believe it is because I have been drained of tears. It's a cliché but there is such a thing as a river of them and I have cried one.

I know I don't show my emotions like I used to. To be deprived of your freedom for something you did not do goes to the very core of the beliefs you have about society and your place in it, your sense of safety and trust. I don't talk to anyone, even Terry, about it all and, while I have tried as much as possible in this book, there are some things I cannot explore with myself or another. I want to move on. I don't want to be heartbroken for ever. I feel we've all suffered enough.

I am not consumed by hate at what has happened to us. Professor Meadow has become the villain of stories like mine in so much media coverage but I am not on a witch-hunt. He was asked for his opinion and gave it. But I do believe that juries don't hear the tiny distinctions made in evidence – they hear the headlines: one in 73 million, the word 'smothering'. There are many medical experts out there who talk as though their theories are facts and something should be done. Child abuse does happen but questions should be asked when families with no history of ill treatment, about whom there are no concerns, with no physical evidence of abuse are accused. I find the arrogance implicit in these cases breathtaking and the reluctance to challenge them disheartening. I am an ordinary woman, without degrees or medical experience, but I know that people should sometimes have the courage to look beyond the supposed facts, refuse to be deafened by the chorus around them and stand up for what they believe in. There are those who did it in my case but it took too long for them to be heard. The medical profession seems unable as ever to admit its mistakes and I believe that to be a truly great doctor you must have humility as well as humanity. I have met many doctors like that and I admire them all.

I am realistic enough to know that the deaths of three babies had to be investigated – it is, thankfully, a very rare event but one that should be looked at. People do harm their children. The police had to make enquiries, doctors had to detail our medical history and, once I came to trial, lawyers and judges had to do their jobs. I will be eternally grateful to the three who gave me my freedom.

But what I cannot accept is how my case got so far. How the Crown Prosecution Service could look at the evidence against me and proceed. That is where everything went so very wrong because no one questioned the basis of the case – the assumption of guilt about deaths that were then, and remain now, a mystery. If statistics can be used to prove anything then people should have been aware that the chance of two babies being murdered in one family is one in 2,200 million. Of course three babies do not die without reason but I agree with the Court of Appeal that everyone involved in my case approached it believing in my guilt – not with an open mind. It was, as Bill said, like a witch-hunt and it amazes me it was not stopped. Even now I believe there should be a public inquiry into what went wrong with cases like mine, but I wonder if there are too many people – in government, the medical and legal worlds – who have too much to lose for that to happen. Someone must have ignored warnings that something was going wrong.

It is not all bad news – many people are working to ensure miscarriages of justice like mine do not happen again. In September 2004 a new set of guidelines was published by the Royal College of Pathologists and the Royal College of Paediatrics and Child Health on how to deal with sudden unexpected deaths in infancy.

It recommended that all post-mortems in SIDS cases were carried out by a specialist paediatric pathologist, with the help of a forensic pathologist if there were concerns about abuse. It also said the decision to prosecute should only be taken after a case review by all professionals involved and called for families to be given better support during investigations. In terms of court cases, inquiry chair Baroness Kennedy of the Shaws said: 'Expert witnesses must present their evidence as experts on a scientific basis. It is not enough to come with a gut feeling.'

Sir Liam Donaldson, the chief medical officer, is also conducting a review of the use of medical experts in the family courts.

Just three of the 297 cases in the Attorney General's review involved SIDS, the others related to other types of death in children under two. Twenty-eight out of two hundred convictions were identified as potentially unsafe. So far three convictions have been quashed, two upheld and two people refused leave to appeal. The other ninety-seven cases related to shaken-baby syndrome – another controversial area in which medical experts are pitted against each other. In January of this year the Attorney General announced that three cases should be referred to the Court of Appeal.

Local authorities, who were asked to review their own family court cases, did so and 28,867 were looked at. The first stage of the review, which looked at 5,000 current cases, resulted in just one care order being changed. Exact figures for the second stage – involving some 24,000 cases – were never published but it is believed just a handful of care orders were altered, compared to the questions in more than 10 per cent of criminal cases. Campaigners say the shroud of secrecy hangs as tightly as ever around the family courts.

Professor Meadow is still held in high regard by many in the medical profession, who pay tribute to his years of experience and pioneering work to protect children, and he has lectured to standing ovations. He went to the High Court in January to appeal against being struck off. His lawyer told the judge he had provided evidence in good faith, which he believed was correct and accurate. The judge agreed, saying Professor Meadow was a first-class paediatrician who had made 'one mistake'. He overturned the GMC's finding of professional misconduct and its decision to strike the paediatrician off. The judge also broke new legal ground when he ruled that experts should be immune from disciplinary hearings except those initiated by trial judges. Critics say this is a charter for doctors to advance controversial theories without fear of scrutiny by their regulator. The GMC is set to appeal the ruling.

My only other anger is reserved for social services. We were constantly told they were protecting Jade's best interests but I, as a mother, do not think they did. I believe the real abuse occurred in the name of the investigation into me, which resulted in a three-year-old child's safe and happy world being ripped apart. Children deserve to feel secure in the knowledge that they are protected by their parents. Of course they will grow up and realise bad things happen but Jade learned too young that her parents couldn't always keep her safe – and that anchor to self-confidence and peace was destroyed. She has lost the ability to be a child, to have fun, and I hope she will one day regain it.

But where I have some sense of optimism about my future with Jade, there is only uncertainty with Terry. I wish I could give you a happy ending but I cannot. We both made mistakes when I came out, he needed softness and I could not give that to him, he shut off from me and would not build bridges. We had both changed and struggled to adjust to the people we found waiting for us. He believes he will see Gemma, Jason and Matthew in another life, but the comfort I found in religion while in prison has not extended to life on the outside. I still find it hard to understand how all that has happened to me fits in with God.

Most importantly, I believe we must learn to move past our sadness and into the future. It will always be a part of us but I worry if we will ever be able to come to terms with it. Terry is still so damaged, so wracked with pain about what has happened, and cannot move on. Where I stopped seeing a counsellor after a year, he continues to receive support. I worry my patience will be stretched too thin as I wait for us to live life, instead of cowering in the shadows. It has been so painful to watch him and all the pain he carries inside. Sometimes I can't see a future but I know there is one out there and I feel it is only us who can make it a happy one. We cannot continue to dwell on what happened, full of blame and rage. We must move on.

For now I simply live my life from day to day. I don't feel I want too much – to see my husband untroubled, my daughter having fun, to work again, enjoy being with each other, to explore without fear holding us back, to be a normal family. I still find it extraordinary that all this happened to me and have to pinch myself that the life that should have been so ordinary has not been. I find it awkward when I meet strangers and it comes up in conversation. When I tell them I lost three babies and was convicted of their murder, I can see the recognition dawn in their eyes. Maybe I imagine it but there always seems to be a moment when they shrink back from me before sympathy overcomes them. I fear many people don't think 'That's the woman who lives up the road' but 'That's the woman who was convicted of . . .' and, while I've never had a negative response, I am aware that one day I might.

I hope this book will convince some of those who doubt me. Maybe it won't, I must accept that, but at least I have been able to tell my story. Always remember that parents wrongly accused in the family courts will never be able to do so.

I watch the countryside race past the window as I sit on the train with Jade. We are on our way to Exeter for a day's shopping and she is writing on a notepad beside me.

'I hope I can find some nice clothes, Mum,' she says.

'Well, we'll go for lunch when we get there and then we can look round the shops and decide what to spend your Christmas and birthday money on,' I tell her.

A cautious optimism fills me as she goes back to her notepad and outside the Devon coast rushes by on the edges of the train tracks – we are nearly there. My new year's resolution was to do more with Jade, and we've gone to the cinema, flown up to

Scotland to see relatives, walked the dogs on the beach and are now on a day out together. I am determined we will have fun, and we are. Going back to school has meant fewer shouting matches – we still have our moments, of course, but things are improving – and we are learning how to be more affectionate with each other. I treasure the moments when she walks up to me for a hug or when we laugh at a joke together. At last she and I are starting to enjoy each other's company.

'Are we nearly there yet?' she asks.

'It won't be long, darling, about twenty minutes,' I say as I smile at her.

She moves across the seat to cuddle into me and I breathe in her comforting smell as I bend my head to hers.

'You know you're the best mummy in the whole world,' she says quietly as she nestles into me.

I'm not sure about that, who could ever be a perfect mother? I know I've made many mistakes with Jade since my release and I'm learning all the time with her. But there is one thing of which I am certain – like Gemma, Jason and Matthew, I will love her for ever. She is my child.